W9-CLI-341

Labor Arbitration in Health Care

About the book . . .

"The principles set forth in . . . [this book] . . . provide a valuable, practical guide to labor and management, both public and private, unionized and non-unionized, as to how impartial arbitrators under collective bargaining agreements and impartial hearing officers under various administrative procedures dispose of disputes submitted to them for adjudication. More important, they give the reasoning and grounds for sustaining either the position of the employee or employer."

. . . from the Introduction
by Jesse Simons

This book is the first published collection of arbitration cases dealing exclusively with employer-employee disputes in the health care field. It provides valuable guidance to hospital and other health care institution administrators, union officials, lawyers, and teachers of employee relations. The editors have selected cases which illustrate the application of accepted labor-relation principles to the many unique situations encountered in health care facilities. The underlying theme which places a different emphasis on the problems encountered is that the "product" of health care facilities is people.

Health Systems Management
Edited by Samuel Levey, Ph.D. and Alan Sheldon, M.D.

Volume 1:
Financial Management of Health Institutions
J.B. Silvers and C.K. Prahalad

Volume 2:
Personnel Administration in the Health Services Industry: Theory & Practice
Norman Metzger

Volume 3:
The National Labor Relations Act: A Guidebook for Health Care Facility
Administrators
Dennis D. Pointer and Norman Metzger

Volume 4:
Organizational Issues in Health Care Management
Alan Sheldon

Volume 5:
Long Term Care: A Handbook for Researchers, Planners and Providers
Sylvia Sherwood, Editor

Volume 6:
Analysis of Urban Health Problems: Case Studies from the Health Services
Administration of the City of New York
Irving Leveson and Jeffrey H. Weiss, Editors

Volume 7:
Health Maintenance Organizations: A Guide to Planning and Development
Roger W. Birnbaum

Volume 8:
Labor Arbitration in Health Care
Earl R. Baderschneider and Paul F. Miller, Editors

Labor Arbitration in Health Care

A Case Book

Edited by

Earl R. Baderschneider

and

Paul F. Miller

both of the American Arbitration Association,
New York, New York

With an Introduction by Jesse Simons

S P Books Division of
SPECTRUM PUBLICATIONS, INC.
New York

Distributed by Halsted Press
A Division of John Wiley & Sons

New York   Toronto   London   Sydney

SPECTRUM PUBLICATIONS, INC.
86-19 Sancho Street, Holliswood, N.Y. 11423

Distributed solely by the Halsted Press division of John Wiley & Sons, Inc., New York

Library of Congress Cataloging in Publication Data

Main Entry Under Title:
Labor arbitration in health care.
  [Health systems management; v. 8]
  Includes indexes.
    1. Arbitration, Industrial -- United States --
cases. 2. Collective labor agreements -- health
facilities -- United States -- cases. I. Baderschnei-
der Earl. II. Miller, Paul, 1923-   [DNLM:
1. Hospital personnel administration -- case studies.
2. Labor unions -- case studies. W1 HE588F v.8/
WX159 L123]
KF3450.H4L3   344'.73'01890413621   76-2612
ISBN 0-470-15037-8

Preface

Public Law 93-360 became effective in August 1974 and amended the National Labor Relations Act so that its coverage extended to all private, profit and non-profit, health care facilities. The increased use of collective bargaining in the past decade by both skilled and unskilled hospital employees played a significant part in the passage of this amendment. The employer-employee relationship in hospitals presents many areas of possible conflict not seen in the industrial environment. Physician and patient, physician and physician, hospital administration and professional or non-professional employees, professional employees and non-professional employees, hospital administration and the public served — these are all potential areas of dispute in health care facilities.

As a result of the established use of arbitration in other industries, a wealth of material has been developed which has been, and continues to be, helpful in guiding people who are responsible for settling employer-employee disputes. Much of this material is applicable to dispute settlement in hospitals and related institutions which are relative newcomers to collective bargaining. However, aspects which are unique to these institutions may require different emphasis in the application of well-established principles.

Literally hundreds of recent awards were available to us. We selected for this volume those which pointed up something unique about labor relations in the health care setting. Underlying these unique aspects is the fact that the "product" of these facilities is people, and every individual is either a consumer or a potential consumer of the industry's service. A well-known labor arbitrator stated in one of the cases reported herein that "nursing assignments cannot reasonably be treated in the same manner as industrial jobs." This statement can be expanded to include all personnel who work in health care institutions. For instance, coarse language, which may be tolerated or condoned as "shop talk" on the loading dock of a factory, would not be permissible in hospital corridors, where vulgarity might have an unsettling effect on patients. Failure to obey orders, excessive absenteeism, and the theft of supplies of seemingly negligible value are also examples of conduct which are intolerable when life and death are at stake. Relatively unimportant matters, such as proper grooming, may assume added significance in the hospital milieu. These are just a few of the issues that are discussed in the awards reported in this book.

At first glance, it might appear that we have selected a disproportionate number of cases pertaining to discipline and discharge (Parts I, II, and IV). The motivation in selecting many of these cases was not concern over the discipline itself, but the unique situations which brought about the disciplinary action — the problems encountered in trying to provide efficient service while contending with such current problems as money shortages, drug addiction, and malpractice suits.

Illustrative of the force which prevailing social problems can exert on a hospital's reaction to a disciplinary matter is the case of a registered nurse who unintentionally alarmed a patient by telling her that the hospital had only twice previously performed the type of operation she was scheduled to undergo. The surgeon's fear of a possible malpractice suit was a major factor in his insistence that the nurse be discharged, notwithstanding her excellent prior record. In another case, the negligible monetary value of hypodermic needles stolen by a security guard would probably have influenced labor relations officials in an industrial setting to impose some discipline short of discharge. However, the hospital's decision to discharge was viewed in light of its need to maintain the security of its drugs and supplies.

Although many of the cases reported do pertain to discipline, we also included awards (Parts III and V) that point up some of the special problems of scheduling, promotions, job assignments, and other working conditions. One of the cases reported, for instance, discusses the problem of scheduling nurses for weekend duties during the summer months. Another case discusses the weight to be given a nurse's ability to get along with others in determining her qualifications for a supervisory position. Each of the cases in these two parts of the book placed common labor relation's problems in a new light because of the hospital setting in which they occurred.

*   *   *   *   *

The range of AAA services to the health care community has widened considerably in recent years in tandem with the economic and social impact of health care on America. The Association's elections work has included a number of representation elections in hospitals, elections for community advisory boards to health delivery agencies, and leadership elections for hospital housestaff organizations. Since 1969, the AAA has administered medical malpractice arbitration demonstration projects at selected hospitals and Health Maintenance Organizations in Los Angeles, and more recently in Seattle, San Diego, Hawaii and Portland, Oregon. New demonstrations are ready for use in Illinois, New York, and Northern California.

The Research Institute of the AAA is also deeply concerned with the role of informal dispute resolution in newly emerging systems of health care delivery — HMO's, prepaid groups, and clinics. Funded by grants from the Commonwealth Fund, the Robert Wood Johnson Foundation, the Henry J. Kaiser Family Foundation, and the Department of Health, Education and Welfare, the Institute will determine whether the installation of democratic processes such as elections, meaningful patient grievance procedures, and consumer and community participation in governance assists these new agencies to accomplish their basic mission — delivery of top quality health care.

*   *   *   *   *

We would be remiss if we did not acknowledge the support we have received from the American Arbitration Association. The financial support of the members and the expertise of the staff have made it possible for us to devote the time necessary in completing this work. A special acknowledgment must also be given to Morris Stone, Vice-President in charge of publications for the AAA. The vast knowledge he has accumulated through 20 years of publishing articles and books about arbitration and dispute settlement proved to be of invaluable assistance to the editors.

Finally, a note of thanks must be given to Teresa Balbo and Joy Correge of the AAA's Publications Department, who not only endured the problems we encountered in selecting the cases to be reported, but who also performed many of the tasks required in preparing the material for publication. Without their dedication and assistance, this book would not have been possible at this time.

It is our hope that this book will become a useful source of reference to all who are concerned with the efficient operation of our health care facilities. By reviewing the problems experienced by others, we are not only looking for methods of settling disputes that may arise in the future, but also methods of avoiding these potential future disputes. The American Arbitration Association is already deeply involved in the health care field, helping to prevent conflict and aiding in the settlement of disputes. Arbitration, mediation, and elections are not used to suppress dissent or to compromise the assertion of new rights. Rather, the aim of the AAA is to create an orderly mechanism for permitting mutually acceptable changes in the system. Successful settlement of disputes will contribute to the national goal of high quality health care for all Americans.

The Editors

CONTENTS

Editors Preface

Introduction by Jesse Simons

Part I — *Improper Professional Conduct*

Case No. 1 — Was it proper to suspend a nurse who unintentionally alarmed a patient by telling her that the Hospital had only twice before performed the type of operation she was scheduled to undergo?
Lakeview General Hospital (Battle Creek, Mich.) and
Service Employees International Union, Local 79
Arbitrator: Leon J. Herman   3

Case No. 2 — Did an RN act as a professional when she refused to take responsibility for more patients than she felt she could adequately attend to without jeopardizing their health and safety? Was the Hospital justified in discharging the nurse who felt her actions were proper and gave no assurance that she would not repeat her behavior?
Flint Osteopathic Hospital (Flint, Mich.) and
American Federation of State, County and Municipal Employees, Council 29
Arbitrator: C. Keith Groty   7

Case No. 3 — Should discharge be upheld in the case of a Licensed Practical Nurse who allegedly refused to administer medication and who behaved "rudely" toward a patient? Was it relevant that the LPN had never been disciplined before, despite several

ix

years of unsatisfactory work, and that she was "upset" over the recent surgery performed on her daughter?

Elizabeth Horton Memorial Hospital (N.Y.) and
Licensed Practical Nurses of New York, Inc.

Arbitrator: Woodrow J. Sandler   13

Case No. 4 — Was a Licensed Practical Nurse who admittedly refused to answer a patient's call and who "backhanded" the head nurse entitled to reinstatement because of the Hospital's failure to follow procedures and give her a hearing prior to discharge?

Women's General Hospital (Cleveland, Ohio) and
Service, Hospital, Nursing Home and Public Employees Union,
Local 47

Arbitrator: Peter DiLeone   23

Case No. 5 — Could a nurse who shared responsibility with another nurse for disobeying a physician's orders to administer medication to a patient be demoted? Was the Hospital barred from taking this action by having promoted the other nurse?

The Youngstown Hospital Association (Youngstown, Ohio) and
The Ohio Nurses Association

Arbitrator: Wayne T. Geissinger   27

Case No. 6 — Did a Hospital policy stating that an employee witnessing an accident must accompany the patient to the emergency room justify the discharge of an employee, who, not having witnessed the accident, refused a supervisor's order to accompany the patient to the emergency room?

City of Memphis Hospital Authority (Memphis, Tenn.) and
American Federation of State, County and Municipal
Employees, Local 1733

Arbitrator: Samuel S. Perry   35

Part II — *Improper Patient and Public Relations*

Case No. 7 — What was the proper penalty to impose on a nurses aide who executed a procedure which only registered nurses are permitted to perform? Was the aide's conduct excusable because the Hospital failed to issue instructions which warn against forbidden procedures and because nurses often gave improper assignments to aides?

Grace Hospital, Northwest Unit (Detroit, Mich.) and
Service Employees International Union, Local 79

Arbitrator: Harry N. Casselman   51

Case No. 8 — Was the Hospital justified in reprimanding a psychiatric aide who refused to obey an order to catheterize a patient? What effect did the aide's lack of academic instruction have on the disciplinary action taken?

Ohio Department of Mental Health and Retardation and
American Federation of State, County and Municipal Employees, Local 1136

Arbitrator: Ivan C. Rutledge   59

Case No. 9 — Did an Orderly's overall record of conscientious dedication to his patients absolve him from slapping an elderly patient who would not get back into bed when ordered to do so?

Oak Pavilion Nursing Home and Rehabilitation Center (Ohio) and
National Union of Hospital and Nursing Home Employees

Arbitrator: Walter G. Seinsheimer   67

Case No. 10 — Was the Hospital justified in suspending a housekeeping aide for making threatening remarks to a patient? Could the employee properly be suspended pending completion of the investigation of charges against her?

Kaiser Foundation Hospitals, et al. (Hayward, Calif.) and
Hospital and Institutional Workers, Local 250

Arbitrator: Leo V. Killion   77

Case No. 11 — Did the Hospital have the right to discharge a nurses aide who was charged with slapping a mentally ill patient and pushing his wheelchair away with undue force? Did the arbitrator have the right to impose a lesser form of discipline, or was the grievant entitled to reinstatement will full back pay and benefits?

Brown County (Wis.) and
Brown County Hospital Employees, AFSCME, Local 1901

Arbitrator: Edward B. Krinsky   83

Case No. 12 — Was there just cause for discharging a nurses aide who had violated a rule against personal contact with tuberculin patients and for other unsatisfactory performance which had been noted in previous evaluations?

Middle River Sanitorium and General Hospital (Douglas County, Wis.) and

American Federation of State, County and Municipal Employees, Local 1146

Arbitrator: Donald B. Lee   91

Case No. 13 — Was there just cause to discharge a security officer who attempted to steal several hypodermic needles from a doctor's supply cart? Was the value of the needles (negligible, in this instance) relevant? Was the offense to be judged in the light of the Hospital's responsibility toward patients?

The New York City Health and Hospitals Corporation and Individual grievant

Arbitrator: Jesse Simons   99

Case No. 14 — Was a five-day suspension justified in the case of an X-ray technician who hit a malfunctioning machine with force sufficient to break a glass panel and jam an indicator needle?

Flint Osteopathic Hospital (Flint, Mich.) and

American Federation of State, County and Municipal Employees, Local 1850

Arbitrator: George T. Roumell, Jr.   103

Case No. 15 — Was a regulation requiring all beards to be closely cropped and neatly trimmed reasonably related to proper exercise of functions of the Hospital in treatment and care of its patients so as to justify the discharge of a psychiatric technician for noncompliance?

St. Mary's Hospital and Medical Center (San Francisco, Calif.) and

Hospital and Institutional Workers Union, Local 250

Arbitrator: David Karasick   115

Case No. 16 — What was the proper penalty to be imposed on a Psychiatric Nursing Assistant who took no action when an unauthorized, intoxicated acquaintance entered her ward and talked to the patients? Was the Assistant guilty of improper patient contact when she talked to a patient who was troubled about the unauthorized visit of the grievant's acquaintance?

Johns Hopkins Hospital (Baltimore, Md.) and
*National Union of Hospital and Nursing Home Employees,
Local 1199E*

Arbitrator: Peter Florey   127

Part III — *Work Schedules and Working Conditions*

Case No. 17 — When the Hospital experienced an unusually low patient census, could it, in the absence of a share-the-work provision, institute a general reduction in the work schedule? Or was it required to lay off employees according to seniority?

Community General Hospital (Sterling, Ill.) and
Nurses Staff Association

Arbitrator: Alex Elson   135

Case No. 18 — After deciding that a night shift nurse needed more supervision of the kind that was available only on the day shift, did a VA Hospital have the right to effect that transfer and replace her with a day shift nurse who preferred not to go on the night shift? Did the need for the original transfer constitute an emergency, justifying the disregard of procedures that would otherwise apply in inter-shift transfers?

Veterans Administration Hospital (Pittsburgh, Pa.) and
American Federation of Government Employees, Local 2028

Arbitrator: Ralph D. Tive   145

Case No. 19 — Where the contract contained a maintenance-of-standards provision, could the Hospital unilaterally change the method of scheduling weekends off for nurses? Was the Hospital relieved of a duty to bargain by the fact that it was contractually obligated to evenly distribute weekend time off?

Marinette General Hospital (Marinette County, Wis.) and
Marinette General Hospital Employees Union, AFSCME

Arbitrator: Douglas V. Knudson

155

Case No. 20 — Did a shortage of full-time nurses during the summer months constitute justification for a Hospital's requirement that part-time nurses agree to work two weekends in four under a collective agreement that did not require them to work weekends? Did full-time nurses have the right to change their status to part-timers for the summer months, the object being to avoid weekend work?

Hurley Hospital (Flint, Mich.) and
Hurley Hospital Registered Nurses Organization

Arbitrator: Leon J. Herman   **161**

Case No. 21 — In an effort to insure the best possible patient care, could a VA Hospital assign LPN's to the night shift against their wishes?

Veterans Administration Hospital (Canandaigua, N.Y.) and
Service Employees International Union, Local 227

Arbitrator: Robert W. Miller   **175**

Case No. 22 — Did a VA Hospital have the right, in an effort to increase efficiency, to relocate the office of a ward clerk (a woman) so as to combine it with the nurses' station? Did the relocation of the grievant subject her to undue embarrassment from patient exposure and increased fear of bodily harm?

Veterans Administration Hospital (Murfreesboro, Tenn.) and
American Federation of Government Employees, Local 1844

Arbitrator: Walter F. Eigenbrod   **181**

Case No. 23 — In an interest arbitration, should Hospital social workers be granted the same number of vacation days as all other Hospital workers, or should they be granted two extra vacation days so that their vacation benefits equal those negotiated for social workers in all other area contracts?

St. Luke's Hospital Center (New York, N.Y.) and
Drug and Hospital Union, Local 1199

Arbitrator: Morris P. Glushien   **189**

Part IV — *Work Stoppages, Concerted Activities and Union Business Disruptive to Patient Care*

Case No. 24 — Was the Hospital justified in discharging an acting steward of nurses aides and orderlies who, when only half the scheduled work force reported for work on a Sunday, threatened the Hospital with a walkout unless the remaining employees were paid at a premium rate not otherwise called for in the contract?

Lahser Hills Nursing Home (Southfield, Mich.) and
Service Employees International Union, Local 79

Arbitrator: M. David Keefe   195

Case No. 25 — Could the Hospital discharge an RN with a good record who actively engaged in picketing for a union representing nonprofessional hospital employees? Was it relevant that the Hospital did not discharge the nurse until more than a month after the strike ended?

Association of Hospitals of Santa Clara County (Calif.) and
California Nurses Association

Arbitrator: Arthur B. Jacobs   201

Case No. 26 — What was the proper discipline to be taken against a head nurse with 27 years of service who was absent for 2 days in protest of her working conditions? Was it disparity of treatment in that lesser penalties were given to nonprofessional co-workers who also withheld their services?

The New York City Health and Hospitals Corporation and
Individual grievant

Arbitrator: Jesse Simons   211

Case No. 27 — Did the absence of four out of five nursing assistants and one unit clerk constitute a concerted refusal to work? Did their failure to present valid medical evidence of alleged illnesses constitute at least misrepresentations of reason for absence?

St. Vincent Charity Hospital (Cleveland, Ohio) and
Hospital, Convalescent and Nursing Home Employees Union, Local 10

Arbitrator: Charles F. Ipavec   219

Case No. 28 — What was the proper discipline to be taken against two off-duty nurses aides who returned to the Facility and engaged in intra-union activity which was disruptive of operations?

Lafayette Extended Care Facility (Flint, Mich.) and
American Federation of State, County and Municipal Employees, Local 1918, Chapter P

Arbitrator: E. V. Ott   229

Case No. 29 — In an effort to prevent patients from becoming involved in internal hospital–union affairs, did the Hospital have the right to prohibit employees from engaging in union activities on its property? Did the Hospital's action infringe on the employees' Constitutional right to freedom of speech?

Metropolitan Hospital and Health Centers (Detroit, Mich.) and *Office and Professional Employees International Union, Local 42*

Arbitrator: George T. Roumell, Jr.   239

Part V — *Discrimination and Bona Fide Job Qualifications*

Case No. 30 — Could a female employee's application for an Orderly vacancy be rejected solely on the basis of sex? Were the business and medical reasons for placing a male Orderly on the night shift sufficient to overcome the Hospital's obligations under the non-discrimination provision?

Jackson Osteopathic Hospital (Jackson, Mich.) and
Hospital Employees Division of the Service Employees International Union, Local 79

Arbitrator: Howard A. Cole   253

Case No. 31 — Did a Hospital wrongfully discriminate against male Licensed Vocational Nurses (LVN) by refusing to assign them to "sensitive personal care" of female patients? After determining that two male orderlies should not have been promoted to LVN because there were not enough male patients for them to work with, did the Hospital have the right to demote them to orderlies again?

Kaiser Foundation Hospitals and Medical Center, et al. (Bellflower, Calif.) and
Hospital, Institutional and Professional Division, Local 399, BSEIU

Arbitrator: Edgar A. Jones, Jr.   259

Case No. 32 — Did the Clinic have the right to refuse to recall an X-ray technician from layoff because she was pregnant? Does a pregnant woman who has accepted the risks of an X-ray technicians' job have the additional right to risk the safety of her unborn child?

Centerville Clinics, Inc. (Centerville, Pa.) and
Office Professional Employees International Union, Local 457

Arbitrator: Alice B. Grant   271

Case No. 33 — Was it discriminatory for a Nursing Home to require male employees in the food service department to cut their hair so that it would not "extend below the collar" while female employees were required only to wear hairnets?

St. Paul's Towers (San Francisco, Calif.) and
Hospital and Institutional Workers, Local 250

Arbitrator: James R. Lucas   277

Case No. 34 — When the State Department of Health recommended that the Hospital establish a new position, was it reasonable for the Hospital to assume that failure to do so immediately might jeopardize its certification? Having unilaterally established the new position, could the Hospital require that it be filled by an LPN?

Benzie Medical Care Facility (Benzie County, Mich.) and
Benzie Medical Employees Chapter of Local No. 1084, AFSCME

Arbitrator: Samuel S. Shaw   287

Case No. 35 — Were the lack of ability to perform the required secretarial functions of the employee health nurse position and unfamiliarity with rules and regulations pertaining to safety and compensation adequate reasons to deny the bids of otherwise qualified employees and fill the vacancy from the outside?

Cooley-Dickinson Hospital (Northampton, Mass.) and
Massachusetts Nurses Association

Arbitrator: Robert F. Koretz   297

Case No. 36 — In view of the fact that a nurses aide's slight physical stature was apparent at the time she was hired, did the Hospital have the right to subsequently terminate her on the ground that she was not physically capable of performing the duties of her job? What restraints are properly placed on management in the exercise of its discretionary power to terminate an employee during the probationary period?

Jackson County Medical Care Facility (Jackson, Mich.) and *American Federation of State, County and Municipal Employees, Local 139*

Arbitrator: M. David Keefe   307

Case No. 37 — Where two applicants for the position of operating room supervisor had equal technical qualifications as to work and day-to-day ability, were a junior nurse's demonstrated superior ability to get along with her associates and her more advanced educational progress valid considerations in determining that she was better qualified for the open position than the grievant?

Williamsburgh General Hospital (Williamsburgh, N.Y.) and *New York State Nurses Association*

Arbitrator: Maurice C. Benewitz   315

Subject Index   321

Index of Arbitrators   323

Introduction

By Jesse Simons

In the last decade, most of the health care field has witnessed rapid and extensive changes in its working environment and in its personnel policies and their administration. These changes consist of new ways in which employees perceive themselves, their rights and their employers; new ways in which management relates to and deals with its employees; and in the way in which management acts and understands its own functions. Much of this change has been the result of recent unionization of health care employees.

In the past, some employees entered the health care service to achieve personal fulfillment of a deep-seated psychic need to care for the sick and the injured. Matters of salary, pensions, hours of work, promotional opportunity, and working conditions in general were not of primary interest to them or to their many professional organizations. Other employees, particularly women and minorities, were drawn to the health care field because they could not obtain jobs elsewhere. Many were unskilled and inexperienced, and some lacked a high-school education.

Consequently, there developed a basically authoritarian structure in these institutions, with power highly centralized at the top and usually held by physicians and only later by professional administrators. As employees organized, and as professional organizations gradually began to take on some aspect of unionism, top management of health care institutions was compelled, albeit reluctantly, to abandon its traditional view of managerial prerogatives as absolute and nonreviewable. Management was also compelled to alter its rules governing employee conduct and duties, administering them so as to accord to employees due process rights and to provide clear definitions of wages, overtime, vacations, job duties, promotional opportunities, and other aspects of working conditions.

Moreover, middle management and line management were unprepared to give leadership to and to manage and direct unionized employees who were not psychically motivated. Even to this day, the bulk of top, middle and line management in the health care field appears to lack the training or education needed to meet the new state of affairs brought on by rapid unionization.

Employees and their spokesmen are equally unprepared. There have been wide changes among employees in a whole range of attitudes. While some employees are still motivated primarily by a feeling for public service, most are predominantly interested in job security, promotion, salary increases, pensions, and the like.

The attitudes of these employees, which are shared by their union shop representatives and officers, reflect a past history of low wages and authoritarian control. There is a backlog of resentment which influences present conduct. It accounts in part for the militant mood of the newly organized. The new unions, for the most part, still need to develop the skills and expertise in representation that unions generally develop only after decades of experience. Thus, in the health care field at present, there is a somewhat higher than normal number of unwarranted grievances and complaints coming to arbitration or coming before administrative review boards.

The high degree of rank-and-file militancy present among the newly organized health care employees often makes it difficult, if not impossible, for the professional or legal staff of health care unions to eliminate unmeritorious complaints and grievances. On achieving stability, they may be able to weed out grievances that lack merit. But this degree of leadership develops slowly and at an uneven rate.

While precise figures are not available, the best informed estimates are that unions represent about 15 percent of the 2,700,000 employees in the approximately 7120 public and private hospitals in the United States. In addition, there are approximately 30,000 to 40,000 specialized institutions for the aged, the mentally retarded, the mentally ill, and the physically handicapped. Some of these specialized institutions are purely custodial, and others perform both custodial and remedial functions. It is estimated that these institutions employ nearly 2,000,000 workers in all classifications, of which perhaps 10 percent are organized.

Following the 1959 and 1962 hospital employees' strikes in New York City, the New York State Legislature modified the State Labor

Relations Act to include health care workers in the private sector. This gave considerable impetus to unionization in New York. In 1974, by Federal Law, non-public health care workers and employers came under the National Labor Relations Act. This encouraged the further unionization of health care employees. It has been estimated that by 1980 the number of employees in unions and the number of contracts will double.

It is believed that 70 percent of health care employees are women and minorities. Both groups are extremely vulnerable and relatively weak and inexperienced in advancing their interests. This fact, plus the lack of coverage under the law until very recently, tended to hinder union efforts to organize. The scope and content of collective bargaining agreements also reflects the peculiar situation in health care institutions. Today's contracts tend to be narrow in scope. This is true not only of agreements with unskilled workers, but also of contracts governing professional employees who do not have a substantial history of bargaining.

Most agreements provide for arbitration of disputes which cannot be resolved through the grievance procedure. Additionally, there are a variety of appeal procedures for public health care employees — federal, state, county, and city — for the hearing and adjudication of employee claims of unfair treatment and/or denial of rights accorded to the employees under law, rules, and regulations. This volume does not strive to fully cover the spectrum of both systems of dispute adjudication. Rather, 37 decisions have been selected which are believed to be of particular interest and use to those engaged in day-to-day employee and personnel relations.

The decisions chosen for inclusion are typical of the health care field in that they deal with issues which would not have arisen elsewhere in quite the same manner. In addition, they were chosen because they set forth dicta and principles which, though derived from the "common law of the shop," are highly relevant to the special problems encountered in this field.[1]

[1]The phrase "common law of the shop" has been used in labor relations for many years. However, its usage attained greater popularity following the Supreme Court's decision in *Warrior & Gulf*. In many major industries, widespread use of a third-party adjudication of employee disputes goes back to the early part of the century. As a consequence, there exists a large body of published awards dealing with disputes in these industries. In many instances, these awards have been collected and indexed by industry or by subject matter, and thus, they are readily available for reference, or have been the subject of specialized volumes.

The principles set forth in these awards provide a valuable, practical guide to labor and management, both public and private, unionized and non-unionized, as to how impartial arbitrators under collective bargaining agreements and impartial hearing officers under various administrative procedures dispose of disputes submitted to them for adjudication. More important, they give the reasoning and grounds for sustaining either the position of the employee or employer.

Although many impartials apply the principles that have emerged out of decades of employer-employee dispute adjudication, they must keep in mind that the purpose of health institutions is to care for the ill, the injured, and the handicapped and this clearly distinguishes this field from other industries. Virtually each and every duty of virtually every employee is one link in a chain of duties any one of which, if not performed in a timely manner or if not performed at all, can literally have lethal consequences on a patient or group of patients.

There are, within most health care institutions, five different services: (1) direct patient care performed by physicians, nurses, and paraprofessionals;[2] (2) diagnostic and laboratory services;[3] (3) housekeeping services such as food preparation, building maintenance, and security;[4] (4) medical and financial record keeping;[5] and (5) auxiliary services, including home nursing care, preventive treatment, community health programs, and social and psychological counseling.[6]

It can readily be seen that financial record-keeping employees and most employees engaged in performing auxiliary services are performing duties that fall outside the category of direct-patient care. Those engaged in duties not directly related to patient care constitute 10 percent of the work force.

At first glance, it might appear that some of the decisions reported in this volume could have arisen anywhere. Theft and pilferage by employees, for instance, is a problem in many industries. But in a hospital, this kind of misconduct has special consequences. Similarly, if housekeeping tasks are not done properly or when scheduled, such

[2]See cases reported in Part I and Part II.

[3]See Case Nos. 14 and 32.

[4]See Case Nos. 8, 13, and 33.

[5]See Case No. 22.

[6]See Case Nos. 15 and 23.

delinquency can lead to spreading of contagious diseases. Theft,[7] destruction, or loss of medical supplies and equipment[8] can result in their unavailability in cases of emergency.

For that reason, most health care institutions apply rigorous standards in judging improper performance or non-performance of duties. Arbitrators, too, take a serious view of misconduct on the part of employees engaged in vital health care duties.

Because no institution can have two standards for dealing with employees, most health care employers apply the single, more rigorous standard across the board, even to those employees whose duties are not directly related to patient care. Moreover, Arbitrators cannot sustain double standards for employees within one institution. Therefore, they tend to apply these more stringent standards to typists, accountants, social workers, and the like.

Grievances submitted to third-party adjudication fall into three categories: (1) grievances concerning penalties assessed for *gross* misconduct; (2) grievances concerning penalties for *minor* misconduct; and (3) grievances concerning a wide range of *incidents of personnel administration*, such as promotion, out-of-title assignments, layoff, rehiring, and vacations.[9]

In adjudicating grievances concerning all forms of misconduct, it is well established that the employer has the burden of proving the specific alleged act or acts of misconduct. In a criminal proceeding, courts require that "proof must be beyond a reasonable doubt." In arbitration, the employer's case must be supported by "a preponderance of the evidence submitted."[10]

The body of arbitration awards issued in the last forty years has clearly distinguished between minor and major misconduct. Generally, it has been held that major misconduct consists of such actions as assault with or without a deadly weapon, possession of a deadly weapon, theft, willful destruction of company property, repeated insubordination, and causing or participating in slowdowns or work stoppages.[11] For such incidents of gross misconduct, discharge

[7]See Case No. 13.

[8]See Case No. 14.

[9]See cases reported in Part III and Part V.

[10]As examples see Case Nos. 10 and 11.

[11]As examples see Case Nos. 3, 24 and 25.

is usually imposed. If a grievance concerning discharge for gross misconduct is arbitrated, the penalty assessed is generally sustained upon the presentation of the required quantum of proof. Absent such proof, the penalty is either reduced or revoked and the grievant is "made whole."

There are, however, a few exceptions to this general rule. For example, in the event the grievant had decades of loyal service unmarred by prior misconduct, and if it was shown that a single act of gross misconduct was an aberration wholly inconsistent with the entire attitude, character, and behavior of the grievant, arbitrators have reduced the penalty. Arbitrators have also generally tended to reduce penalties where a blow occurred as a result of clear provocation, or was struck in "self-defense," when both flight and obtaining aid were clearly not possible, or where the penalty assessed or proposed was discriminatory in that one person was penalized while others equally involved were not penalized at all.

While application to health care employees of the traditional definition of gross misconduct, albeit on a more rigorous basis, is proper, it is necessary to add one further category of misconduct to the list, namely, failure to perform a "key duty." Examples are the failure of a nurse or a paraprofessional to respond to call because they are asleep while on duty, the failure of a nurses' aide riding in an ambulance to provide proper first aid because of drug or alcoholic intoxication, or the failure of an employee to properly identify and deliver the specific cylinder of gas ordered.

In almost any industry, the refusal or failure of an employee to obey a direct work order is regarded as a grave offense. However, most private and public employers usually do not discharge an employee who has not properly performed his duties unless the duty is of a critical nature or the employee is an habitual offender. However, in a hospital setting, the failure to perform a "key duty" has or could have grave consequences and, therefore, constitutes gross misconduct warranting severe discipline. Similarly, even the common faults of absenteeism, lateness, refusal of overtime, etc., which in manufacturing industries might be regarded as mere misdemeanors, may be capital offenses when committed by persons on whom the welfare of patients depends directly. It is precisely because of the more stringent standards of penalties justifiably applied by health care institutions that both arbitrators and hearing panels extend the fullest possible degree of due process to employees and grant them the widest latitude possible as to arbitrability of issues, admissibility of evidence, and presentation of testimony.

In cases of absenteeism, lateness, early departure, and absence from the place of duty,[12] arbitral dicta has held that discipline should be essentially corrective and graduated, and dismissal is warranted only when incorrigibility has been demonstrated by full applications of these procedures. The same principle, with one addition, is applicable in the health care field. The absence or tardiness of one employee may put an excessive burden on another, who necessarily will perform with something less than his full attention and energy. This too has an impact on the quality of patient care. Thus, there is justification for strict administrative procedures and expeditious application of graduated discipline on an ascending scale somewhat more steep than might be warranted elsewhere. Most arbitrators and impartial hearing officers realize this need for greater stringency.

Although it might appear that a disproportionate number of cases reported pertain to employee misconduct, such a result might be expected given the narrow scope of non-disciplinary subjects presently covered in collective bargaining agreements. In the public sector health care agreements, non-disciplinary matters are frequently governed by federal, state, county or city civil service laws and regulations, and therefore, are not permissible subjects for bargaining. In the private sector health care field, the number of matters covered is narrow because collective bargaining is still a relatively new process. In many instances, the reasonableness of a work rule is tested only after disciplinary action has been taken against an employee for non-compliance with the rule.

The number of disputes concerning working conditions or rules adjudicated in the health care field to date is not sufficiently great to permit a judgment to be made as to what is the most common grievance concerning matters other than employee misconduct. In all probability, the caseload mix will follow that of other labor-management relationships.

Despite the health care field's existing lack of experience and expertise in the area of labor relations and dispute adjudication, both parties have used the impartial tribunal for "marginal bargaining." This

[12]See Case Nos. 26 and 27.

phrase is used to describe the process whereby, through the grievance and arbitration procedure, either party seeks to obtain in the decision some incremental improvement which did not heretofore exist. To the union, it would probably be a marginal improvement in working conditions; to the management, it would probably be greater flexibility in manpower deployment. Experienced impartials readily become aware of this concealed effort to obtain a marginal bargaining advantage. Impartials usually avoid such subversion of the adjudicatory process by issuing the narrowest possible award.

In this connection, the axiom that "hard" cases make bad law also applies in third-party adjudication of labor-management disputes. On occasion, the parties will either avoid a particular dispute or will withhold grievances from submission to final adjudication until there appears a most extreme or "hard" case. Management may have committed a particularly egregious error, or an employee or a union may seek some benefit under a fanciful construction of a contract or rule. Usually an impartial arbitrator or hearing officer will avoid the dangers implicit in such "extreme cases" by limiting his opinion and award to the maximum extent possible so as to minimize the "bad-law" consequences to the parties of the "hard" or extreme cases presented for adjudication.

In any event, while most impartials give considerable weight to previous decisions, they are not bound by them. Thus, the parties are protected from a decision containing an unfortunate construction of contract language or of a rule based on an extreme set of circumstances.

With regard to the future of the dispute settlement and adjudication process, it is believed that the current inflationary trend with its enormous impact on health care costs, taken in combination with the desire of legislatures and governmental executives to reduce budgets and avoid tax increases, will require that health care services be curtailed as to budget, manpower, education, training, and construction. While all in the community pay obeisance to the need to maintain the present level of services, recipients of all other services simultaneously insist that the critical services provided to it, public or private, should continue at the present level. Something must give and will give. Therefore, it is not unreasonable to expect contraction of the work force resulting in an increase in disputes concerning seniority, layoff, and rehiring rights.

The present social and economic climate will tend to speed up the process of unionization and, correlatively, the consummation of more labor-management agreements, resulting in a more vigorous presentation of employee claims by any and all means. Thus, it can be expected that third-party adjudication of health care labor-management disputes will increase in number.

The very existence of unions has already produced significant changes, and it can be anticipated that both labor and management will develop, out of the conflicts and disputes that were and are occurring, increased sophistication in the utilization of third parties in the adjudication of their disputes. However, increased knowledge and skill in labor relations does not necessarily mean a reduction in the use of the adjudicatory process.

Arbitration decisions do not constitute binding precedents. But they are persuasive and educational. By making this volume available, it is hoped that a modest contribution will be made to the everyday practitioners of labor-management relations in the health care field who are seeking knowledge, all of whom need every bit of practical guidance they can obtain in this new, growing, contentious, and complex field.

About the citations . . .

Most of the thirty-seven cases have been previously reported in one or more of the award-reporting services commonly used in the labor-management community. Two of the services from which the cases were selected are published monthly by the American Arbitration Association. *Summary of Labor Arbitration Awards* contains private sector awards. A typical citation reads 190 AAA 11, which means the eleventh case in the 190th monthly issue. *Labor Arbitration in Government* is AAA's monthly publication reporting awards involving federal, state, or local government agencies. The reports are numbered consecutively. LAIG 386 therefore means the 386th case reported in that publication.

The Bureau of National Affairs, a commercial publishing company in Washington, D.C. reports awards which are cited by Labor Arbitration volume and page number, as in 64 LA 96. The Commerce Clearing House, a somewhat similar commercial publisher, headquartered in Chicago, cites its cases by a number which indicates the year of publication, and a paragraph number, as in 73-1 ARB ¶8198.

E.B.
P.M.

Part I

Improper Professional Conduct

Case No. 1

*Was it proper to suspend a nurse who unintentionally
alarmed a patient by telling her that the Hospital had only twice
before performed the type of operation she was
scheduled to undergo?*

Lakeview General Hospital (Battle Creek, Mich.)
and
Service Employees International Union, Local 79

Arbitrator: Leon J. Herman
Date of Award: January 17, 1972
Citation: LAIG 386

Grievant L—, 22-years old, has been employed at the Hospital for four years. She has worked the 8–11 p.m. shift four days per week.

One of the patients under grievant's care on September 7, 1971 was a Mrs. Harmon, who was scheduled for an operation the next day for laryngoscopy with possible vocal chord stripping. Her surgeon, Dr. Hirt, talked to Personnel Manager Gibson that night about 10 p.m. He was very angry because a nurse had told the patient that the Hospital and the doctor had had only two or three cases of this type in the past. He said the patient had become very apprehensive, questioning his ability to perform the operation and fearful that she was being treated as a guinea pig in the Hospital. The doctor was worried about a possible malpractice suit against him. He asked that the nurse be fired and that the incident be published in the Hospital, so that it not be repeated.

A check revealed that grievant was the nurse charged with making the statement to the patient. Mr. Gibson talked to her and suggested that she write out a statement of the facts as she saw them, and that she submit it to the Hospital administrator. She followed his instructions. Her statement read:

Sept. 9, 1971

To Whom it may Concern,
   On Tuesday, Sept. 7, I had charge of Rm. 43, therefore including Mrs. Harmon.
   During the course of the evening, Mrs. Harmon expressed a interest in her pending surgery. I explained to her that I had no idea as to what was going to be done, and stated that there have only been 2–3 cases done in the hosp. I did not, however, state that Dr. Hirt had only done a few surgerys of this type. I'm sorry if Mrs. Harmon misunderstood my statement. But she did not appear overly apprehensive to me. Each time I entered the room she seemed in good spirits, leaving no doubts in my mind.
   Around 10:00 p.m., I was charting at the station, and I overheard snatches of Dr. Hirt's conversation. I knew the pt. involved, when Dr. Hirt finished, I inquired as to the procedure and was unable to pronounce one word. Dr. Hirt seemed upset about something and stated: "When you can say it, I'll tell you".
   I had no idea what Dr. Hirt was mad about, until I arrived for duty at 2:45 p.m. Sept. 8.

—LPN

In a discussion on September 14 at about 1 p.m. between administrator Simmons, Mrs. McMasters, the night nursing supervisor, and grievant's mother, Mrs. B, also a nursing supervisor, Mr. Simmons suggested that she quit her employment. She refused to do so. After some discussion he proposed a one month leave of absence without pay, to be reviewed after two weeks. She would then be placed in a division of the hospital other than surgical. Grievant and Mrs. B both felt at the time that this was a fair disposition.
   Thereafter grievant filed a grievance protesting the suspension, and asking for reinstatement with full back pay. The grievance was denied. A hearing on the grievance was held with the personnel director on about September 20, at which time Mr. Gibson offered to reduce the suspension to two weeks on condition that she withdraw her grievance. The Union rejected the offer and the matter was brought on to arbitration.
   At the hearing grievant testified that she had considered the 30-day suspension fair at the outset but changed her mind later and decided that it was not fair, since she felt she had done nothing wrong. She testified that Mrs. Harmon had asked her how she would feel after surgery.

Grievant replied that her throat would be a little sore, but that she couldn't tell her much because only two or three such operations had been performed at this hospital. She insisted that she made no mention of Dr. Hirt nor of his experience in the field.

Grievant admitted that she had used poor judgment in discussing the case with Mrs. Harmon. She had studied nursing ethics while at LPN school and had been taught not to talk to patients about their cases. She knew this was an unwritten rule in the hospital, although it has never been included in the book of rules which the hospital has printed and distributed to its employees.

Grievant's only previous discipline had been a verbal warning concerning an incident in March, 1971 when she had dropped the cap from a sterile bottle to the floor and had picked it up and replaced it on the bottle.

The Hospital argues that the penalty should be permitted to stand. The doctor–patient relationship is a delicate one. Patients, particularly those who are about to undergo surgery, are usually apprehensive. Poor judgment in discussing their cases can only increase a patient's tension and fears. Grievant was familiar with the LPN code of ethics and knew that she should not have discussed her case with the patient. When the discipline was proposed she was given a fair opportunity to present her side of the matter and had admitted at the time that she thought that the discipline was fair. The grievance should therefore be denied.

The Union contends that the grievant's state of mind at the time is the aspect which should be considered. She had no intent to discuss the case with the patient. She merely professed ignorance of the pending operation because she did not know anything about it and quite naturally gave as a reason that it was not often done. She was denying her knowledge, not discussing the case. She had contributed no comment relative to the doctor. It was not her fault that the patient misunderstood her. The penalty was expressly made severe because the Hospital had to appease Dr. Hirt. Even if a penalty were to be deemed proper in the circumstances, certainly it should have been limited to the two calendar weeks or 9 working days following which the hospital offered to reinstate her. The balance of the penalty is unreasonable.

I agree with the Hospital and with the concession made by grievant that she used extremely poor judgment in the comments she made to Mrs. Harmon. It does little to relieve a patient's anxieties to be informed that the Hospital has had very little experience in this type of operation. I believe grievant's statement that she made no comment in reference to the doctor. It is easy to understand, however, how a patient about to undergo surgery would metamorphose such a statement into the conviction that the surgeon himself had had almost no experience with such an operation and that she was about to become a subject for experimental and training purposes. Grievant's remark to the patient was improper, uncalled for and utterly unjustifiable.

It is true that the Hospital has no written rule with regard to discussion of a patient's illness with a patient. As a licensed practical nurse, grievant is pursuing a profession which has a high standard of ethics. One of the courses she took at school was a study of the ethics of the nursing profession. She well knew that such discussions were improper. A confession of poor judgment after the fact does not alleviate the apprehension which the patient underwent because of her injudicious remarks.

I am satisfied that a disciplinary suspension of 30 calendar days was both fair and reasonable. Had the Hospital been content to let this penalty stand I would have confirmed it without hesitation. However, the Hospital administration appears to have been of the opinion that two weeks was a reasonable penalty. In assessing the penalty the Hospital Administrator stated that he would review the penalty after two weeks with a view towards reducing it to that period. The personnel manager again offered to reduce the penalty to two weeks in the course of a grievance hearing. The condition he attached to the offer of reduction was not proper. His offer was made subject to the withdrawal of the grievance. This he had no right to do. In effect, he was proposing that the grievant waive her rights under the contract. If grievant was entitled to a reduction of penalty to two weeks she should have received it without precondition. She should not be asked to give up rights which the Union has obtained by its contractual arrangement with the Hospital. The condition was improper and was properly rejected by the Union.

I feel that I am bound by the administration's own admission that a two calendar week penalty was fair in the circumstances. I must therefore rule that the penalty be reduced to two calendar weeks.

AWARD

The grievance of L— is sustained to the extent that her suspension is reduced to two calendar weeks. The Hospital is directed to reimburse grievant for all work days beyond that period which she lost while she was under suspension.

Case No. 2

Did an RN act as a professional when she refused to take
responsibility for more patients than she felt she
could adequately attend to without jeopardizing their health
and safety? Was the Hospital justified in discharging the nurse
who felt her actions were proper and gave no assurance that
she would not repeat her behavior?

Flint Osteopathic Hospital (Flint, Mich.)
and
American Federation of State, County and Municipal Employees,
Council 29

Arbitrator: C. Keith Groty
Date of Award: April 20, 1975
Citation: Previously unreported

Statement of the Issues

1. Did the grievant act improperly by refusing to accept an assignment on July 21, 1974 and proceeding to leave the premises of the employer?
2. If the behavior of the grievant was unjustified, was her termination of employment justified by the nature of the violation?

Pertinent Contract Clauses

ARTICLE 4—*Recognition of the Hospital's Right to Manage*

The Union recognizes and agrees that the Hospital retains the sole right to manage and operate the Hospital in all respects and as to all matters in connection with the exercise of such right, subject only to the employee's right to grieve, in accordance to the procedures later provided in this Agreement, if action taken by the Hospital may be claimed, reasonably and sensibly, to be contrary to this Agreement.

All management rights and functions except those which are clearly and expressly abridged by this Agreement, shall remain vested exclusively in the Hospital. It is expressly recognized, merely by way of illustration and not by way of limitation that such rights and functions include, but are not limited to: 1) full and exclusive control of the management of the Hospital, the supervision of all operations, the methods, processes, means and personnel by which any and all work will be performed, the control of property and the composition, assignment, direction and determination of the size and type of its working forces; 2) the right to determine the work to be done and the standards to be met by employees covered by this Agreement; 3) the right to change or introduce new operations, methods, processes, means or facilities and the right to determine whether and to what extent work shall be performed by employees; 4) the right, to hire, establish, and change work schedules, set hours of work, establish, eliminate or change classifications, assign, transfer, promote, demote, release and lay off employees, consistent with other provisions of this agreement; 5) the right to determine the qualification of employees, and to suspend, discipline and discharge employees for just cause and otherwise to maintain an orderly, effective and efficient operation.

ARTICLE 10, Section 3—*Terms and Conditions of Arbitration*

The arbitrator shall have no authority to add to or subtract from or otherwise modify any of the terms of this Agreement.

Except as otherwise provided and limited by this Agreement, no grievance claiming back wages shall exceed the amount of wages the employee otherwise would have earned less any remuneration or payment she may have received during any period of suspension from employment with the Hospital.

ARTICLE 13—*Discipline and Discharge*

Disciplinary action shall include the following: Warning, Written Reprimand, Suspension, and Discharge.

If the employer has reason to formally discipline an employee, it shall be done in an area away from other employees, patients or the public. An employee may be represented by her steward at any time during the disciplinary procedure.

The employer agrees to promptly notify a disciplined employee's steward of such discipline. Notice shall be in writing. A discharged or suspended employee shall, if so instructed, immediately leave the work area and shall not return. The employee will be allowed to discuss her discharge or suspension with her steward for a reasonable period of time before leaving the Hospital. The employer will make an area available for such discussion. The Union may file a grievance concerning a discharge or suspension starting at the fourth step of the grievance procedure. The grievance must be filed within five (5) days of the discharge or suspension.

The employer may review all disciplinary action and in consideration of the employee's record and hospital discipline policy adjust such discipline. If the discipline is increased, the employee will be notified in writing of such and the reasons for such action. Such increase itself shall be subject to grievance. No discipline may be increased after three (3) days from the date of the original discipline except the three (3) day period may be extended by mutual agreement.

Statement of the Facts

There is no basic disagreement between the parties as to the specific facts surrounding the incident which occurred on July 21, 1974. The grievant is a registered nurse employed by the Flint Osteopathic Hospital from June, 1970, until her dismissal July, 1974. Prior to her last assignment with the employer as a staff nurse she was employed as an in-service training program supervisor for the employer.

On July 20, 1974, the grievant reported for her assignment to the second shift. After appearing for work she called the supervisor of her shift and stated that she could not work as the only R.N. on the shift team because of the number of patients and their conditions. After discussing the situation with Ms. Carlson, her supervisor, another R.N. was reassigned to work with her.

After reporting to work the following day, July 21, 1974, she again realized that she was to be the only R.N. on the ward team. She again called Ms. Carlson and told her that she would not accept the responsibilities for the ward by herself. When the grievant was not offered any additional registered nurse assistance on her shift, she reported to Ms. Carlson's office and told her that she could not give the necessary care and therefore would not accept the responsibility for the patients on the ward. The grievant then proceeded to "punch out" and leave the premises of the employer.

By calling in an off-duty supervisor, borrowing another R.N. from the cardiac intensive care unit, and spending more than the normal period of time attending to the patients in the grievant's assigned area, the supervisor of the shift covered the duties which the grievant had refused.

Upon report of the incident to the Assistant Nursing Director, the grievant was given a 3-month suspension. Several days later, after having conferred with representatives of the union, Assistant Administrator, James King, increased the 3-month suspension to termination. Following notification of the termination a grievance was filed leading to the present arbitration proceeding.

Position of the Empoyer

The Hospital's position rests on its management rights to determine the staffing needs, standards of care, and personnel. They argue that the Hospital has the full and absolute right to assign personnel and that there is nothing in the contract contrary to that power. They point to the failure of the Union and the grievant to properly utilize the grievance procedure prior to the grievant's "self help" behavior which they maintained posed a serious threat to the health and welfare of the patients.

The employer argues that claims involving health and safety factors are not related to the grievant and would be the only recognized exception to the duty of an employee to perform the functions of their job and file a grievance later if unhappy. They further point to the conflicting testimony between professional nurses as to whether or not the conditions were potentially unsafe even for patients.

In addressing the discipline review conducted by Mr. King, Assistant Administrator, the Hospital argues that the decision to increase the discipline from 3-months' suspension to termination is justified as fair and reasonable since there was no assurance that the grievant would not repeat her behavior, acceptance of such conduct could lead to similar behavior by other employees, and the grievant had no remorse for her acts but felt fully justified.

Position of the Union

It is the position of the Union that the grievant acted as a professional in refusing to take the responsibility for more patients than she felt in her judgment she could adequately attend to without jeopardizing their health and safety. They argue that the grievant was justified in her actions since the employer was negligent in providing adequate registered nursing staff.

It is argued the situation was not new but had existed and been brought to the attention of the Hospital administration prior to July 21, 1974.

Attention is drawn to the grievant's work history to show that she is both extremely competent and without past disciplinary history.

Findings and Conclusions

There is no dispute between the parties as to the specific facts surrounding the actions that took place on July 21, 1974 involving the grievant. The grievant arrived for work at the regular time of 3:00 p.m. and perceived that she was the only R.N. assigned to work in the unit for her shift. She informed the shift coordinator that unless another registered nurse was assigned to that unit for the shift, she would not accept the responsibility but would leave and go home. When no additional registered nurse was provided in the unit for the shift, the grievant left the Hospital. This occurred at approximately 3:15 p.m.

It was the testimony of the supervisor, Ms. Carlson, that no other R.N.'s were available for reassignment, and in her opinion, the grievant could adequately provide the nursing care necessary in the unit. Conflicting testimony was provided by subsequent witnesses as to whether or not the grievant was assigned responsibilities beyond her capacity to perform and whether there was danger to the health and safety of the patients and the grievant. Ms. Beverly Hampton, Assistant Director of Nursing, testified that in her opinion the grievant was able to adequately give nursing care for the number of patients in the unit. Ms. Helen Malandrinos, Director of Nursing, echoed this opinion when she testified: "[S—] was capable. She was one of the most competent people on our staff."

Contrary evidence was offered by Ms. McCloud who testified "one registered nurse could not give adequate care to any unit with 42 patients." In her opinion she stated "patients would not be safe." She went on to testify that the nurse would be endangering herself because more than one patient could be going into crisis at the same time. Witness Ms. LaVone Suski supported this testimony by offering her opinion that one R.N. could not carry out the care of 42 patients.

While the testimony indicates that there is a difference of professional judgment in the capacity to care for the number of patients in question, the question of the employee's health and safety was given only passing consideration. It is particularly important when judging the actions of the grievant to consider not only professional standards, which are obviously in dispute, but the employment standards by which an employee seeks remedy through "self help" behaviors. The arbitrator is unable to find throughout the testimony that there was immediate danger to the health and safety of the grievant. Attention is drawn to a discussion of this issue of safety and health on pages 672-675 of *How Arbitration Works*, Elkouri and Elkouri (The Bureau of National Affairs; Washington, D.C.) 3rd Edition.

The grievant's "self help" action, where there was no immediate danger to her health and safety, was inappropriate and produced a greater threat to the patients under her care. Although she might have disagreed with the adequacy of the staffing level of registered nurses, the remedy was to file a grievance, not to initiate "self help." The action of the grievant was inappropriate for the conditions and strong disciplinary action was indicated.

In reviewing the level of discipline, attention must be given to the testimony offered by employer witnesses indicating that the "grievant is a very competent nurse" (Carlson), "[S—] was capable. She was one of the most competent people on our staff" (Malandrinos). Attention is also directed to the grievant's employment record which indicates no prior discipline.

AWARD

Based on testimony and evidence, the grievant is found to have acted improperly when she refused to complete her assignment on July 21, 1974 and left the premises of the employer.

In reviewing the discharge discipline, the arbitrator finds, based upon the employee's employment record, that the grievant should be reinstated within ten days following the date of this award with these restrictions: 1) No back pay; 2) Temporary loss of seniority for three months while the grievant serves a probationary period and cannot exercise seniority for job or shift assignment.

Case No. 3

Should discharge be upheld in the case of a Licensed
Practical Nurse who allegedly refused to administed medication
and who behaved "rudely" toward a patient? Was it relevant
that the LPN had never been disciplined before, despite several
years of unsatisfactory work, and that she was "upset"' over
the recent surgery performed on her daughter?

Elizabeth Horton Memorial Hospital (N.Y.)
and
Licensed Practical Nurses of New York, Inc.

Arbitrator: Woodrow J. Sandler
Date of Award: December 18, 1974
Citation: 64 LA 96

The Relevant Contract Provisions

Section 1.03—Management of the Hospital—A. Except as otherwise
provided in this Agreement, the Association agrees that the management of the Hospital, the direction of its working force, and the
exercise of the ordinary and customary functions of management,
whether or not exercised by the Hospital prior to the execution of
this Agreement, shall be in the sole discretion and in the sole responsibility of the Hospital, and the same shall not be subject to
arbitration. Without limiting the generality of the foregoing, the
Hospital shall retain the exclusive right to hire, fire for cause, lay
off. . . .

* * * * *

B. Among the Hospital's prerogatives retained hereby shall be
the right to continue its present employment practices. If a physician

of the Hospital shall certify that any regular LPN constitutes a danger to the health, safety or welfare of the residents of the Hospital, this shall constitute grounds for temporary suspension or discharge, providing the LPN shall have the right to contest same as provided for in Section 1.09 hereof.

Section 1.09—Grievance and Arbitration—A. All grievances of LPN's or disputes over the interpretation, application or performance of the terms of this Agreement shall be processed as follows. . . .

❋ ❋ ❋ ❋ ❋

Step III: If no satisfactory settlement is reached in STEP II, the grievance may then be submitted to arbitration before the New York State Board of Mediation by an arbitrator, staff or panel, duly designated by said Board. Either party may require a panel arbitrator. Demand for arbitration shall be made within two (2) weeks after receipt of the reply of the Administrator in STEP II.

❋ ❋ ❋ ❋ ❋

D. The decision of such arbitrator shall be final and binding on the parties hereto. The arbitrator designated pursuant to the above provisions shall have no right to add to, subtract from, or in any other way modify the terms and provisions of this Agreement. The party shall pay the costs and expenses of their own attorneys, witnesses and stenographers, if any, but the fee and expenses of the arbitrator and of the arbitration shall be divided equally by the parties.

❋ ❋ ❋ ❋ ❋

Section 1.10—Discipline and Discharge—The Hospital shall have the right to discipline or discharge employees for just cause, subject to the grievance and arbitration procedures herein.

The Issue

"Did the Hospital have just cause in the discharge of R— on September 5, 1974? If not, what shall the remedy be?"

R— was hired by the Hospital in October, 1971, as a Licensed Practical Nurse (LPN). She was originally assigned to a medical, surgical floor. Her rating for her work during the first few months of her employment was not good.

A "performance appraisal report" for the period October 4, 1971, to December 15, 1971, made out by a Rose Kujawski, R—'s then supervisor, contained the following comments, typical of the whole: "Does not relate to team leader or head nurse. Does not appear to show any enthusiasm for her job." Appears to be thoughtless at times to patients' needs. . . . If she comes upon a patient who is obviously upset or crying, she appears to have no compassion or even try to find out why the patient may be in this state." "If she has . . . 4 patients assigned to her she may do an excellent job in giving bath and making bed but in such a slow manner the other patients may lack for care until someone is available to finish her assignment." "In conference with employee regarding her performance she does not seem to be aware of any shortcomings on her part. She was unaware of the resentment toward her by other employees. . . ." ". . . she told me she had a hearing problem which she has never to anyone's knowledge, mentioned before . . ." The Report is counter-signed by the assistant director of nursing, who adds: "I concur with both evaluations (two supervisors) and do not feel that any negative comments made were done with any personal feeling. R— has shown some improvement and I would like to see her evaluated in 3 months." Annexed to the appraisal report is the following enigmatic comment by R—: "I have . . . discussed this with my supervisor (printed). I agree with the Task Evaluation because I did not feel free to personal communication. R—." Possibly she overlooked the printed portion and was trying to say that she didn't feel like discussing the report.

Sometime early in 1972, R— was transferred to obstetrics and gynecology. The reasons were that (a) it was a smaller department (b) the patients there were not "sick." Mrs. Mary Bendlin, head nurse of the department, testified that at the time of the transfer, she was told by Mrs. Kujawski that R—'s work was poor, and that she had a poor response to supervision.

In her new department, R— showed some improvement, though qualified. Her first rating sheet for the period ended October 4, 1972 states in part: "R—'s general effectiveness has improved somewhat in the past few months. . . . She is a willing worker and with direction will perform and complete tasks as required. She seems to have a good theoretical background but has difficulty getting her day's work organized, becomes sidetracked very easily, getting involved with other patients. . . . She is capable of calculating dosage of drugs and generally dispenses medicines without difficulty. However, she is hesitant about procedures that should be very routine to her by now." The report was signed by Mrs. M. Bendlin in March, 1973.

A report dated May 1, 1973, signed by Mrs. Grace Barnes, assistant head nurse, who directly supervised R—, states in part concerning the latter: "She never offers to pick up breakfast trays." "The clerk reported to me today that she found her (R—) reading in Room 206 when everybody else is so busy. . . . She is sitting or talking out in the lounge entirely too much when she should be helping with patient care."

Mrs. Bendlin testified at the hearing that R—'s performance deterio-rated during the last year of her employment. She testified that R— "didn't relate well to patients; had a poor bedside manner; that several patients asked to have R— taken off their cases; she required more than normal supervision; and resented supervision."

She testified further that she discussed these matters with R— on numerous occasions, to try and ascertain the reasons, but that R— "often walked away," or else denied the charges. On one occasion, June 14, 1973, she threw an assignment sheet at Mrs. Bendlin. Bendlin further testified that R— didn't carry her normal load[1] and that the other LPN's and nurses aides on the "team" complained about this.

Bendlin further testified that the incidents became more frequent as time went on, and that she would speak to R— about them immediately. The response was usually to deny the charges or to walk away.

She further testified that around August of 1974 she asked R— if she liked the job and the answer was that she did; and that R— didn't seem to be bothered by the fact that some patients asked to have her taken off the case.

Bendlin further testified that R— functioned best with routine pa-tients, but that she was not empathetic; that she never referred to a pa-tient by name and "didn't seem to want to become totally involved;" and that her manner was gruff and unfeeling when she became pressured and upset.

Bendlin, in her testimony, was apparently not relying on her memory, as she and Mrs. Barnes had kept notes of all these "incidents" together with the date they occurred. These notes were all received in evidence at the hearing. It would be repetitious to detail all of them, but some typical entries are summarized herein: On June 14, 1973, R— refused to admit a patient and said someone else, should do it. Bendlin told her if she con-tinued to refuse she would be reported to the nursing office. On August 26, 1973, R— was asked to give a patient a suppository (she was seated in the lounge at the time). She must have refused, because Bendlin told her if she didn't comply with the request, she would report to the nursing office immediately. R— gave the medication.

Mrs. Grace Barnes, assistant head nurse, testified that R— "was never willing to do anything extra" and that she would "walk away" when Barnes remonstrated; that she didn't like R—'s "rough manner" and that she "often had to be quieted down."

---

[1]Bendlin testified that R— took "45-minute breaks."

Two incidents precipitated R—'s discharge. The first, on August 25, 1974, involved a Mrs. K—, who had a stillborn child. R— refused her codeine medication early in the afternoon, which caused the patient to cry. Mrs. Dorothy Ross, nursing supervisor of the entire hospital, testified that Dr. Levinson,[2] Mrs. K—'s physician, called her to complain about this. In a discussion with Mrs. Barnes, R— said she "must have" given the medication, but in view of all the other testimony and the uncertainty of her denial, I find she did not. In a report of the incident, Mrs. Ross stated in part: "She (R—) had not given the patient the medication . . . and failed to report to the charge nurse that the patient was upset and crying."

The second incident occurred on September 1 or 3, 1974. Two patients in Room 210 were in tears and stated that this was because R— had been rude to them. Mrs. Virginia Bruyn, a nursing supervisor, heard from Mrs. Barnes that the two patients, Mrs. A— and Mrs. S—, complained that R— had thrown their towels on their beds and told them to take showers. On the same day, Dr. Allan Rubinstein told Mrs. Bruyn, "I'm sick and tired of patients crying because of R—."[3] Mrs. Bruyn called R— to her office, where the latter denied any provocative behavior. Mrs. Bruyn told her to stay out of Room 210 and "work with a smile."

On the same day, R— refused to do some routine clerical work. She was sent to see Mrs. Bruyn who discussed with her the "professional behavior" required of her. R— "accepted the admonition to control her behavior."

The actual decision to terminate R— was made final on September 5th by Mrs. Edna Wetmore, Director of Nursing Service, and it was based not only upon the incidents of August 25th (Mrs. Kelsh) and September 1st or 3rd (Mrs. Arnold and Mrs. Smith), but on "mistreatment of patients" generally. Mrs. Wetmore testified that she felt that R— had been given "enough rope."

She spoke to R— on September 3rd and told her of the decision to terminate her. R— explained that she had been upset by her daughter's illness.

The discharge was appealed to Mr. John Norton, Administrator of the Hospital. He discussed the matter with R—, who denied that she had thrown the towels down in the manner specified. He also met with Mrs. Wetmore, Barnes, Bendlin, Bruyn, and Drs. Levinson and Rubinstein.

---

[2]Dr. Levinson did not testify, but it was stipulated that the physicians, if called, would confirm the hearsay testimony concerning them.
[3]See previous footnote.

The decision was that R—'s "professional standards were not up to the Hospital's" and that her discharge must be upheld.

The following are relevant excerpts from R—'s final evaluation by Mrs. Bendlin:

> "*Attitude*—seems to be unhappy and irritable a good part of the time on duty—generally resentful of supervision—has a bad effect on team effort in that she is not often willing to help others . . . ." "*Dependability*—cannot be relied on to execute assigned tasks . . . . Does not recognize problem situations or cope with them—cannot be depended on to make a professional decision on a routine problem . . . ." *Response to Supervisors*—Sometimes balky and unresponsive to supervision—When criticized for poor workmanship she may react with casualness or become very vocal and antagonistic. *Potentialities* —Appears to have low potential for future professional growth—Has had adequate time to prove any talent or ability for leadership— Does not attend to development of unit efficiency or productivity. *Personality Limitations*—Possesses a personality that antagonizes some patients and at times fellow staff members—Cannot relate well to patients, lacks capacity for empathy. Her bedside manner and language imply lack of interest. Mechanical in her manner at times. Seldom refers to patients by name—"Bed # 2 with red hair" or "Bed # 1 with the lame husband." Critical of her patients. *General Effectiveness*—Her workmanship, especially in relation to her nursing care has been unsuitable for the unit. She has not been able to handle her work load and pull her weight on the unit, having had more than adequate time to prove herself. *General Comment*—Since the last written evaluation for R—, there has been a definite deterioration in her performance as a staff LPN on the obstetric and gynecology unit. I have not been able to uncover a substantial reason for this from her as a result of confidential conferences. However—needless to say, in view of anecdotes submitted I believe R— to be unsuited to give nursing care on this unit and also unsuited to the position she holds as a staff member.

The Appraisal Report contained the following ratings of R—, as of the beginning of September, 1974:

Attitude—Unsatisfactory
Dependability—Poor
Initiative—Poor
Response to Supervision—Unsatisfactory
Potentialities—Poor
Personality—Poor
General Effectiveness—Poor

The Defense

R— did not testify at any time during the hearing. I draw no inference of any kind from this fact. Her failure to take the stand could conceivably have had no bearing on the issues, but might have stemmed from sheer apprehension.

Nevertheless, her failure to testify leaves the Hospital's testimony undenied, except where the Hospital's own witnesses testified that R—, when confronted, denied certain of the specifications against her. This type of denial does not weigh as heavily as if it had been repeated from the stand, with the customary opportunity for cross-examination.

R—'s one witness was an LPN, Mrs. Emma Barrett. She was asked only about the incident involving Mrs. K— which occurred on August 25, 1974. She testified generally that she saw Mrs. K— during the early part of the day, that she seemed composed and didn't cry or complain about the fact that she had lost her baby. (Mrs. K— had two stillborns before this and also had one normal child). Later on in the day, Barrett said, Mrs. K— was "in pain." Mrs. Barrett then corroborated the Hospital's contention that K— had asked for "medicine" and was given only aspirin (presumably by R—, who was in charge of K—'s medication). Nevertheless, Barrett testified that Mrs. K— had not complained about R— to any supervisor.

At 2:30 P.M., Barrett heard Mrs. K— crying, but didn't ask her why. Dr. Levinson had just left as Barrett entered the room. (He had also been in the room around 9:30 A.M.)

To the extent that Barrett helped R—'s case, her testimony is diluted by the fact that she obviously didn't remain in the room, but was in and out several times during the day.

In other respects, she corroborated testimony that R— had refused codeine and instead gave Mrs. K— aspirin; that Mrs. K— was crying around the time of this refusal; and that Mrs. K— was not crying in the morning.

In extenuation of R—'s behavior, the Association attorney pointed to the fact that, according to the testimony, R—'s daughter had been a patient in this very Hospital in the Spring of 1974, for surgery and this fact had upset R—.

The Association attorney also argued that, by implication, since the Hospital hadn't disciplined or discharged R— at any previous time over the three year period, despite a procession of "incidents", she couldn't have been that bad a nurse. After all, Mrs. Bendlin did testify that R— "got along well with some patients," and some of the testimony does deal with intangibles such as a "bedside manner," "compassion," "empathy," etc.

He argued moreover that even if R— was "at fault" termination was too drastic a remedy. She could have been disciplined and perhaps transferred to another department.

Argument

Apparently, the Hospital does not lightly take steps to terminate an LPN. During the year prior to R—'s termination, only one other LPN was terminated, for absenteeism, and this decision was rescinded.

The supervisory nurses' explanation for the nonimposition of discipline on R— for such a long time was that they hoped, by befriending R— and having confidential chats with her, that she would "shape up" and improve her patient care. After all, the hospital isn't a "factory." It's "product" is human life—recovery from illness and patients' comfort. One nurse less and, in a situation where constant pressure exists, the loss would surely be felt. Better to keep helping, training, in the hope of having one more LPN to assist in this work. If an LPN such as R—, doesn't fully relate to patients, refers to them by bed number rather than by name, is short, or brusque or unsmiling, and is not cooperative generally, possibly she can be helped to attain what is essentially a good nurse's state of mind and attitude by frequent and nonhostile repetition of the conduct deemed desirable.

Ultimately, it is the patients' well-being that is the primary concern of any hospital. They, collectively, more than any individual nurse, are inclined to be irritable, upset, afraid, and often depressed. Their spirits are revived and their recovery speeded by nurses who are interested in them, who enter the room smiling, neat as a pin, and who utter words of encouragement and busy themselves making the patients comfortable.

So, in this case, the supervisors, without apparent rancor, fought to the end of the line to solve the puzzle of R—, and make her into one more smiling, dedicated, cooperative, sympathetic LPN. That they failed appears to be as much to their distress as it no doubt is to R—'s.

Their demeanor in testifying was devoid of resentment or any hostility toward R—, and was, outwardly at least, completely objective. Their words were spoken, like the ghost of Hamlet's father, "more in sorrow than in anger."

The fact that they waited three years before deciding to terminate R— should not and does not militate against the validity of the decision when made. To hold otherwise, I would deem most unjust. R— could not have been lulled into a false sense of security, in view of the numerous times she was spoken to. She must have known about the various "incidents" testified to, as they are called to her attention and corrected as soon as they occurred. By giving her more than average help, over a longer period of time, her supervisors should be praised—not faulted.

Nor could it be alleged that the Hospital was out to "get" R—. It would be a strange way to "get" an employee, to keep her on the job for three years when valid grounds for discipline existed long prior to that.

As to the argument that at most R— should have been disciplined and possibly, transferred, it should be recalled that R— originally was assigned to another department and was transferred to obstetrics because of the same personality traits that she exhibited later. Also, Mrs. Bruyn had testified that R— was sometimes "floated" (loaned) to other departments, but that invariably they complained about her. R— was lacking in fundamentals—basic "musts" for a good nurse in terms of good patient care, and these defects apparently adversely affected her work no matter where in the hospital she was an LPN.

As to her daughter's surgery, it is not clear how long the girl was confined, but certainly it didn't even come close to the three year period of R—'s employ. I believe it occurred towards the end of R—'s employment.

Was There "Just Cause"?

Was temination too drastic a penalty? Did the Hospital have "just cause" for discharging R—?

I find that the decision was not a hasty one; that it was made with full knowledge of the facts; that it was not arbitrary, capricious or discriminatory; that it was made with due deliberation at all levels of management; that the discharged employee was given an opportunity to be heard; that there was no evidence of bias; no "heat" or lack of emotional balance in making the decision; that it was made in good faith after weighing the interests of all concerned—staff, patients and the employee.

The hospital supervisors could reasonably have felt that lesser discipline would have accomplished nothing. On her past record, they could anticipate that R— might very well return from a suspension more hostile than ever. I do not find in the record a syllable to indicate that R— ever felt that any criticism of her was justified; on the contrary, her actions and statements consist solely of denials, self-justifications or indifference.

AWARD

I therefore find and decide that the Hospital had just cause for discharging R—.

Case No. 4

Was a Licensed Practical Nurse who admittedly refused to answer a patient's call and who "backhanded" the head nurse entitled to reinstatement because of the Hospital's failure to follow procedures and give her a hearing prior to discharge?

Women's General Hospital (Cleveland, Ohio)
and
Service, Hospital, Nursing Home and Public Employees Union, Local 47

Arbitrator: Peter DiLeone
Date of Award: November 30, 1973
Citation: LAIG 1028

Submission

This matter was heard October 5, 1973 by the Arbitrator in accordance with the submission agreement referred to in the Clark, McDaniels, and Christian cases. The issue for determination is:

Was the discipline which was administered by the Hospital in the L— matter imposed for just cause?

All parties interested in this matter were present to give evidence and argument. Each of the witnesses for both sides were examined and cross-examined as was the case in the Clark, McDaniels, and Christian cases.

At the conclusion of this case also, the parties wished to file post-hearing briefs which were received in accordance with the agreement reached at the hearing.

L—, the grievant, was employed by the Hospital in 1970 as a Licensed Practical Nurse in the Progressive Patient Care Unit (PPC), under supervision of the Unit's Head Nurse, H. Kisis.

On the afternoon of August 4, 1972, two patients were brought to the PPC Unit. Head Nurse Kisis took the report on the patients and then ordered the grievant to take the "vital signs" of one of them. The grievant did not *immediately* comply, nor did she respond to a patient's bell when ordered to do so moments later. For these reasons, she was charged with insubordination.

Thereafter, according to the Hospital, the grievant was obstreperous and behaved in a progressively insolent manner. The continuing dialogue culminated in an altercation in which the grievant slapped the Head Nurse. It is contended by the Hospital that when Kisis told the grievant to "hush up," the grievant slapped her in the face, which assault, the Hospital claims, is intolerable under any circumstances. The Hospital says that no matter what the record of the grievant, the severity of this conduct justifies discharge without prior warnings as distinguished from anticipated discipline in instances of ordinary insubordination.

The Hospital charges that the grievant's assault upon the Head Nurse was without cognizable provocation.

The grievant testified quite to the contrary. She said that she "backhanded" the Head Nurse only after Kisis had grabbed her by the nose; that her act was an immediate and spontaneous reaction to this unpardonable humiliation.

The incident was reported by the Head Nurse to the Nursing Supervisor, and without hearing or supplemental investigation, the grievant was summarily discharged.

Who is at fault, and is discharge the proper penalty?

The testimony of the grievant appears to be the most creditable. The grievant's account of what happened bears out the fact that heated exchange of words occurred when she declined a direct order near the end of her workday. Her own testimony bears witness to the fact that she disobeyed her superior, refusing to follow instructions concerning a patient's calls. Now it may be that the Head Nurse was overtly impatient with the grievant. It may even have appeared to the grievant that she was being taken advantage of so near the end of her workday. But the inescapable fact is that she did not follow reasonable instructions; and for this, discipline is merited.

The grievant testified that the Head Nurse grabbed her nose and told her to "go *now*" to the patient. The evidence on behalf of the

Hospital denies that such insultingly provoking conduct occurred. Even if we accept the story of the grievant as to what occurred, this Arbitrator does not believe that slapping or backhanding the superior was justified. At the same time, this Arbitrator does not believe that the circumstances of this case warrant the severest penalty.

In retrospect, this entire incident might have been easily resolved had Nursing Supervisor, Miss South, conducted an investigation which could have brought the two employees face to face. It surely was her responsibility to make certain that all employees' rights were safeguarded, including those of the grievant.

It is my judgment that Miss South chose her course of action without a responsible review of the facts. In her high position as a supervisor, she was duty bound to check the truthfulness of the Kisis story before making any decision, and because of her failure to do so, this Arbitrator must overturn the discharge.

The grievant's conduct was reprehensible, but the denial of her right to a fair hearing prior to discharge was fatal to the discipline.

Both parties contributed to the difficulty; Kisis was unreasonably impatient; the grievant was obstreperous and insubordinate. Because the Hospital, through its Supervisor South, failed to conduct an immediate investigation to determine fault and mitigation, the grievant will be reinstated to her job without loss of seniority; and further, because the evidence in this case tends to support the proposition that there could have been an avoidance of the severest penalty if proper steps were taken by the supervisor in the investigation of this case, this Arbitrator must grant partial back pay to the grievant.

AWARD

The discharge is overturned; the grievant shall be reinstated without loss of seniority. But due to the negligence of South, this Arbitrator is awarding one month's back pay.

Case No. 5

Could a nurse who shared responsibility with another nurse
for disobeying a physician's orders to administer medication to
a patient be demoted? Was the Hospital barred from taking
this action by having promoted the other nurse?

The Youngstown Hospital Association (Youngstown, Ohio)
and
The Ohio Nurses Association

Arbitrator: Wayne T. Geissinger
Date of Award: March 31, 1972
Citation: LAIG 605

The Grievance

Under date of January 29, 1971, R—, R.N., filed a grievance stating in part:

* * * * *

DETAILS OF GRIEVANCE: "Demotion from Assistant Head Nurse to General Staff Nurse. Violation of ONA-YHA contract Article 12, Section 2."
RELIEF REQUESTED: "Reinstatement to Assistant Head Nurse."

* * * * *

Pertinent Contract Provisions

ARTICLE I—*Management Rights*
Section 1—The management of the Hospital, the control of the premises, and the direction of the nursing force are vested exclusively with the Hospital. The right to manage includes, but shall not be limited to, the right to hire, transfer, promote, suspend or discharge nurses for just cause. . . .

✿   ✿   ✿   ✿   ✿

ARTICLE XII—*Discipline*

Section 1—The Hospital shall have the right to discipline or discharge any nurse for cause.

Section 2—The Hospital will notify ONA in writing within twenty-four (24) hours of the discharge or suspension or disciplining of any nurse, which notice shall give the reason for the disciplinary action taken.

Section 3—The Hospital recognizes the right of a nurse to appeal disciplinary action through the Grievance Procedure provided for in this Agreement including the reasonableness of any work rule involved. Any grievance relating to a discharge, suspension, or other disciplinary action must be filed by the close of the second (2nd) working day following the working day on which such discharge, suspension, or other disciplinary action occurred or the grievance shall automatically be disallowed. Such grievance shall be placed at Step 2 of the Grievance Procedure and a representative of the ONA may be present at such hearing. If as a result of the processing under the Grievance Procedure the disciplined nurse is found to have been justly dealt with, then the action shall be final; if it is found that the nurse was unjustly suspended or discharged, she shall be reinstated to her former status as of the date of such disciplinary action and, unless otherwise agreed to, paid for all time lost, less the following:

(a) Any unemployment compensation received which she is not obligated to repay as a result of her claim against the Hospital being allowed.

(b) Compensation earned outside the Hospital during the period covered by back-wages allowance.

In the case of a discharge or suspension, the Hospital will recognize a grievance timely initiated by ONA where it can be shown that the nurse affected was unable to file a grievance within the time limits provided because of her incapacitation.

Facts and Background Summarized

The grievant, R—, R.N., was employed as a General Staff Nurse in February, 1960. She was promoted to Assistant Head Nurse in June, 1967. In December, 1970, due to the illness of Head Nurse Reapmaster, the grievant took over the duties of Head Nurse and on January 6, 1971 was temporarily promoted to Acting Head Nurse, a nonbargaining unit position, with the expectation that she would continue in that position as long as the regular Head Nurse was absent on sick leave. In accordance with a joint decision of the Hospital Administrator and the Director of Nursing the grievant was awarded extra pay upon assuming the duties and responsibilities of Acting Head Nurse, contrary to usual and normal practice in cases where an Assistant Head Nurse was called upon to temporarily replace the Head Nurse. No Assistant Head Nurse was assigned during the period the grievant served as Acting Head Nurse.

Beginning with her promotion to Assistant Head Nurse in 1967 the grievant served under and her job performance was evaluated by Head Nurse Reapmaster. It is undisputed that prior to April–May, 1970, the grievant was evaluated as a highly satisfactory and even "exemplary" Assistant Head Nurse. During the April–May period there occurred a series of so-called "incident reports" involving the grievant, relating to the manner in which she performed her duties. These "incidents," their nature, and reasons for them are in dispute and evidence concerning them is conflicting. It is undisputed, however, that the grievant was never formally warned or disciplined in connection with these "incidents" and that the Head Nurse had noted "improvement" prior to going on sick leave in December, 1970. Prior to February 1, 1971 the grievant had never been disciplined as far as the record shows.

On or about February 1, 1971, the grievant was removed as Acting Head Nurse and demoted from Assistant Head Nurse to General Staff Nurse. The "trigger incident" was the so-called "Tomlin Case" of January 23, 1971, wherein the patient was not given medication as ordered by the attending physician. The prescribed medicine was not sent from Pharmacy. Medication Nurse Beda did not notify the grievant. The parties are in complete disagreement as to the relative responsibilities of the grievant and the medication nurse in connection with this incident.

A somewhat similar incident involving the grievant, the so-called "Marioti Case" occurred circa November 27 to December 10, 1970, in which the patient received one instead of two insulin injections as ordered by the physician, due to an improperly prepared medication ticket. Again the relative responsibilities of the grievant and the nurse are in controversy.

Positions of the Parties Summarized

It is the basic position of the *Employer* (The Youngstown Hospital Association) that beginning in early 1970 the grievant's performance fell off rather dramatically in that she became careless and irresponsible in carrying out her duties as Assistant Head Nurse. As a result and in an effort to correct the situation, Head Nurse Reapmaster counseled with the grievant and recorded specific derelictions on so-called "incident reports" in such a manner as to leave the grievant in no doubt that her performance was becoming unacceptable. In December, 1970, when Head Nurse Reapmaster went on sick leave, the grievant as Assistant Head Nurse was in the normal and regular line of progression to fill the resulting vacancy. The duty and obligation of the Assistant Head Nurse to so act is spelled out in the job description for that position and the Employer was simply following routine administrative procedure. The "Tomlin Case" of January, 1971, was the culmination of a series of events which cumulatively justified demotion of the grievant to General Staff Nurse from Assistant Head Nurse. The errors and derelictions were of a sufficiently serious nature to justify removal of the person responsible to a position of lesser responsibility. The demotion was fully justified because the grievant was not meeting the standard of care required of nurses on her floor, much less the standard of care of one in the position of supervisor of other nurses.

The Employer maintains that the demotion was a proper exercise of its contractual rights and should be sustained.

*   *   *   *   *

The Ohio Nurses Association, on behalf of the grievant, does not question the right of the Employer to establish standards for non-bargaining unit, management positions (here, Acting Head Nurse) and to unilaterally remove such management personnel. It concedes the Employer had the right to remove the grievant from the position of Acting Head Nurse for whatever it considered sufficient reason.

It is the basic position of the Nurses Association that the grievant was fully qualified for and had satisfactorily performed the duties of her regular classification, Assistant Head Nurse and that she did nothing to justify a disciplinary demotion from Assistant Head Nurse to General Staff Nurse. Under the contract, the most the Employer could do under the circumstances of this case was to return the grievant to her former position of Assistant Head Nurse. It is not permissible for the Employer to now discipline the grievant for an alleged failure to meet the additional management responsibilities which it unilaterally visited upon her.

It is the further position of the Nurses Association that there was no cause for demotion from Assistant Head Nurse to General Staff Nurse. The grievant had been generally rated "exemplary" over an 11-year period by Head Nurse Reapmaster and less than a month prior to her demotion had been temporarily promoted with extra pay to Acting Head Nurse with approval of the Hospital Administrator and the Director of Nurses. There is therefore no basis for a conclusion that she was not competent and qualified to hold the position of Assistant Head Nurse. The grievant was never disciplined prior to February 1, 1971, and was never told to improve her performance if she expected to avoid discipline. The demotion was improper, arbitrary and unreasonable and the grievant should be reinstated as Assistant Head Nurse and compensated for lost wages.

The Issue

Was the demotion of R— from Assistant Head Nurse to General Staff Nurse for just cause?

Opinion

In arriving at my decision I have given full and careful consideration to the voluminous transcript of the hearing and the excellent briefs of counsel. I have made no effort to restate the testimony and other evidence in detail. I have, however, carefully reviewed the evidence concerning the numerous "incident reports" and the more serious Tomlin and Marioti cases in reaching my conclusions.

Both parties concede that there was a "conflict of personalities" between the grievant and Head Nurse Reapmaster and both draw different conclusions. I have no desire to referee that contest. In view of the general importance to the future relations of the parties I feel it is fair to state that in my opinion the grievant was probably less than cooperative and that the Head Nurse as a result probably applied extra effort to maintain and insist upon high standards of professional performance. Both women doubtless resented each other. It is my conclusion that in her position as Head Nurse Reapmaster had not only the right but the obligation to insist upon high performance standards by all nurses under her, including the grievant. It may well be that her reaction to the grievant as a person caused her to become overzealous in writing up "incident reports" during the April–May period but there doesn't appear to be much question that incidents were as recorded.

There isn't enough evidence available to determine whether Mrs. Reapmaster was unfairly overlooking derelictions of other nurses similar to those charged to the grievant.

It further appears that during the years that Mrs. Reapmaster gave the grievant high marks for performance her ability to evaluate the grievant's performance was not questioned. If, as appears to be the case, the grievant became careless and less efficient in the opinion of Mrs. Reapmaster it is not surprising that Mrs. Reapmaster would feel constrained to write up "incident reports" and otherwise call her deficiencies to the attention of the grievant. I am not persuaded that Mrs. Reapmaster and the Director of Nurses were necessarily engaged in a "plot" or improperly motivated to "get" the grievant. Clearly, they were not satisfied with the grievant's level of performance at the time of the incidents as reflected in Mrs. Reapmaster's documentation. It is also true that the "incident reports," as such, were not disciplinary measures and no formal disciplinary measures were taken. The parties agree that Mrs. Reapmaster runs a "taut ship," demands high performance standards, and that there was a "personality conflict". A personality conflict is a two-way street and the evidence will not support a finding that because of possible personal dislike the grievant was required to meet higher standards than normally required of others.

This case, however, does not turn on the "personality conflict" issue. It is clear from the evidence that, in December, 1970, the grievant had not been disciplined or otherwise penalized for poor or substandard performance and that Mrs. Reapmaster, her immediate superior, appeared to feel that she was showing improvement. There is nothing in the record to indicate that the grievant was on the verge of demotion from Assistant Head Nurse to General Staff Nurse or that she had been given reason to believe that she was. She certainly must have been aware that Mrs. Reapmaster was not entirely satisfied with her overall performance during a large part of 1970 but there was nothing to indicate that formal disciplinary action was imminent.

It is undisputed that the grievant took over as Acting Head Nurse when Mrs. Reapmaster went on sick leave and that on January 6, 1971 she became temporary Acting Head Nurse with a grant of extra pay not required by contract or normally given in such cases. If, as contended by the Employer, this was not a true promotion but simply a routine extension of the regular job duties of an Assistant Head Nurse, why the additional pay? Had the Employer simply required the grievant to fill in as Head Nurse until another could be selected, the contention that the grievant had an unsatisfactory, substandard performance record would carry more weight. The only conclusion I can draw is that, with all her sins, the grievant was considered competent and qualified to serve as Acting Head Nurse at that time, whether you call it a promotion or not. I find it hard to accept that an Assistant Head Nurse of dubious ability would be advanced to Head Nurse unless on an interim, emergency basis. There is nothing in the evidence to indicate that this was the case here. I think the conclusion must be accepted that as of January 6, 1971 the grievant was considered by her Employer to be a qualified, competent Assistant Head Nurse, of sufficient experience and ability to serve as temporary Acting Head Nurse. Admitting that her "exemplary" halo may have slipped a bit during 1970 it does not follow that her performance fell below levels required for retention as Assistant Head Nurse. She may not have been as good as she could have been but she wasn't bad enough to justify demotion at that time or she wouldn't have been made Acting Head Nurse.

The next question is whether the "Tomlin Case" of January 23, 1971 was sufficient justification for demotion from Assistant Head Nurse to General Staff Nurse. It is my conclusion that both the grievant and Medication Nurse Beda were at fault. The Medication Nurse was at fault in the first instance but unquestionably the grievant had the ultimate responsibility for errors of her subordinates. The evidence further shows that following the grievant's demotion a few days later, admittedly triggered by this incident, Medication Nurse Beda was promoted to the vacancy as Assistant Head Nurse. I can accept as reasonable the removal of the grievant as Acting Head Nurse for her part in the incident, but not her demotion from Assistant Head Nurse to General Staff Nurse. The Employer, by elevating Medication Nurse Beda to Assistant Head Nurse quite obviously did not consider the Tomlin error, as such, a disqualifying factor for the Assistant Head Nurse position. Further, the Tomlin incident took place at a time when the grievant was the de facto Head Nurse and did not have the help and support of an Assistant Head Nurse.

It is undisputed that the position of Head Nurse is a nonbargaining unit position not covered by the Agreement or the "just cause" requirements. There is no contention that the Employer did not have the right to remove the grievant from the position and title of Acting Head Nurse. When so removed she reverted to her regular position and/or classification of Assistant Head Nurse and the demotion from Assistant Head Nurse to General Staff Nurse must meet the requirements of the Agreement. In other words the demotion must be for "just cause".

The Employer's decision to demote was based on the principle that the Tomlin incident was the "last straw" in a series of incidents which cumulatively constituted just cause for demotion. The reasonableness of this decision must be weighed against the record which shows that although the grievant's standard of performance had declined earlier in the year, there had been subsequent improvement to the extent that the grievant was in effect promoted to a position of higher responsibility. This action is not consistent with a position that the grievant was on the verge of discipline and demotion for unsatisfactory performance as an Assistant Head Nurse.

It is my finding that demotion of the grievant from Assistant Head Nurse to General Staff Nurse was not for "just cause" within the meaning of the Agreement.

AWARD

The grievance of R— is sustained for the reasons given in the opinion.

It is awarded that she be reinstated as Assistant Head Nurse and reimbursed for the difference between the pay of Assistant Head Nurse and General Staff Nurse from the date of her demotion and the date of reinstatement.

Case No. 6

*Did a Hospital policy stating that an employee witnessing an
accident must accompany the patient to the emergency room
justify the discharge of an employee who, not having witnessed
the accident, refused a supervisor's order to accompany
the patient to the emergency room?*

City of Memphis Hospital Authority (Memphis, Tenn.)
and
American Federation of State, County and Municipal Employees,
Local 1733

Arbitrator: Samuel S. Perry
Date of Award: November 12, 1974
Citation: LAIG 1211

The Grievance

The grievance was submitted to the Impartial Arbitrator by Memphis
Public Employees, Local #1733 AFSCME, Grievance Form, dated March
15, 1974 (Joint Exhibit #2) which states as follows:

Aggrieved Employee Name Mrs. F—
Address 1877 Patrick Rd. Phone 743-3043 Dept. Blood Bank.
Class. (Title) L.P.N. Phlebotomist. Shift 8-4. Date Employed 1-9-60.
Art. and/or Section of Contract Violated Arts. 7 Sec. 4, Art. 3.
Brief Statement and Nature of Grievance—Mrs. F— was unjustly
terminated. Remedy or Disposition Requested: That Mrs. F— be
reinstated with no loss of pay or any other benefits.

The Hospital submitted its Third Step Grievance Response (Hospital Exhibit #1) to the Union by letter dated April 5, 1974, which stated as follows:

1. Nature of Grievance: Violation of Articles III and VII. In that Mrs. F— was unjustly terminated.
2. Disposition Requested: That Mrs. F— be reinstated with no loss of pay or other benefits.
3. Disposition of Grievance: The grievance is denied. The employee refused a direct request to take a patient to the Emergency Room and it is widely known among the hospital employees that refusal to perform a work assignment is a dischargeable offense. It is commonly recognized that when an employee is given an order or a direction with which he or she disagrees, he or she is to perform that order and then later file a grievance. The employee's flat refusal to carry out the order is insubordination which justifies discharge. In this case, the order given to the employee involved what the physician felt could be an emergency situation and which could have literally meant the difference between life and death. Insubordination or refusal by an employee to carry out orders to care for patients can have disastrous consequences both for the patient and for the hospital which would be liable to civil suit for neglect of duty. Mrs. F—'s action in this case was simply inexcusable. The Hospital would have been derelict in its duties to the patient as well as to Mrs. F—'s fellow employees had it not invoked the discipline it did in this case. Care of patients is the Hospital's sole reason for existence. If the Hospital were put into a situation where it could not act *immediately* in response to patients' needs, its ability to care properly for the patients would be severely jeopardized.

The Union submitted a letter to the Hospital by certified mail dated April 18, 1974, wherein the Union alleged that the Hospital has violated Article 5 of the Agreement. (Joint Exhibit #3) The letter states as follows:

Dear Mr. Lipes:
The Agreement between the Hospital Authority and Local 1733, Article 5, is very clear as to the time in which the Union and the Administration are to present and answer grievances.
On March 21, 1974, at 10:00 A.M., a grievance hearing was held for Mrs. F—, in which you had ten (10) days to answer the grievance.
The Administration has violated Article 5, because we received your response on April 17, 1974, nineteen (19) working days after the hearing, therefore, we are demanding that the grievance be

upheld in favor of the aggrieved employee, (Mrs. F—) at arbitration. Your cooperation in this matter is appreciated.

Issue

Whether grievant, F—, has been discharged in accordance with the provisions of the agreement between the Hospital and the Union and with just cause (Joint Exhibit #1).

Pertinent Provisions of the Contract

ARTICLE 3—*Employee Rights*

The union and the employer agree that no employee shall be discriminated against or discharged because of Union membership, sex, marital status, race, religion, creed, national origin, political affiliation or for exercising the use of the grievance procedure.

Nothing in this Agreement can be construed to require an employee to join the Union or any other employee organization. Neither the Union nor the Authority shall coerce or intimidate any employee in the exercise of his right to join or not to join the union. Neither shall either party to this Memorandum coerce, intimidate or in any other manner discriminate against any employee who exercises his rights to join or not to join, or to continue or not to continue, membership in the union. No employee shall be denied promotion or any other benefit because of his membership in the union. Nothing, however, shall prevent an employee, acting in his individual capacity, from presenting any grievance to his supervisors. The terms of any settlement reached pursuant to the grievance procedure herein shall be filed in the appropriate personnel office, with a copy to the union, and shall be available as a matter of public record. (Joint Exhibit #1, page 5)

ARTICLE 5—*Grievance Procedure*

Section I. Any grievance or dispute which may arise between the Authority or its representatives and employees covered by this Agreement, over the application, meaning or interpretation of this Agreement, shall be settled in the following manner:

Step III. If the grievance still remains unsettled, it shall be presented by the Union representative, Chapter Chairman, Chief

Steward and aggrieved employee to the Administrator or his designated representatives, within seven (7) days after the response of the department head in Step II. If the grievance is not appealed to the Administrator or his designated representatives within seven (7) days, the grievance will be considered settled on the basis of the department head's answer in Step II.

The Administrator or his designated representative, has *ten (10 days)* (italics added) to respond to the grievance. If the Administrator or his designated representative *fails to meet and respond within ten (10) days* (italics added) the grievance shall be upheld in favor of the aggrieved at arbitration. (Joint Exhibit #1, page 5)

ARTICLE 7—*Discipline and Discharge*

Section I. Disciplinary actions or measures shall involve only the following:
  A. Oral reprimand
  B. Written reprimand
  C. Suspension, not to exceed ten (10) days
       (notice to be given in writing)
  D. Discharge

Section II. A formal oral reprimand may be given to an employee, but must be given in the presence of a steward, and said discussion will not become a part of his record.

Section III. The employer shall not suspend or discharge any employee without just cause. In any case involving discharge, the employee may contest the suspension or discharge and may elect to use the grievance procedure or the Civil Service procedure.

Section IV. The employee, his steward, and the union will be notified in writing that the employee has been suspended and is subject to discharge. The notice should set forth the reasons for the disciplinary action. Notice to the employee and the union shall satisfy technical complaints.

Section V. If the employee goes twelve (12) months with no disciplinary action having been taken against him, all previous records of disciplinary action shall be void for the purpose of administering progressive discipline.

Section VI. The employee and his steward shall have the right to take the suspension or discharge to the third step of the grievance procedure and the matter shall be handled in accordance with this procedure through the arbitration step, if necessary. (Joint Exhibit #1, pages 9 and 10)

ARTICLE 37—*Management Rights*

Nothing contained in this or other articles of this Memorandum of Understanding shall be construed to limit the Authority's exclusive rights of management, including, but not limited to, the exclusive right to determine the purpose and duties of each of its agencies; to set the standards of services to be offered to its citizens; to enter into any contracts for hospital business; and to exercise control and discretion over its organization and employees, so long as the determination does not violate this Memorandum of Understanding.

It is also the right of the Authority to direct their employees; to hire, promote, transfer, assign, or retain employees in positions within an agency or department: *and to establish reasonable work rules. However, any work rule change that affects an established system shall be discussed with the proper Union committee in advance of the change.* (italics added)

The Authority also has the right to suspend, demote, discharge or take appropriate disciplinary action against its employees for *just cause and in accordance with the provisions of this Memorandum of Understanding.* (italics added) or other applicable ordinances. regulations and statutes, and to relieve its employees from duty in the event of lack of work, funds, or for other legitimate reasons; provided, however, that nothing contained in this article shall be deemed to deny the right of any employee to submit a grievance concerning the application or interpretation of this Memorandum of Understanding of a claimed violation, mis-interpretation, or mis-application of the rules or regulations of the Authority affecting the terms and conditions of employment.

Nothing set forth in this Memorandum of Understanding shall be deemed a waiver of authority granted to the Memphis and Shelby County Hospital Authority pursuant to the laws of the State of Tennessee, County of Shelby, or City of Memphis. (Joint Exhibit #1, pages 28 and 29)

Facts and Background

The Grievant, F—, has been employed by the Hospital for approximately 14½ years. She is a Licensed Practical Nurse–Phlebotomist and has been employed in the Donor Area of the Blood Bank in the Hospital. The Grievant testified that she was considered to be the Charge Nurse in the Donor Area and received a $25.00 per month differential in pay. The Grievant further testified that her duties in the Donor Room included training of personnel working in the Donor Area and that the other Licensed Practical Nurses working in the Donor Area were considered to be under her supervision.

On or about March 5, 1974, while Grievant was on duty in the Donor Room of the Blood Bank, a donor, who had given blood, became faint and passed out. It was determined that the donor required further medical examination and a request was made to the Grievant that she accompany the donor to the Emergency Room. It is alleged that Grievant refused to accompany the donor to the Emergency Room and as a result of her alleged refusal, the Grievant was discharged from her employment with the Hospital. Grievant denies that she refused to take the donor to the Emergency Room.

From this disagreement, the parties completed the grievance procedure which culminated in this arbitration.

Position of the Union

The position of the Union is that the Hospital violated the provisions of the Agreement (Joint Exhibit #1) when the Hospital discharged the Grivant, F—, for what the Hospital has alleged to be a dischargeable offense, to-wit: refusal of Grievant to perform a work assignment (Hospital Exhibit #1).

The Union further contends that the Grievant was not discharged pursuant to Article 7 of the Agreement (Joint Exhibit #1) and that the Hospital has not complied with the provisions of Article 5, Section I, Step III of the Agreement (Joint Exhibit #1), in processing this grievance and therefore the grievance should be decided in favor of the Grievant.

Position of the Hospital

The Hospital contends that the Grievant, F—, was discharged in accordance with the provisions of the Agreement for insubordination in that Grievant refused to perform a job assignment and that the refusal of Grievant to carry out an order to care for a patient could have led to disastrous consequences both for the patient and for the hospital.

The Hospital further contends that they have complied with Article 5, Section I, Step III of the Agreement (Joint Exhibit #1). The Hospital alleges that with the acquiescence of the Union, they interpreted Article 5, Section I, Step III of the Agreement (Joint Exhibit #1) to mean ten business (not calendar) days to respond to the grievance.

The Hospital further contends that in the months prior to the incident on March 5, 1974, the Grievant had become a disgruntled, emotional, and increasingly unreliable employee.

The Hospital further contends that the Grievant's charges of racial discrimination were unfounded.

Discussion and Opinion

The issues to be resolved in this case are: (a) whether or not the discharge of Grievant by the Hospital has been done pursuant to the Agreement (Joint Exhibit #1); (b) whether or not racial discrimination may have had any bearing on this discharge and to what degree the tension growing from such racial discrimination, if there be any, may have influenced the actions of the parties involved; and (c) whether or not the Hospital has properly interpreted Article 5, Section I, Step III, of the Agreement (Joint Exhibit #1).

The Hospital has offered testimony through Aaron D. Carter, Assistant Chief Medical Technologist in the Blood Bank, that he has been the Assistant Chief Medical Technologist in the Blood Bank since February 12, 1973; that the Blood Bank included a Donor Room, which was staffed by three Licensed Practical Nurses and one Medical Technologist. On or about March 5, 1974, Grievant was on duty in the Donor Room. Mrs. Marie V. Washington, another Licensed Practical Nurse was also on duty, having arrived for duty approximately twenty minutes before the incident which is at issue in this arbitration occurred.

According to other testimony, the Grievant had started work in the Donor Room on March 5, 1974 at 7:45 a.m., and worked alone until 10:00 a.m. at which time Mrs. Marie V. Washington, one of the other Licensed Practical Nurses assigned to the Donor Room, reported for duty.

Testimony further indicates that just prior to the incident which is the subject of this arbitration, there were Donors in all of the chairs in the Donor Room (6 chairs) who had just completed giving blood, and these Donors were then being paid by Marie V. Washington, LPN. Grievant, at this time, was not physically present in the Donor Room, but was in an adjoining office with Rosie M. Fowler and Edith Burford. Marie V. Washington was present and at approximately 10:20 a.m. as she was paying the Donors, one of them became faint, fell to the floor striking his head. Marie V. Washington saw the man fall and went for a stretcher. Grievant heard the Donor fall and rushed from the office to the Donor Room to assist the Donor. Shortly thereafter, James R. Barnawell, MD, the medical doctor who was assigned to the Blood Bank arrived and made an examination of the Donor while he was still on the floor.

The Doctor made an examination of the Donor; checked his vital signs, eyes, heart, etc., and determined that Donor was in no immediate distress. The Doctor was told that the Donor had become faint and hit his head. The Doctor examined Donor's head for cuts and whether it was safe to transfer Donor to another location in the Hospital for a more thorough examination. The Doctor was of the opinion, after the examination, that the Donor should be transported to the Emergency Room on a stretcher for further examination. The Doctor recommended that someone trained in medical technique should accompany the Donor to the Emergency Room.

There does exist within the Hospital a messenger service which is generally used for the transporting of patients, but the messenger service personnel are not medically trained.

Testimony indicated that the Secretary, Rosie M. Fowler had been told to call messenger service and had done so. Messenger Service had not arrived when Aaron D. Carter, Assistant Chief Medical Technologist told the Grievant that Donor had to be taken to the Emergency Room and requested that Grievant accompany the Donor to the Emergency Room.

According to the testimony of Aaron D. Carter, the Grievant stated that she did not have a job description in the Blood Bank, did not feel this was her responsibility and requested that a Union Steward be called.

According to testimony by James R. Barnawell, MD, he heard Grievant say, "I can't, I'm too busy or I have something else to do." The Doctor stated that he was not certain these were Grievant's exact words.

According to testimony offered by Rosie M. Fowler, Aaron D. Carter asked the Grievant to take the Donor to the Emergency Room and she heard the Grievant ask for a Union Steward.

The Grievant testified that she told Carter she was busy and Carter said let the Donors wait and Grievant said, I have been working by myself, can't you take him to Emergency; wait just a moment, let me call the Stewardess and Carter said that's ok F—, I'll carry him myself and Grievant said that's ok I'll carry him and Carter said that's ok and Doctor Barnawell and he carried him (Donor) to the Emergency Room.

As a result of this dispute as to the transporting of the Donor to the Emergency Room, the Grievant was discharged as an Employee of the Hospital by the Chief Medical Technologist for insubordination in not giving proper patient care.

It is generally conceded by witnesses for both the Hospital and the Union the Grievant was considered to be the "Charge Nurse" in the Donor Room and other LPN's employed in the Donor Room were under the supervision of the Grievant.

Testimony elicited further indicated that Grievant had been a long term employee (approximately 14½ years) and generally had a rather exemplary work record, including a letter of excellence from the Mayor of the City of Memphis for drawing blood. The work record of the Grievant contains no record of previous reprimands, oral or written, although Diane Poe McAfee, Chief Medical Technologist, who is in charge of the Blood Bank, including the Donor Room, testified that although she had never previously formally disciplined the Grievant, she had counselled her.

Testimony seems to indicate that until approximately July, 1973, Grievant was an excellent worker and her work was well done. In June of 1973, Grievant was placed on medical leave and when she returned in July, Grievant seemed unable to handle pressure-type situations, especially situations involving racial matters. No action was taken by the Supervisors of the Grievant, other than counselling her.

Testimony has been offered of an incident which occurred on or about Saturday, February 16, 1974, relative to taking the blood from a proposed Donor. It seems the Grievant initially refused to take blood from the Donor because in the opinion of the Grievant, the Donor was too pale. The proposed Donor then went to William D. Marbury, Assistant Director of Engineering, who was serving as Duty Administrator on that day and inquired as to why his blood could not be taken. Mr. Marbury then contacted Rita Robbins, Associate Administrator–Head Nurse and Doris Walker, Director of Nursing, and asked whether a person could look at a person and tell whether to take his blood without a test. The Nurses indicated this was not possible. Mr. Marbury went to the Blood Bank with the proposed Donor and talked to the Grievant about taking the blood of the proposed Donor. A Doctor Shively was called about the blood level (hemoglobin). This test had not been made and after the blood level was checked blood was taken from the Donor. A report of this incident was made to the Administrator, by the Duty Administrator, but no action was ever taken against the Grievant.

Throughout this oral hearing, testimony seems to indicate an undercurrent of racial discrimination existing in the Blood Bank which was being practiced in a very settled manner. Testimony was offered that there had been discussions going on for sometime between the Union and the Hospital as to such alleged practices. Testimony by witnesses offered by both parties indicates that there was tension in the Blood Bank directly related to racial matters. It appears that all parties employed in the Blood Bank were aware of these racial tensions and both the Chief Medical Technologist and Assistant Chief Medical Technologist had on occasions counselled with the Grievant, although no formal action was ever taken against the Grievant, nor were steps taken to alleviate the tension situation which was developing in the Blood Bank.

The Union also contends that the Hospital has violated Article 5, Section I, Step III, of the Agreement (Joint Exhibit #1) in that the Hospital has failed to respond to the grievance within ten (10) days and the grievance should be upheld in favor of the aggrieved for this reason.

It is the opinion of this Arbitrator that it would be a very narrow and technical decision to hold in favor of the Grievant, if there does in fact exist a violation of this Article 5 by the Hospital.

The Arbitrator in this case, must agree with the argument set forth in the Brief of the Hospital as to time limitation contained in Article 5, Section I, Step III of the Agreement (Joint Exhibit #1). The contractual language is ambiguous as to the time limitation.

As set forth in the Brief of the Hospital and as stated by Paul H. Sanders, Arbitrator, *In Re: Globe-Wernicke Company (Cincinnati, Ohio) and Allied Industrial Workers, Local 382*, 33 LA 555:

> It is a well-known rule of construction that language should be construed strictly to avoid forfeiture. This does not mean that the plain language of a contract should be set aside, but it does mean that any doubtful question of interpretation should be resolved against a forfeiture rather than in its favor. The parties in this instance have provided some specific time limits for the processing of grievances and it is recognized that such contractural arrangements should be rigidly carried out where the facts fall within the clear language of the Contract. Nevertheless, there is an underlying purpose to such provisions which should be kept in mind—that is, that they are inserted for the purpose of preventing delay in processing. They are not designed primarily with the idea of being a trap for the unwary.

Time limitations such as the ten (10) days limitation in Article 5, Section I, Step III, of the Agreement (Joint Exhibit #1) requiring the Administrator or his designated representative to respond, are in effect, "statutes of limitations" imposed by the parties upon themselves, and under ordinary circumstances they should be strictly observed. In the instant case, testimony has been offered that there were extenuating circumstances which might have made it impossible for the Hospital to comply with the time limit (Union office closed on April 4, 1974, for Martin Luther King, Jr. Day March).

The Hospital has offered testimony that the Union has previously acquiesced to the Hospital's interpretation of the time limitation.

The Hospital further contends that the Union has failed to resolve any doubts as to the interpretation of the contractual time limits in previous cases and this should preclude the Union from raising this issue at this proceeding.

The Union has offered no evidence or testimony to deny the allegations made by the Hospital as to the time limitations.

The Arbitrator has reviewed Article 5 of the Agreement (Joint Exhibit #1) and the argument offered by both parties in their Brief.

The Arbitrator is of the opinion that Article 5 of the Agreement (Joint Exhibit #1) lacks clarity and that the language should more clearly spell out as to whether the parties are speaking of "ten (10) working days" based on a five (5) day work week or ten (10) consecutive calendar days, so as to clearly set forth the intent of the parties as to "time limitations."

In reviewing the Agreement (Joint Exhibit #1) and the letter from the Union to the Hospital, dated April 18, 1974 (Joint Exhibit #3), it appears to this Arbitrator that should the time limit be interpreted to mean ten (10) calendar days, the Hospital response was due on March 31 and should the time limit be interpreted to mean ten (10) working days based on a five (5) day work week, the Hospital response was due April 4.

It is the contention of the Union that they received the response from the Hospital nineteen (19) working days after the hearing. This contention has been borne out by testimony from witnesses offered by both the Hospital and the Union and by evidence offered by the Union (Union Exhibit #1—letter from Hospital to Union dated April 5, 1974 with note from Jane Martin).

Because of the lack of clarity in the contractual language as to the time limit limitations and the prior acquiescence of the Union to the Hospital's interpretation of the time limitation, it is the opinion of this Arbitrator, that it would be in the best interest of the parties that this matter be decided on its merits to insure labor peace, rather than on narrow, technical grounds.

The Arbitrator finds that when the donor fell and struck his head in the Donor Room, the incident was witnessed by Mrs. Marie V. Washington, that the Grievant was not present to see the incident when it occurred.

Hospital policy dictates that the hospital employee who witnessed the incident should accompany the patient to the Emergency Room. Hospital policy further dictates that the employee who witnesses the incident should prepare the incident report.

In the instant case, the person who witnessed the incident was not requested to accompany the patient to the Emergency Room and the incident report was not prepared by the person who witnessed the incident.

Considerable testimony has been offered by witnesses for both parties which would tend to indicate that there existed considerable tension within the Blood Bank because of racial differences. It would seem that positive action would or should have been taken by the persons administratively in charge of the Blood Bank to solve or at least to alleviate the situation. Testimony seems to indicate that from time to time, the persons involved were counselled or "talked to" but no action was ever taken openly to "set the tone" for the entire Blood Bank, to let all employees know that racial harmony was the policy of the Hospital.

An incident has been recited by William D. Marbury, wherein the Grievant initially refused to take the blood of a prospective donor because in the opinion of the Grievant, the donor appeared too pale or too "white".

It would seem to this Arbitrator that Grievant in drawing blood from a donor when a medical doctor is not present on the premises of the Blood Bank may be exceeding the limits of her training, duties and responsibilities. Testimony has been offered by the Hospital that a medical doctor should be present in the Blood Bank when blood is being taken.

It is the opinion of this Arbitrator that there were extenuating circumstances in this case, surrounding the discharge of the Grievant, which must be considered. The Grievant was a long term employee (14½ years) and she previously had an "unblemished" record.

Article 7 of the Agreement, Section I (Joint Exhibit #1), sets forth what this Arbitrator interpreted to be "progressive discipline," with discharge being the final step.

The Grievant did not witness the incident for which she was discharged. The Medical Doctor testified that based on his examination of the Donor, the Donor was in no immediate distress. The policy of the Hospital appears to be that in case of an emergency, any employee may accompany a patient to the Emergency Room. The Supervisory personnel in the Blood Bank were fully aware of the Grievant's ability after her return to duty from medical leave in July, 1973, to handle pressure type situations, especially where the situation related to racial conflicts and yet no formal action was taken by the Supervisory personnel, prior to March 5, 1974. With this in mind it is the opinion of this Arbitrator that discharge in this case is too severe. The Grievant should have received a lesser penalty. It must be concluded that the Grievant was improperly discharged and without just cause.

AWARD

The grievance of F— is sustained. In light of the evidence presented, a penalty of a Written Reprimand is deemed to be more reasonable and proper to correct the employee's deficiencies.

It is therefore awarded that the discharge penalty be vacated and converted to a Written Reprimand; that Grievant be reinstated to her job with full back pay and benefits; that the Hospital prepare a written reprimand to become a part of grievant's personnel record, pursuant to Article 7 of the Agreement (Joint Exhibit #1); that said Written Reprimand shall be effective March 6, 1974.

Part II

Improper

Patient and

Public

Relations

Case No. 7

*What was the proper penalty to impose on a nurses aide
who executed a procedure which only registered nurses are
permitted to perform? Was the aide's conduct excusable
because the Hospital failed to issue instructions which warn
against forbidden procedures and because nurses often gave
improper assignments to aides?*

Grace Hospital, Northwest Unit (Detroit, Mich.)
and
Service Employees International Union, Local 79

Arbitrator: Harry N. Casselman
Date of Award: November 10, 1971
Citation: LAIG 330

Issue

Did the Hospital have just cause for discharging Grievant I—
from her job as a nurses aide in the latter part of February or early
March, 1971? If not, what is the appropriate remedy?

Pertinent Contract Provisions

Preamble

It is the purpose of this Agreement to reduce to writing the
understanding of the parties regarding wages, hours and working
conditions of employees of the Hospital's Central and Northwest
Units who are covered by this Agreement. The parties agree that
the total welfare of the patients of the Hospital is of paramount

importance. Both parties pledge to devote their best efforts to serving the patients of the Hospital. All employees of the Hospital shall be of fit character and shall conduct themselves in a proper manner.

The Hospital recognizes that its employees covered by this Agreement are entitled to and should receive such wages, hours and working conditions as are consistent with efficient and economical administration of the Hospital and the rendering of optimum services to patients.

ARTICLE XVII—*Hospital Rights*

Section 2. The Hospital, in addition to the rights set forth in Section 1 above, shall have the right to promote, assign, transfer, suspend, discipline, discharge, lay off and recall, to make and establish work rules and rules of conduct and fix and determine penalties for violation of such rules, to maintain discipline and efficiency among employees, and to establish and assign relief personnel; provided that such rights shall not be exercised by the Hospital in contravention of any of the express provisions of this Agreement. All of the rights of the Hospital set forth in this Section 2 shall be subject to the grievance procedure set forth in this Agreement.

Grievant, L—, has been employed at Grace Hospital as a nurses aide for approximately five years. At the time she started to work, there was no training program for aides, but Grievant has voluntarily attended training sessions on sterile techniques, bedside care of patients and other matters related to her work. Grievant testified without contradiction that she has never been reprimanded or disciplined concerning her work and had been commended and praised by Mrs. Hugill (R.N.), her floor supervisor and by others for diligence in patient care beyond the call of her normal duty.

The instant case involves an Obstetrical patient in bed (1), Room 251, Northwest Unit, Grace Hospital. This patient had been recently delivered of a baby. On the day in question, in late February, or early March, 1971, which was not specifically fixed by the testimony, Grievant was assigned the care of this patient among her duties. In accordance with Grievant's uncontroverted testimony, at about 4:00 p.m., the patient notified Mrs. L— that she had not urinated since 2:00 p.m. and was uncomfortable. Grievant reported this to the charge nurse, Mrs. Hugill (R.N.) who told Grievant not to worry. Shortly after 6:00 p.m. Grievant again saw this patient. Again the patient complained about her failure to urinate and complained of stomach pain after having consumed four glasses of water and pop. She assisted the patient to the bathroom, but she could not void. Grievant again reported the situation to Mrs. Hugill and was again told not to worry. Shortly before 10:00 p.m., Grievant again saw the patient in question, her complaint still continued. Grievant again reported to Mrs. Hugill who said she would give the patient a sleeping pill and a pain pill and she would be all right.

Shortly afterward, Grievant overheard Mrs. Hugill direct Mrs. May Wells (LPN) to catheterize the patient in Room 251, Bed 1. Grievant went to her utility rooms to clean sinks as assigned; when Mrs. Wells asked her to help with the catheterization, Grievant remarked that the job was Mrs. Wells' and not hers. Mrs. Wells told her to come since it was her patient. Grievant complied.

Mrs. Wells brought in a catheterization tray and directed Grievant to have the patient drink more water. Grievant told her how much water the patient had consumed, but Mrs. Wells insisted that she drink more and that Grievant assist her to the bathroom. The patient drank five more glasses and yelled that she didn't want Mrs. Wells in the room. The trip to the bathroom was unavailing. Finally, Mrs. Wells tried to insert the catheter, but was unsuccessful in two attempts. Grievant suggested Mrs. Hugill be called, but Mrs. Wells said, "No, not her." She then sent Grievant for another tray. Again her probing attempts were unsuccessful.

Mrs. Wells asked Grievant to call Miss Sorrentino, a student nurse. The latter is in her fifth year at Wayne University, and expects to receive her bachelors degree next year. Miss Sorrentino has been employed at the hospital for one and one-half years as a nurses assistant.

A third catheter tray was brought in by Grievant and Mrs. Wells asked Miss Sorrentino to try to relieve the patient. Miss Sorrentino stated that she had very little experience, but would try.

The testimony at this point is controverted. Grievant testified that Miss Sorrentino got the catheter part way in, but it would not go the necessary distance into the bladder without resistance. Mrs. Wells then left the room to get an OB nurse experienced in catheterizing patients. According to Grievant, Miss Sorrentino said, "L—, you try." Sorrentino told the patient to push on her abdomen. Grievant testified that the catheter was part way in, she pushed the catheter one-half an inch and put the other end into the urine cup. Miss Sorrentino said, "There's urine in the cup."

According to Mrs. Wells' testimony, Grievant interrupted her effort to get an OB nurse by yelling, "You couldn't do it, the student nurse couldn't, so I did it." She returned and accused Grievant of catheterizing the patient; she did not chart the procedure because she didn't perform it and she was upset as to who would chart it. Mrs. Wells told Grievant that she intended to report her.

Miss Sorrentino testified that she observed Mrs. Wells attempt the procedure and meet resistance and that she encountered the same problem when she tried with a new catheter which she withdrew. She testified that she looked around to locate Mrs. Wells and when she looked again, Grievant had her hand on the catheter and urine was draining into the tray. Grievant then called Mrs. Wells and made the statement, "You couldn't do it, the student couldn't do it, but I did it." She testified in answer to her inquiry, she told Mrs. Woloshin, nursing supervisor, that Grievant had inserted the catheter, using the same catheter she had used.

She testified that two weeks later, Grievant approached her and said, "You had better change your mind about what you said." Miss Sorrentino testified that she said, "I'm sorry, I can only tell the truth about what I saw and what happened."

Grievant testified that when Mrs. Wells refused, she measured the urine and found 400 cc's. Grievant testified she later asked Mrs. Wells if she reported her as she had threatened and she said, "Yes, I'm protecting my job, L—." Grievant denied that she performed the procedure, except to assist Sorrentino who had already inserted the catheter. Grievant asked Sorrentino if she reported her and the latter said, "I'm not involved."

Mrs. Woloshin confirmed, in answer to Grievant's inquiry, that Mrs. Wells and Miss Sorrentino had stated that she performed the catheterization and told her to see Mrs. Vreatt tomorrow. She went to Mrs. Vreatt's office the next day accompanied by her steward; Wells was also present. After some discussion in which Grievant denied acting on her own initiative, Mrs. Vreatt then said, "The two nurses said you did and as far as I'm concerned, you did." Grievant said, "I did what I was told, please give me another chance." Mrs. Vreatt said, "No." Grievant asked if she was discharged and Mrs. Vreatt said, "Yes, you're fired as of now." Grievant started to cry and blacked out. She later awoke in "Emergency" and was told by Mrs. Woloshin to go home, after receiving treatment.

The next day Grievant went to the patient's room. The patient said she was fine and was going home. Her husband gave Grievant a bottle of cologne for her care of the patient.

Grievant denied telling Miss Sorrentino to change her story and denied the statement attributed to her when she recalled Mrs. Wells.

She later met with the Union on the grievance. Subsequently she went to see Mr. Schmoekel, personnel director and asked for a reference. He said he could not give her one. Grievant told him the other hospitals where she applied for work advised her that they would contact her former employer and she was told by at least two hospitals that she did not have proper recommendations. She applied at Ford, Harper, Receiving, Sinai, Mt. Carmel, Beaumont, St. John and Holy Cross Hospitals, but could not get work.

The Hospital stipulated for the record that there was no issue raised that Grievant did not diligently seek other work.

Grievant testified that on some occasions she was asked by Mrs. Wells and Mrs. Hugill and others to discontinue intravenous procedures and blood transfusions by removing the needle and sterilizing the area.

Mrs. Wells denied such assignments on rebuttal. (Mrs. Hugill was not called as a witness.) Mrs. Wells testified that there was a bulletin board memo with things LPN's can and cannot do and that she followed it. One of the rules requires RN's to be consulted before IV's are discontinued.

Grievant also testified and her testimony was not controverted, that she was never given a list of things, orally or in writing, that she could, or could not do and was never specifically told that she could not catheterize a patient.

Mrs. Vreatt, director of nursing services, testified that aides have a regular training program currently relating to bedside nursing of the classroom variety, but it includes no sterile procedures or catheterization. She did not deny that Grievant had not received regular training. She testified that forcing a catheter is very dangerous, since it can puncture the urethra, bladder or cause infection.

She testified that she received a written report of the incident and that the written reports and Grievant's statement to her were the basis of the discharge.

On cross-examination, she agreed that retention of urine was dangerous, but was vague as to the danger, she did suggest the possibility of a bladder rupture, but was unsure of other possible results. She testified that only Grievant was disciplined.

The patient involved in this proceeding went home and as far as is known, had an uneventful recovery.   ·

Opinion

Management, having effected the discharge, has the burden of establishing just cause therefor. Although the agreement does not specifically deal with this problem, it is clearly imbedded in the great body of labor arbitration awards that the right to discharge in the absence of contrary contract language, not found here, is dependent on the proof that the discharge is supported by just cause. The Hospital has made no contrary claim.

The principal evidentuary problem is the issue of determining whether or not Grievant was requested by Miss Sorrentino to attempt to catheterize the patient. I was impressed with Grievant's forthright testimony and her obvious conscientious service. I am also convinced that Miss Sorrentino was not engaged in a deliberate fabrication. It would have been absurd for one with her theoretical background to have intentionally authorized Grievant to perform the procedure in question. I, therefore, conclude that Grievant misunderstood Miss Sorrentino in her zeal to assist the patient. The issue is indeed important, but its precise resolution in behalf of either party is unwarranted on the record.

It is clear on the record that Grievant was highly patient-oriented and conscientious. She was obviously concerned with the patient's condition and suffering and it is clear from the medical authority cited in the Union brief that there was serious reason to be concerned about the patient's inability to void from 2:00 p.m. to after 10:00 p.m., a period in excess of eight hours. In the light of this fact, Mrs. Wells' failure to call a person experienced in the procedure, an RN, OB nurse, or the charge nurse as suggested by Grievant, rather than a student nurse, with little practical experience by her own frank admission, bespeaks a greater concern for her own position than the patient's welfare. For this reason, I find her testimony slanted to support her own protestations of propriety, rather than convincing against Grievant.

It is noteworthy that Grievant testified that she had never been told which procedures for patient care were permissible and which were not; nor had she ever been told not to catheterize a patient. While it is true that much of what is expected of an aide is routine and is doubtless absorbed over a period of time, nevertheless, it seems negligence in the extreme for the hospital's nursing administrators to have failed to make it expressly clear to Grievant and other aides and those engaged in related functions, what functions or procedures were definitely not to be performed by them. Grievant's testimony in this respect was not controverted. Grievant also testified that she had been told by RN's and Mrs. Wells, an LPN, to terminate intravenous and blood transfusion procedures. Mrs. Wells admitted that this procedure is forbidden to aides and denied that she had asked Grievant to perform them. Grievant named other nurses who were RN's who issued such orders, none were called to contravene her testimony.

It is rather clear that what is involved is a double standard for Grievant and some of the professional or semiprofessional employees.

It should be obvious that if high regard for the patient's welfare is to be demanded of aides, and of that there can be no question, the same standards must be enforced throughout the Hospital.

Grievant's excellent record was known, or should have been known, the fact that she received no training or advice as to forbidden procedures, was known, or certainly should have been known, to those enforcing standards of patient care. In these circumstances it was highly improper to apply the supreme penalty, particularly, when there is credible evidence that procedures also dangerous to patient care, such as termination of intravenous and transfusion procedures, were being assigned to aides by professional nurses.

While it is not the Arbitrator's function to assess fault beyond a judgment of Grievant's culpability, it is apparent that what has happened in this instance is closely related to the "old army game" of the general passing the blame to his subordinate, and so on down the line to the point where there is no subordinate and the blame remains fixed. Such a practice hardly squares with the standard imposed by the concept of "just cause."

I in no way wish to deprecate the *extremely important* goal of good patient care. There isn't much point to a Hospital without it. Nor is there any doubt that medical procedures, such as catheterization and sterile technique, must be limited to those deemed qualified by the Hospital on pain of discharge.

I simply would point out that in the particular circumstances, in which the Hospital was *more* culpable than Grievant for failure to train her and specifically warn against forbidden procedures, and to uniformly enforce rules on limitation of procedures to those qualified, there was no just cause for her discharge.

At most it must be felt that Grievant, as an intelligent person, should have realized from working around the Hospital that there were dangers in the procedures in question and that she should not have participated in them even if she was asked.

Under all the circumstances, corrective discipline would require no more than a warning notice. The discharge must be rescinded and Grievant reinstated with full back pay less interim earnings and unemployment compensation, if any (Section 4, Article IV, Agreement of the parties).

AWARD

There was no just cause for Grievant L—'s discharge in late February or early March of 1971.

The Hospital shall reinstate Grievant within a week of the date of this Award with full seniority and all contract benefits that she would have received if not discharged. She shall be paid wages she would have received if not discharged, from the date of her reinstatement, retroactive to the date of her discharge, less wages earned in any other employment during the period of her discharge, less unemployment compensation, if any.

Grievant's record shall be cleared of any reference to her discharge, but shall contain a notice limited to a record of written warning against catheterizing patients.

Case No. 8

Was the Hospital justified in reprimanding a psychiatric aide who refused to obey an order to catheterize a patient? What effect did the aide's lack of academic instruction have on the disciplinary action taken?

Ohio Department of Mental Health and Retardation
and
American Federation of State, County and Municipal Employees, Local 1136

Arbitrator: Ivan C. Rutledge
Date of Award: December 31, 1974
Citation: 63 LA 1258

What the grievant describes as a misunderstanding and the hospital authorities as insubordination lies at the bottom of this submission. The representatives of the State of Ohio and the Union agree that the matter is submitted for final and binding arbitration, that there are no questions of arbitrability, and that the question submitted is whether the discipline imposed upon the grievant, a letter of reprimand, is for just cause.

According to the grievant, when she was asked to do a catheterization on a female patient she demurred on the ground that she hadn't sufficient experience to handle this patient, or any patient, in inserting a Foley, because her prior exposure consisted entirely of demonstration on a mannikin. According to the State, the whole process, including the letter of reprimand, is the education of an insubordinate psychiatric aide who stubbornly refuses, when the occasion presents itself, to advance her training beyond that for which she was given the mannikin stage of catheterization. It is common ground that when called upon to do the operation the grievant did refuse and telephoned her supervisor for help. Her supervisor was in another building where the patient's bed was and from which the grievant had taken the patient to Hyde, the building from which grievant called her supervisor. Her supervisor asked grievant to put the nurse conducting the catheterization on the line and when she came on offered to leave her post and go to Hyde and minister to the patient. There is no dispute but that the nurse at Hyde declined the offer, said she would attend to it and there the telephone conversation terminated.

The parties' theories of the facts diverge radically at this point. Grievant's testimony is that she went from the telephone to her patient and saw her through the operation, holding the patient's body so that another employee could insert the catheter, and in so doing applied substantial force in accordance with her training as a psychiatric aide. Her refusal to take the other role was based upon her having had no training for it other than the mannikin demonstrations some two years earlier. The nurse's testimony is that the grievant three times refused to do the operation whereupon the nurse assigned two other employees to do it. Her testimony is that she had unequivocally called upon grievant to do it, that she offered to supervise the grievant in the interest of advancing her learning, notwithstanding that she was busy with other duties and taking time to supervise her would have been a hardship.

Neither party offered testimony that clearly established how much skill is required for the actual insertion of the Foley. The grievant's testimony tended to show that in the case of the patient in question it was much more difficult than taking blood, and her testimony was that no psychiatric aide was permitted to take a specimen of blood. Testimony on behalf of the State compared it closely to taking a specimen of blood and tended to show that practical experience under supervision in one or two operations would qualify a psychiatric aide to continue without supervision. State's testimony characterized removal of wax from the ear as much more difficult and grievant's testimony tended to show that the operation on the patient in question would be difficult because the patient was incontinent and uncooperative. The grievant's testimony about the patient's inability to give an informed consent and about aides being forbidden to obtain blood specimens was uncontradicted.

The State did, however, produce testimony flatly contradicting that of the grievant about her part in the operation. It tended to show that the grievant stood away from the scene, although nearby the patient, where the grievant could not observe the procedure, and that the grievant rendered no active assistance.

The State submits that grievant's refusal to catheterize the patient would not in and of itself constitute insubordination but that a psychiatric aide not adept in catheterization should accept the opportunity to be supervised in doing so, and that lack of practical experience on the part of the aide is not a sufficient reason for refusal to be supervised in the proper technique. That catheterization is within the duties appropriate for assignment to the aides, says the State, is established by testimony that it has been so considered in hospitals of the Ohio Department of Mental Health and Retardation. In the absence of evidence that a particular assignment of such duty was arbitrary or unreasonable, according to the State's contention, the practice of the department and the opinions of the appointing authority and three nurses, one a licensed practical nurse and two registered nurses, that catheterization is a duty properly assigned to an aide (Psychiatric Aide I) should not be overruled.

Moreover, the grievant signed an undated form entitled "Job Description and Worker Characteristics" in which three blocks under the instruction, "To be completed by Employee" were inscribed, albeit not by the grievant. The first is marked under "Rank" as "I" for 75% and includes "catheterization and irrigation" along with taking pulse, bathing and grooming, x-ray and lab work, observation of patient's behavior, positioning and turning, and numerous other duties. The second rank, at 20%, appears to be aptly summarized as housekeeping, such as putting away supplies. The third, at 5%, appears to deal with errands to other wards, including "sitting with patient for Lab-test housed on other wards." The State's submission is that the grievant's execution of this form supports the inference that catheterization is grouped with the primary duties of this aide, that such employees properly perform this function, and that they are well aware of the appropriate nature of this assignment within their classification.

The State submits that catheterization is a subject for progressive instruction, from the classroom stage of demonstration on a mannikin to practical experience under the supervision of a qualified instructor, but that grievant refused such supervision when instructed by a person who had supervisory responsibility for the time being and as a registered nurse the requisite educational qualifications. Thus did the grievant, according to the State, manifest a clear disregard for the opportunity to further her nursing experience as well as a clear disregard for the imminent needs of her patient and her own responsibilities in accompanying the patient to another building for medical attention.

The grievant did not make any response when shown the incident report form dated December 26, 1973, by way of notation thereon, although it states that she refused to be supervised. The supervisor who signed the form noted that the grievant had refused to sign it and had stated that it was "all a misunderstanding." This notation also includes the supervisor's observation that the grievant appeared to resent having to leave her cottage, where they were short of help, to take the patient to the other building. Under these circumstances, urges the State, the appointing authority's letter of December 28, 1973, reprimanding the grievant for insubordinate and improper conduct was reasonable.

The Union's position is twofold. First, the supervisor's instructions did not amount to a proper order as to which there could be insubordination; and second, that there was no work rule in effect justifying a catheterization assignment to an aide accompanying a patient transferred from one cottage to another.

On the second branch, the Union cites from an Agreement of the parties a provision stating:

> Work rules will be reduced to writing and a copy of such work rules shall be furnished the Union within six (6) months of the effective date of this Agreement. Copies of newly established work rules or amendments to existing work rules will be furnished the Union at least fourteen (14) days prior to the effective date of the rules.

On the first part of the Union's argument, it is submitted that the supervisor's instructions must be very clear and must be understood by the employee to be an order. The supervisor must clearly state the penalty for failure to comply. Moreover, the employee did not willfully disregard a proper order but was merely protesting for her patient to have proper medical attention.

The second branch, relating to reduction of newly established work rules to writing and furnishing them to the Union before their effective date, does not appear to apply to this grievance. If it is assumed that the instruction of aides in their duties is a topic germane to work rules, nevertheless there is no evidence tending to show the establishment of new work rules or amendments thereto. Rather, the contention of the State, that the configuration of duties assigned to aides has remained constant, appears to be shown without substantial conflict in the evidence.

However, on the first branch, which includes the contentions that an employee must understand that the supervisor is issuing an order and the supervisor must clearly state the penalty for disobedience, hangs the center of the issue submitted here. That is, what was the grievant's understanding, or what should it have been, of what was expected of her from her temporary supervisor? Did she in good faith and with adequate grounds for reasonable belief proceed to help in the catheterization under the impression that the Hyde registered nurse was not going to insist upon her being the one to insert the Foley? She testified that her part in the operation was muscular, that with difficulty and much use of strength she held the patient still so that another could proceed to obtain a sample of urine. She had maintained from the time of the incident report that it was "all a misunderstanding" even if her testimony fell short of describing the misunderstanding.

Or was the grievant determined to be instructed by her own regular supervisor, if at all, and so uncooperative away from her own cottage that during the operation, although she did in a sense attend her patient she stood near the head of the bed so that she could not see what was going on and lifted no hand to help?

Either party seeks to draw inferences from the failure of the other to call one of the two active participants in the operation, the other testifying to grievant's nonparticipation. However, were it established that the other witness was no longer in the employ of the State, it would become clear that inferences should be drawn against the Union from its failure to call this witness. As it is, no inference should be so drawn, nor should it be drawn against the State, which is not liable to the inference that it made a choice of witnesses on the basis that it chose the witness whose testimony would be favorable (as it was) but did not call the other witness because her testimony would be unfavorable.

The credibility crunch thus posed is, it must be said, not essential to the resolution of the disciplinary question posed by the submission, which goes back to an earlier stage, while the temporary supervisor was present, meeting with resistance, indeed downright refusal, of the grievant. It was clear that she was asked to catheterize and she made it clear in response that she could not perform the operation. It is not clear whether she agreed to undertake it under the supervision of her regular supervisor or sought to enlist the regular supervisor so she could help and observe. In any event, the evidence is subject to no substantial conflict in this regard and tends to show that grievant was being difficult, disagreeable, and insubordinate.

Moreover, no principle in labor relations is better established than that the employee should agree now and grieve later. It is no less applicable in the employment aspects of a hospital, which is no more than an industrial environment a place for debate. The respect due supervisory authority is essential to the functioning of an institution like the one in question where resources are thin for meeting even minimal obligations to patients. Both grievant and temporary supervisor were firm in their testimony to time-pressure in their respective assignments, the temporary supervisor with much to be done rather than stop and instruct, and the grievant with the challenge of getting her patient's urine sample ready in time to meet the schedule of the laboratory.

It would be a grievous error were the arbitral process to accentuate such burdens with an award that might be taken either as a vindication of insubordination on the part of the grievant or of impatience on the part of supervision, but there is no escape from the risk of misinterpretation of an award, because of the necessity of choice. To minimize the risk of interpretation, the following observations are offered.

There are well established exceptions to the principle of work then grieve, such as the case when a supervisor requires an employee to do something dangerous to life or limb. This exception is not here applicable, because the alleged danger was not to the grievant but to her patient. The operation of a hospital would quickly become impossible were each aide to become the protagonist of her patient in defiance of the authority structure of the hospital. Such structures are essential and in the instance of the temporary supervisor here it is crucial to an understanding of her role that it does not exclude what might appear to the outsider, at least superficially, as errors. All roles for human beings include the making of mistakes in their performance. Hence the grievance herein may not be sustained, nor is the Union understood so to contend, merely on the basis that the arbitrator disagrees, nor is the grievance to be dismissed because of agreement, with the supervisor's judgment that instruction of the grievant in catheterization had become timely. It was the supervisor's judgment to make.

That conclusion, however, does not require dismissal of the grievance which is based upon the ensuing formal written reprimand for the grievant's refusal, repeated more than once, to go along with the supervisor's offer of instruction. As indicated above, this refusal was the subject of no misunderstanding; it betokened unwillingness to honor the supervision. The Union's contention that the demand of the supervisor would not be effective as an order unless it carried the threat of the reprimand is not persuasive, and the evidence is susceptible of the interpretation that the grievant understood what the nurse was asking, whether it was that the grievant actually insert the Foley or otherwise participate in the operation.

On the other hand, there is one compelling consideration that supports sustaining the grievance. The parties took it as fact that grievant had completed the first academic phase of instruction so as to be prepared for the practical instruction offered herein. By contrast, the hearing disclosed without equivocation that the grievant's instruction was lacking in purely academic terms. The grievant showed that she did not understand wherein catheterization differed from taking a specimen of blood, which she understood to be beyond the competence of any aide. Also, apparently supervision was so lacking in confidence in her ability to write down a description of her duties it was written down for her. And finally, for whatever contribution to confusion this description may have made, it describes in the third rank sitting with as distinct from catheterizing a patient under the instant circumstances.

The policy of the State making this distinction, mysterious as it is to an outsider, is understandably puzzling to the grievant and quite adequate to warrant her apprehension for the welfare of the patient under the difficulties which burdened the patient. When it came, then, to determine what sanction was appropriate, a determination that failed to take into account the grievant's lack of instruction on this mysterious policy and her concern for the welfare of the patient would go amiss. The dubious value of a formal reprimand for educational purposes under such circumstances is so apparent as to justify characterizing its use as unreasonable. An informal oral explanation, explaining how and to what extent on the next occasion grievant would be required to go forward with catheterization and the difference between that and taking blood would be the maximum discipline reasonably appropriate.

AWARD

Accordingly, the grievance is sustained, and the records of reprimand are to be held for naught in the record of the grievant's service for any purpose, including the event of future discipline.

Case No. 9

*Did an Orderly's overall record of conscientious
dedication to his patients absolve him from slapping
an elderly patient who would not get back into bed
when ordered to do so?*

Oak Pavilion Nursing Home and Rehabilitation Center (Ohio)
and
National Union of Hospital and Nursing Home Employees

Arbitrator: Walter G. Seinsheimer
Date of Award: July 16, 1973
Citation: 73-1 ARB ¶8198

This case involves the discharge of J— for having *"struck a patient on
February 4, 1973."* The Union filed the grievance now before me for
arbitration on behalf of Mr. J— on February 8, 1973.

It reads as follows:

Above Employee was terminated without just cause and management
exercised its rights under Article XVIII, Section 1, in a capricious and
arbitrary manner.

The grievant was an Orderly in the Nursing Home, which had about 120
patients of whom *"95% to 99% . . . would be geriatric patients."* The average,
according to the Administrator of the Home *"would approximately be 70 to 75
years old."* Many of the patients are senile and require a great deal of care and
assistance.

Mr. J— started to work for the Home as an Orderly on July 4, 1968, so that at the time of the incident for which he was discharged, he had been with the Home slightly over 4½ years.

The events leading up to his discharge started on Sunday morning, February 4, 1973 and were related by Mrs. [R.], the Day Coordinator.[1] According to her, at about 10:40 a.m. she was walking down the west corridor of the second floor and as she approached the door to the shower and toilet facility, she *"heard Mr. J— say rather loudly 'get back in that bed.' "* As she got to the door of the Shower Room, she said she looked through it and across the east corridor and into a patient room. In the room, a patient, Mr. S, was sitting at the foot of his bed, his legs over the side and facing the door. Mrs. [R.] then testified as follows:

> Mr. J— was in the process of walking around the end of — the foot end of the bed toward the door, and the door started closing. I didn't see Mr. J— make a movement to close the door but the door started closing. Just prior to the door closing, I saw Mr. J— hit Mr. S . . . on the right side of his forehead with the open part of the back of his hand, his right hand.

She testified further that the Orderly was standing *"almost directly in front of the patient, but off to the right side of him."* She also stated that she did not *"actually see Mr. J—'s hand touch Mr. S . . .'s forehead,"* but she said she did see Mr. S . . . flinch. At this point, she said, the door closed and she saw nothing further.

Mrs. [R.] then testified that she was so upset by what she had seen that she went back to her office and attempted to contact by telephone (unsuccessfully) her superior, Mrs. [B.], the Director of Nursing. Following this, she instructed a Nurses Aide, without explaining why it was needed, *"to take Mr. S . . .'s vital signs."*[2]

Mrs. [R.] again called Mrs. [B.] and this time was successful, and reported to her what she had seen. She stated that *"Mrs. [B.] and I decided that since I was unsure of my position as to whether to dismiss him immediately or not, we would wait until Monday and discuss the situation with Mr. [L.]."* On being questioned as to why she was unsure of her *"position,"* she answered, *"I was still rather new at the facility and was not familiar with the policy regarding patient abuse."* This may well have been true as far as Mrs. [R.] was concerned, but I feel I must comment at this point that this excuse *cannot* be applied to Mrs. [B.].

---

[1]Mrs. [R.] was a new employee of the Home, having started only a month before.
[2]i.e., his blood pressure, pulse and pupil reaction of his eyes.

In any event, nothing was done further about the matter on Sunday and Mr. J— continued to work his shift that day, as he did the next day. On Monday morning, Mrs. [R.] *"took a written account of the incident to Mr. [L.]"* (the Administrator) who told her he would take care of the matter from that point. He also informed Mrs. [B.], after discussing the matter with her, that he'd made up his mind what he would do and that he would take care of it.

Mr. [L.] testified that he then tried to contact Mr. [W.], the Union's Representative, to tell him that he was going to discharge Mr. J—. The reason for this, according to [L.], was: *"We had some weeks before discussed the situation that before I would suspend or terminate an employee I would talk to him."*

He finally reached Mr. [W.] around 4:00 p.m. (after Mr. J— had left the Home) that day and told him the situation. Mr. [W.] apparently told [L.] to go ahead and terminate, but that a grievance would be filed on behalf of the employee.

According to Mr. J—, the first he heard that he had been discharged was from Mr. [W.] while attending a Union meeting on Monday evening. He testified that he couldn't believe it and came to the Home about 4:30 p.m. the next day (which was his day off) to find out what it was all about. It was at this time that he was given the letter of termination, which was cited previously.

Pertinent and Cited Contract Provisions

ARTICLE XVIII — *Management Rights*

1. Except as in this Agreement otherwise provided, the Home retains the exclusive right to hire, direct and schedule the working force; to plan, direct and control operations; to discontinue, subject to the provisions of paragraph 3 of this Article, or to reorganize or combine any Department or Branch of operations with any consequent reduction or other changes in the working force; to hire and lay off Employees; to promulgate rules and regulations, to introduce new or improved methods or facilities regardless of whether or not the same causes a reduction in the working force and in all respects to carry out, in addition, the ordinary and customary functions of management. None of these rights shall be exercised in a capricious or arbitrary manner.

*   *   *   *   *

ARTICLE XX — *Discharge and Penalties*

1. The Home shall have the right to discharge, suspend or discipline any Employee for cause.

2. The Home will notify the Union in writing of any discharge or suspension within twenty-four (24) hours from the time of discharge or suspension. If the Union desires to contest the discharge or suspension, it shall give written notice thereof to the Home within ten (10) working days, from the date of receipt of notice of discharge or suspension. In such event, the dispute shall be submitted and determined under the grievance and arbitration procedure hereinafter set forth, however, commencing at Step 3 of the grievance machinery.

*   *   *   *   *

Argument and Discussion

It was the Employer's position that the grievant did strike Mr. S — and, in addition, another witness, a Nurses Aide, testified that she had seen Mr. J — not only strike other patients, but she felt he handled some of them rather roughly.

It was also pointed out that neither of the witnesses who testified concerning having seen him strike patients had "*any interest aligned with the Employer*" because the Nurses Aide was a fellow employee and member of the Union, and the Day Coordinator no longer was an employee of the Home "*and has no interest to protect here.*"

It was also the position of the Home that J— "*is filled with a quick temper*" and Employer's counsel went on to say:

I think that has been demonstrated by his leaving jobs at [Q.] and at [Z.], where he simply would not conform to the regulations, the policies being followed by those homes. He has got his own way of doing things. Everything has its place and everything should be in that place regardless of the consequences, and if it isn't I think he certainly gets irritated and strikes out.

What apparently bothered the Employer was that even though J— had probably never struck a patient a hard blow, was the fact that the patients were quite old and "*are totally frail and helpless in most cases*" and, counsel continued,

who are within minutes or hours or weeks of the expiration of their lives. They are totally frail and helpless in most cases, certainly in the cases of all these three or four patients that we have heard about today.

They are helpless, virtually vegetable cases. He is the sole — practically was the sole person in charge of their well-being. It just takes perhaps a minor slap with knuckles on the forehead to give these people a stroke and make these people pass from this world. Who can say whether a blow with the knuckles can do that or not.

It was further argued that:

The Home is very concerned about their patients, but principally the home has a public trust, and that's trust to their patients, and they simply cannot permit this man to be doing this, regardless of what he would say in an investigative discussion on Monday morning, after the fact. Once the director of the home believes he had done this, it is like the commission of murder — you either believe that he did or he didn't. And if he did, nothing in the administrator's mind could change the fact that he should no longer be working at Oak Pavilion. So the decision was made to discharge.

Counsel for the Home also pointed out that the testimony indicated that "*J — has done this over a long period of time, has abused these patients, has endangered their lives.*" Reference was made to the fact that he had "*sat through in-service programs where it has been pointed out . . . that the home's policy is gentle care for these persons that are helpless*" but that he had "*totally ignored these kind of instructions.*"

In connection with the just above, reference was also made to an Evaluation of July 4, 1971 made on the grievant by a former Nursing Director on which, while giving him high marks for Attendance, Judgment, Nursing Skills, Patient Relationship & Staff Relationship, it was added:

I feel that he needs to control his temper and to lower his tone of voice when discussing problems, care, etc., with the Nurses, other Orderlies and Aides, as well as patients. I think a good suggestion is for him to listen to what [next few words were not readable, but the paragraph concluded with] *Mr. J   has a tendency to keep on the move instead of stopping and listening to what people have to say.*

The Employer concluded that to reinstate the grievant "*would absolutely destroy the morale of the other employees. And once this gets out, as it is bound to get out, it will destroy the morale of the patients.*"

The Union counsel's position was essentially that the grievant denies all the charges of striking patients, and that this presents the Arbitrator "*with a flat contradiction.*"

Counsel went on to point out that not only did the former Nursing Director believe he was "*Excellent*" and/or "*Above Average*" on the attributes previously mentioned, but the Nurses Aide who testified to having seen him strike other patients, said he was the best Orderly in the Home. It was also pointed out that she testified that she had seen other employees of the Home *"slap patients."*

Another area attacked by the Union had to do with what it called *"the peculiar way in which the Employer proceeded in this case."* It was pointed out that he (the grievant) *"was not accorded the simple decency of being confronted with what happened, and being allowed at least to make a denial, an explanation or whatever, at the time it happened."* Union counsel went on to state that he thought:

> A confrontation between J— and Mrs. [R.] was essential at the earliest possible moment, for the purpose of one, getting at the truth, and, two, considering whether or not some alternative to discharge existed.

To the above comments Union counsel added that he found:

> It rather incredible that a guy who could be permitted to continue to work around patients was not a person to whom some discipline short of discharge could not have been administered.

The paragraph in Union counsel's closing statement in which the preceding was set forth, exposed what was, in my opinion, an indication that Union counsel also may have thought the grievant had very possibly been guilty of slapping Mr. S . . . on Sunday, February 4, 1973. This was further reinforced when the paragraph concluded with: *"Certainly there has been sufficient time elapsed for the Arbitrator to impose some disciplinary layoff, and I think that is the appropriate course to take."*

The Union continued its defense in behalf of the grievant by pointing out that J— had an excellent record with the Home, and that perhaps his main problem was that he *"may suffer from an excess of zeal[3]"* but, counsel added:

> I think an employee who can be efficient with patients is certainly an employee who can be trained or disciplined correctively in a fashion that he can continue to be efficient with patients, perhaps with less zeal.

Counsel's final plea was that to uphold the discharge would mean that *"because of a precipitous action on the part of management"* that *"a dedicated employee"* would be *"taken out of the nursing care field where I would think his presence would be highly valued."*

---

[3]Here again is a statement indicating that possibly the Union counsel believed the grievant could have been guilty of slapping a patient.

Discussion and Opinion

It seems to me that there was not only a peculiar handling of this situation, but there is some question in my mind as to whether Mrs. [R.] saw what she claimed she saw. Taking up the latter first, there are a number of questions that are raised in my mind concerning her testimony.

First of all, if the slap was as strong as Mrs. [R.] demonstrated at the hearing and the patient was as old and tottery as earlier described, wouldn't he have fallen back in bed after he was struck?

Considering the fact that Mrs. [R.] was as far away as she described and was looking *through* a room 15 feet wide across a corridor 6 to 8 feet wide and into another room, I question how she could determine that the slap was *"more a slap of punishment?"* Or even how she could tell how strong the blow was? Or that he flinched? Or, as she affirmed under further direct examination, that the blow *"might have caused an abrasion or discoloration"* on the patient's head?

Finally, on the subject of the *"slap,"* Mrs. [R,] said that in her *"professional opinion"* it was not necessary for Mr. J — *"to strike Mr. S — to control him."* I question her ability to determine this from over 26 feet away and after observing only the alleged slap. She certainly could not have known what had gone on before she heard Mr. J— tell the patient to get in bed or observed the slap. Considering the fact that she claimed to have been so upset that she just left the scene without checking what happened, I am left with grave doubts as to her ability to judge anything about the situation in an objective manner, or for that matter, even in a subjective manner.

Furthermore, I found Mrs. [R.'s] explanation of what she saw to be rather confused. For example, she said she could see the patient sitting at the foot of the bed and that J— was *"almost directly in front of the patient, but off to the right side of him (the patient)"*. Then she stated she saw the *"movement"* of J—'s hand and that the patient *"flinched backward just after Mr. J—'s hand had passed . . ."*, but then she said she didn't *"actually see Mr. J—'s hand touch Mr. S —'s forehead."* She testified she *"saw his hand cross his forehead and at that moment I heard the noise (of the slap.)"*

To return to what I called *"peculiar handling,"* it is my opinion that the Employer's actions,. or lack of action, beginning with that of Mrs. [R.], followed by that of Mrs. [B.], and concluding with that of the Administrator, was to say the least inexcusable.

While it is true that Mrs. [R.] had been with the Home only one month prior to the day of the incident, I can't help but be shocked that she didn't immediately check, *herself,* on the condition of the patient who she claimed had been slapped. After all, she claimed to have had previous experience as a *"day coordinator"* in another nursing home, as well as previous supervisory positions in hospitals and, therefore, it seems to me, she should not only not have been so *"shocked,"* but should have known what action to take, even if it was only to investigate. This was bad enough, but I also find it extremely strange that her *"experienced"* supervisor, Mrs. [B.], didn't seem to know what to do other than to discuss it on Monday with the Administrator. Not to have instructed Mrs. [R.] to go to the patient's room immediately after claiming to have seen an Orderly slap him is, in my opinion, dereliction of duty.

In a sense, even worse than the above, was the Administrator's lack of action the following day. It seems extremely strange to me that he made no effort to talk with Mr. J— or anyone else, for that matter, other than Mrs. [R.] and Mrs. [B.]. The fact that he had agreed with Union Representative [W.] not to *"discharge"* any employee before talking to the Union Representative, hardly coincides with other testimony that for violation of the rule concerning abuse of patients, Mr. J— could have been discharged on the spot and/or could have been suspended until further investigation. Under the circumstances of the claim of the seriousness of J—'s offense, the apparent inaction (allowing J— to work all day Monday without contacting him) is surprising, to say the least. The suggestion that J— would deny *"striking an old man"* is to my mind no excuse not to confront him with the accusation of that action and that he was going to be discharged as a result.

There are numerous other examples of Management's apparent confusion. If Mrs. [B.] was so disturbed about the slapping of the patient and believed it to be such an unconscionable act, why didn't she order Mrs. [R.] to suspend him immediately, subject to investigation? And if the action was so terrible that the continued employment of J— was considered a danger to patients, why did the Administrator allow him to work a whole shift after he had been told of the incident?

It seems rather obvious from other testimony that these Management representatives didn't really believe that J— was a danger to the patients. As an example, I noted that Mrs. [B.] testified that *"it didn't occur to me that he . . . would strike another patient."*

With the above in mind, it should be obvious that I agree with the Union counsel that the grievant should have been confronted by his accuser and that this should have occurred at the earliest possible moment. In other circumstances, such an error on Management's part could well have led to the grievant's reinstatement.

The testimony of Mrs. [K.], a Nurses Aide, was in many ways very damaging to the grievant's case. Yet, on the other hand, she also testified *"I think Mr. J— is the best Orderly we had."* This on the face of it seems contradictory yet after examining her testimony, as well as others, including J—'s, it becomes apparent that he was a conscientious (perhaps overly conscientious) Orderly, who sincerely cared (perhaps to a fault) about the well being, cleanliness and rehabilitating of the patients with whom he worked. This, of course, brings us face to face with the basic question before me, and that is:

Whether this conscientiousness and dedication to his patients absolves him from having slapped the patient, Mr. S —?

As I have said, Mrs. [K.'s] testimony was damaging, since frankly, based on Mrs. [R.'s] testimony and the subsequent lack of immediate action by her and others with management responsibility, I might well have considered that the evidence lacked substance. But with Mrs. [K.'s] testimony, it became apparent that J—, in addition to being the *"best Orderly"* was so conscientious and so wound up in what he thought best for the patient that he neglected to understand and remember that gentleness with the patients was a prime requisite.

J—, perhaps without realizing it, explained why it becomes understandable to believe that he had slapped this patient as well as others. He indicated that he considered himself very efficient and that *"he had a metaphor"* which he said was *"I think everything has a place and everything in its place."* This, along with other testimony by the grievant, indicates that J— is a compulsive individual and that when things don't go the way he thinks they should, that he becomes upset. This was further reinforced by *his* explanation of why he quit his job at the State Hospital and at another Nursing Home. Even Union's counsel recognized that J— had problems in this area when he stated that *"J— may suffer from an excess of zeal."*

All of the above must finally lead to the fact that Mr. J— was discharged for the slapping of Mr. S — on Sunday, February 4, 1973 — not for what Mrs. [K.] said she saw him do prior to that day. Therefore, the only value of Mrs. [K.'s] testimony is that it lent credence to Mrs. [R.'s] accusation. Obviously, it had no merit beyond that. In fact, the Employer didn't even know of the previous incidents until two days before the hearing. Consequently, the only question to be determined is whether J — struck (slapped) the patient in question on February 4, 1973.

I must admit that if it hadn't been for Mrs. [K.'s] testimony, I would have found it more difficult to accept Mrs. [R.'s] testimony. Not that I don't believe she believed she saw J— slap the patient; I'm sure she believes she did. And at this point I am inclined to believe that he did.

I am not a Psychologist and neither were the counsels for the parties, but they both, as I do, sensed something about the grievant's personality that seemed to explain the very good possibility that he could have slapped a patient. Under the circumstances, therefore, I can see no alternative but to uphold the discharge.

Some of the circumstances to which I refer are that I am convinced that despite the confused testimony of Mrs. [R.], that he did slap Mr. S —. Secondly, the reason for his discharge has undoubtedly become known around the Home and thus, as the Employer's counsel pointed out, to put him back to work *"would destroy the morale of the other employees. And once this gets out, as it is bound to get out, it will destroy the morale of the patients"* and, I must add, that of the relatives of the patients.

I can't think of any case I've decided in over 20 years of arbitration wherein I found myself as reluctant as I am now in upholding a discharge. This man undoubtedly has been an excellent, dedicated Orderly and, while it is true such individuals are hard to get, a Nursing Home cannot condone nor accept the slapping of a patient under any circumstances.

While the Home had no published rules against slapping or abusing a patient, it was not, in my opinion, necessary for such a rule to be posted — any more than it is necessary to post a rule that employees shall not steal from the Employer or fellow employees without being discharged. There are certain basic rules which are recognized in a civilized society that must be abided by, and the individual who doesn't abide by them subjects himself to recognized and understood penalties.

AWARD

Based upon the discussion and opinion above, it is my decision that the discharge of Mr. J— was for just cause and, therefore, his grievance is denied.

Case No. 10

*Was the Hospital justified in suspending a
housekeeping aide for making threatening remarks
to a patient? Could the employee properly be
suspended pending completion of the investigation of
charges against her?*

**Kaiser Foundation Hospitals, et al. (Hayward, Calif.)
and
Hospital and Institutional Workers, Local 250**

Arbitrator: Leo V. Killion
Date of Award: February 8, 1973
Citation: 72-2 ARB ¶8673

The issue in this case is whether Grievant's two weeks suspension was for just cause.

The operative facts are found to be that Grievant was employed as relief Housekeeping Aide (maid) at Kaiser Hospital, Hayward, California. Her hire date was July 27, 1969.

On the date in question, a police officer was a patient in Room 406. He had been in an automobile accident four days before. He had bodily injuries, including a bleeding kidney. His admission date was the date of injury and he was moved to Room 406 the following day. Three days later there occurred the following event which precipitated the issue Grievance.

Grievant entered this patient's Room 406 to clean it. She and the patient recognized each other as having previously met. They spoke. Grievant remembered him as one of two Union City police officers, who had arrested her son and who on one occasion used such physical force to subdue him that he had to be hospitalized. Grievant described this in her Hearing testimony.

He arrested him. He tied him up and then he beat him until he was unconscious. I had to put my boy in the hospital on account of that.

Next, she testified:

So I said, "Oh, so you are one of those. Now I got you where you had [her son] remember?" He said, "I don't want you in my room. Will you please get out. Get out."

He right away remembered where he had my boy.

At this time there was also in this room a Nurse's Aide (NA) who was a member of the bargaining unit. She was not present at the Arbitration Hearing but had signed as a witness to the patient's written report of this event and had also executed an official hospital form entitled "Report of Unusual Occurrence" in which she stated (in portion asking for details of incident) that when she entered this police officer–patient's room to answer his light she heard a conversation between Grievant and patient

in which she stated he was "one of those dirty U.C. cops" and "to be careful she didn't poison him." The patient requested to see [Grievant's] Supervisor immediately and [Grievant] not be allowed in his room.

In the room at the time of this happening there was also another nurse (LVN) (member of bargaining unit not present at Hearing) who likewise signed as a witness to the patient's written report. She likewise executed a "Report of Unusual Occurrence." Said she under caption "Details of Incident":

While caring for the patient I heard the maid [Grievant] say "You'd better watch out because I'm going to slip you some poison." The patient requested that [Grievant] not be allowed in his room again.

The patient filed a written report which stated in pertinent part:

[Grievant] reacted hostile and advised me she would get even with me. I advised her I'd rather not talk to her due to my condition. She related to me as she exited the room, while two nurses were present, that they best watch out because she might poison me.

At the Hearing the police officer testified that his report was correct, that he believed that Grievant had threatened to poison him and at the time felt that she might very well have been able to carry out her threat and therefore was concerned over his welfare. He said that he did not take her threat "as a joking gesture."

The incident was investigated immediately by the Head Housekeeping Aide [Grievant's immediate Supervisor] and by the Head Nurse. The written statement of the patient was given to the Executive Housekeeper who immediately interviewed the patient. At the Hearing, he testified that the patient verified his complaint and stated that he requested the Grievant to leave the room several times but she refused and continued with her argument before finally leaving. The patient stated he resented being threatened.

After visiting the patient, the Executive Housekeeper then had a conference with the Head Nurse in her office. She told him that two of her nurses had completed "Unusual Occurrence" reports which verified the fact that the patient was correct in his charges.

Next, the Executive Housekeeper called Grievant into his office and asked for her side of the story. She denied being hostile toward the patient or making threatening remarks to him. She, however, admitted saying to him that he had arrested and beat up her son and that now she had him where he had her son.

At the conclusion of this interview, the Executive Housekeeper gave her a suspension pending further investigation. He told her that she would be notified. She was suspended about two hours after the incident occurred.

A Grievance was filed immediately thereafter, the Shop Steward claiming that a work suspension pending further investigation was unjustified; that the Grievant should have been temporarily transferred to another area of the hospital until the charge of unsatisfactory patient relations was substantiated.

The Union Steward was told by the Executive Housekeeper at the Step One Grievance meeting that the preliminary investigation strongly substantiated the charge of unsatisfactory patient relations and therefore the suspension was justified. The Steward was also told that if the charges should be proven false, the Grievant would be made whole with no loss of pay and all evidence of the incident removed from her file; that Grievant would be notified of any further action at the appropriate time.

The suspension was later converted into a two weeks suspension.

The Third Step Hearing was held two months after the incident occurred. Just prior thereto each of the two bargaining unit nurses executed further statements. The LVN stated:

I didn't hear the complete conversation, all I heard was [Grievant] saying "You had better watch out for him, because I'm going to slip him some poison." I got the feeling she wasn't serious in her comment.

The NA stated in pertinent part that she answered a call light in the patient's room and:

. . . upon entering, the patient and the Housekeeper [Grievant] was involved in a verbal argument in which I was not in on the beginning of. The gist of what I heard was L— said "Oh, you're one of those U.C. cops. If you aren't careful I might poison you." I felt like the tone of her voice was joking about this. Apparently the patient did not and asked me to call the Housekeeper's Supervisor which I proceeded to do.

The Chief Shop Steward testified at the Hearing that the NA told her the day of the incident that she felt Grievant's tone of voice was joking when she said: "Oh, you're one of those [dirty] U.C. cops. If you aren't careful, I might poison you." This Steward also testified that the LVN likewise told her on the day of the incident that she got the feeling Grievant wasn't serious in her comments when she said "You had better watch out for him because I'm going to slip him some poison."

There is no evidence in the record that Grievant, at the time she was interviewed by the Executive Housekeeper, claimed that she was "joking" when she told the patient that she had him where he had had her son. At the Hearing, she testified that she was "just joking" when she said to the patient, "Oh, so now I got you where you had [my son] remember?" At the Hearing she denied saying to the patient anything whatsoever concerning "poison." She testified that neither of the two nurses was in the room when she had her conversation with the patient; that she was out of his room cleaning the room across the hall when these nurses came into this patient's room.

Opinion

It is the opinion of the Arbitrator that the Employer has met its ultimate burden of persuasion that the Grievant uttered menacing words to this police officer-patient which caused him apprehension for his personal safety.

The patient testified that Grievant spoke words which put him in concern of his physical welfare. The patient and two members of the nursing service testified that Grievant said words to the effect that the patient better take care because she might poison him. This testimony the Arbitrator finds to be credible. The Grievant herself admitted that she told the patient that she had him in a helpless condition.

It is further found that the Union has not met its burden of persuading the Arbitrator that the above words were said other than out of a feeling of hostility toward this patient. The evidence from the two nurses contained in their "Unusual Occurrence" reports is that Grievant said that she might poison the patient. Later these nurses said they felt that Grievant wasn't serious in her said words; that the tone of her voice was joking (although the patient did not think so.) The nurses' latter statements only create a conflict in the Union's evidence on this point. The Grievant's testimony was that no such words were spoken at all. The Arbitrator finds that this conflicting evidence has small weight when balanced against the positive testimony of the patient that the Grievant was hostile toward him and the conceded fact that Grievant's son had been beaten by the police officers. There is nothing in the record to serve as a reason why Grievant should here be in a joking mood or should be other than hostile. Months later at the Hearing, the Grievant was very emotional at the point in her testimony when she testified that the patient–police officer had beaten her son.

Issue

The issue thus becomes one of determining whether the Employer had "just cause" for suspending the Grievant for exhibiting hostility to this police officer–patient in telling him that she had him in a helpless condition and might poison him.

I have given long and serious consideration to this case and have concluded that the Employer not only had the right but further had a duty to suspend the Grievant under the circumstances here presented. One of its employees had threatened to poison a patient. It was under a duty to protect that patient. It did not know as a certainty whether or not the employee meant what she said. The Employer could not fulfill its duty by standing idly by and waiting to find out what the real intentions of the employee were and whether she meant her words as spoken. It must take affirmative action. And transferring the employee to another part of the hospital would not have been sufficient action to have prevented the threatened harm.

Thus, the question which had to be answered at the time that the Executive Housekeeper was compelled to make his decision was whether there was an absolute certainty that the Grievant would not attempt to carry out her threat. The hospital had been put on notice that its employee had used menacing words and the duty thus became an absolute one to prevent this employee from bringing harm to the patient. Because of these verbal acts of the employee, the Employer, in addition to its humane duty, was put in a position where it would incur the liability of an insurer if any harm were to come to the patient from the employee. If it did not hold the employee out of service during the time the patient was in the hospital and any harm came to the patient, the hospital would be deemed to have condoned and even ratified the actions of the employee and would be liable for punitive damages. There was even the further possibility of the personal liability of the Executive Housekeeper which had to be considered; if the Grievant would possibly have attempted to carry out her threat, the Housekeeper could possibly have been guilty of criminal negligence, including manslaughter. These possibilities might seem far fetched in an after-the-fact analysis, but are important in evaluating the case on a just cause basis. All of these matters are the things upon which a just cause determination must necessarily have been made, and that evaluation must, of course, have been made on the objective facts as known at the time the suspension decision was made. To repeat, those facts included the fact that the Grievant had said that she might poison the patient. Whether or not she meant what she said could not be determined to a certainty. Hence, it is seen that the hospital, after notice of the Grievant's language toward this helpless patient, came under an absolute duty to protect the patient from this threatened harm. And in these circumstances it would seem only reasonable that the Employer should have the right to protect itself from punitive tort liability and its Executive Housekeeper from possible criminal liability by the procedure of suspending the Grievant for a reasonable time when in so doing it would also be protecting the Grievant from the possibility of committing a dischargeable offense which might result if she should again confront the patient in the hospital.

The situation which resulted in the poison threat was not caused by nor did it grow out of Grievant's employment. It was brought about by a personal matter between the police officer and the Grievant. It stemmed from a personal grudge beyond the control of the Employer.

The two weeks suspension is not found to have here been unreasonable under all of the circumstances or an abuse of discretion. For it there was justifiable cause.

The evidence in the transcript, the parties' exhibits and the arguments of counsel have been thoroughly reviewed and studied.

For the reasons set forth above and upon all of the evidence, the Award is as follows:

AWARD

The Grievance is denied.

Case No. 11

*Did the Hospital have the right to discharge a nurses
aide who was charged with slapping a mentally ill
patient and pushing his wheelchair away with undue
force? Did the arbitrator have the right to impose a
lesser form of discipline, or was the grievant entitled
to reinstatement with full back pay and benefits?*

Brown County (Wis.)
and
Brown County Hospital Employees, AFSCME, Local 1901

Arbitrator: Edward B. Krinsky
Date of Award: April 10, 1970
Citation: LAIC 48

Contract Language

"The Employer shall adopt and publish reasonable rules which may be
amended from time to time. Except for rules, regulations and directives from
the State of Wisconsin, approving agencies such as the American Hospital
Association, or other governmental agencies having jurisdiction over the
institutions, such rules and regulations shall be submitted to the Union for
its consideration.

Action to amend or alter or otherwise change said rules and regulations
shall be taken through the grievance procedure in this Agreement."

Facts

On Monday, November 3, 1969, the grievant, E—, was working her
normal 3:00 to 11:15 p.m. shift as a Nurses Aide on Unit 2 of Brown County
Hospital. She has been employed at the Hospital for approximately five years,

four of which have been spent as a Nurses Aide on Unit 2. Unit 2 is a chronic men's ward containing male patients who, according to the Registered Nurse who supervises the Unit, probably will be there the rest of their lives because they suffer from "emotional instability or mental problems." At approximately 7:00 p.m. on November 3, the Registered Nurse, Wawerka, witnessed the events which caused her to report them to higher levels of supervision and which led to the grievant's discharge on November 7. There is conflicting testimony regarding some of the events which took place.

The grievant was supervising the bathing of a patient in the bathroom of the Unit. She was being assisted by another patient named O'Bern. A third patient, Verhagen, was sitting in his roller chair outside of the bathroom. Verhagen is confined to the roller chair and moves himself by planting his feet in front and pushing backwards. This sends the chair in a reverse direction, and the patient can maneuver the chair in the direction he wishes to go. He is unable to communicate verbally although he can point and make gutteral sounds.

On November 3, Verhagen was pushing his chair from the hallway toward the bathroom, and in so doing, according to the grievant, was banging his chair into the legs of O'Bern. At least twice, according to the grievant, she asked Verhagen to refrain from pushing his chair into O'Bern and each time she pushed Verhagen's chair back into the hallway. Verhagen persisted and made efforts to move his chair back to the bathroom. The grievant testified that she attempted once again to push Verhagen's chair back into the hall but Verhagen planted his feet firmly on the floor, thus interfering with the forward movement of the chair.

At approximately this time nurse Wawerka appeared in the hallway from the medicine room approximately 50 feet down the hall from the bathroom entrance. At that point, Wawerka testified, the grievant was positioned at the side of Verhagen's chair with her back toward the direction from which Wawerka was coming. Wawerka's testimony relates that she then saw the grievant, from a position in the hall approximately 40 feet away, strike Verhagen once on the back and side of the neck with her right hand which she swung from waist level. She testified further that the slap so delivered was a hard one and that she heard the impact but she did not see the patient react to the blow. She testified that the grievant then gave Verhagen's chair a hard push into the adjoining alcove.

Wawerka indicates that she entered the hallway from the medicine room because she heard loud noises and shouting coming from the direction of the bathroom, and she went to investigate. After seeing the striking of Verhagen, Wawerka alleges, she approached the grievant and confronted her with what she had seen. She testified that the grievant was agitated and told her the circumstances related above regarding Verhagen's repeatedly pushing O'Bern with the roller chair and that she was trying to push Verhagen out of the way and prevent him from doing it again. Wawerka testified that Verhagen, while not reacting to the slap, was agitated at this time and that he kept his hand placed on his neck and was pointing at the grievant and making gutteral noises.

Wawerka testified that she did not examine Verhagen's neck to see what if any injuries he had sustained. She testified that all one might expect from a slap of the kind delivered would be a reddened area and that the patient involved had a skin condition on his neck which caused it to be red. She indicated that because the neck was already reddened it would have been difficult to see further reddening caused by a slap. She indicated that there was no blood or other mark of injury. Wawerka reported her observations of the foregoing events to the Director of Nursing.

The grievant's version of what happened differs from Wawerka's. She testified that when she was unable to push Verhagen's chair she went behind it and lifted the front wheels in order to push the chair. She says she was behind the chair and not on the side of it when Wawerka appeared. She denies that she struck the patient. According to the grievant's testimony, she was not aware of Wawerka's presence until Wawerka was within approximately six feet of her at which time she heard a noise. She testified that she was aware that Wawerka was talking to her about what had just happened although she denies hearing what Wawerka was saying since she claims to have had an ear infection which was interfering with her hearing that day.

The grievant and Wawerka agree in their testimony that in the process of moving Verhagen's chair out of the way the grievant pushed his chair forcefully into the adjoining alcove.

The following day, November 4, the grievant and Wawerka, as well as the Director of Nursing, the Local Union President, and the Assistant Hospital Administrator, were called into the Administrator's office for a meeting. The Administrator had received the report submitted by Wawerka to her supervisor. At that meeting the grievant was suspended pending an investigation into the facts of the case. Both Administrator Lucia and his Assistant, De Prey, as well as Wawerka testified that at that meeting the grievant neither admitted nor denied striking the patient when she was asked by Lucia whether she had done it. She said in effect, according to them, that she did not recall having struck the patient. According to the grievant as well as the Union President, the grievant firmly denied at said meeting that she had struck the patient, although the latter's testimony is somewhat confusing regarding what was said.

On November 5, the Administrator and his Assistant consulted with the Board of Trustees about their investigation and sought support for their actions. There is testimony by the Assistant Administrator that as part of the investigation he went to Unit 2 and viewed the surroundings and had Wawerka indicate to him what she had seen.

Having concluded the investigation, the Administrator called the grievant to his office on November 7 and told her of the Hospital's decision to discharge her. He asked the grievant to sign a letter of discharge which the grievant declined to do. Said letter reads as follows:

Dear Miss [E—]:

After careful and complete investigation of the incident of striking a patient, it has been decided that your services are terminated, effective this date.

As you are well aware of Wisconsin Statute 340.58 (sic) "Abuse of inmates of institutions," this was of such serious nature that this in no way could be condoned.

Sincerely,

BROWN COUNTY HOSPIAL

Lynn O. Lucia /s/
Lynn O. Lucia, Superintendent

Lucia admitted at the hearing that the statute number indicated in the letter was erroneous and should have read 940.29 which reads, in relevant part, as follows:

940.29   Abuse of inmates of institutions. Any person in charge of or employed in any of the following institutions who abuses, neglects or ill-treats any person confined in or an inmate of any such institution or who knowingly permits another person to do so may be fined not more than $500 or imprisoned not more than one year in county jail or both:

(3)   A hospital for the mentally ill; . . .

Subsequently a grievance was filed and the parties being unable to resolve the issue requested arbitration.

During the course of the hearing the Panel observed the premises of Unit 2, including a view of the patient Verhagen. He showed his recognition of both Wawerka and E— by pointing at them, grasping their hands when offered them and making some gutteral noises. The Chairman of the Panel observed the back of the patient's neck and did not observe any particular reddening. He was told by Wawerka at that time the patient's skin condition was much improved over what it was in November at the time of the alleged striking.

The testimony with regard to the grievant's past work record indicates that at no time previously has she been disciplined or reprimanded in any way for physical abuse of patients. There was testimony that on at least two prior occasions the grievant received an oral reprimand from the Administrator for what the Administrator termed "verbal abuse" of patients. The grievant received no written warnings or other type of discipline in these instances.

During the course of the hearing counsel for the Employer indicated that he wished the Panel to take additional testimony from two patients in Unit 2 regarding two past circumstances which he said they would testify to of other instances in which the grievant had struck patients. This testimony would not have related to the incident on November 3 and would have been introduced for the purpose of indicating a pattern of behavior. A majority of the Panel felt that such testimony would have been of questionable competence since it would come from mental patients on the ward with no substantiation from any other source. Neither of the instances which were to be testified to had been reported to employees or supervision at the time of their occurrence. A majority of the Panel indicated to counsel for the Employer that such testimony would probably not be considered relevant or given much weight regarding the disposition of the instant grievance. Given that judgment, counsel for the Employer elected not to have the witnesses testify.

Discussion

The grievant, E—, was discharged for striking a patient. The right to discharge an employee is clearly vested in management under Article I of the labor agreement quoted above provided that such discharge is for "proper cause."

The judgment of what constitutes "proper cause" for discharge is always a difficult one to make. It is all the more difficult where, as here, the alleged misconduct may be considered criminal conduct, whether or not criminal prosecution has taken place or is contemplated.

The Panel is of the opinion that where criminal or criminal-equivalent conduct is alleged the burden of proof required must be substantial. This is essential because the effect on the future working life of an employee may be just as serious where an arbitrator upholds a discharge for criminal-equivalent conduct as where the employee is actually convicted in a court of law. It is unlikely that either those who might otherwise be employers of a discharged employee or residents of the community at large will distinguish between an arbitrator's upholding a discharge for "patient abuse" and the criminal conviction for same when evaluating the person involved.

The strongest burden which might be applied in a criminal-type case such as this is proof "beyond a reasonable doubt." The Panel in this case is not convinced "beyond a reasonable doubt" that E— struck Verhagen. The question remains, therefore, whether the evidence is deemed by the Panel to be strong enough to warrant upholding the discharge and finding the grievant guilty of criminal-equivalent conduct.

The alleged slap was viewed from a distance of 40 feet or more. While the hallway was unobstructed and the grievant was in full view of the nurse, Wawerka, there are two factors which complicate the picture. The first is that the grievant's back was to Wawerka, *i.e.*, the grievant was between the patient and Wawerka. This fact would not in itself have prevented Wawerka from viewing Verhagen if he were sitting up and were visible at the grievant's side. The second factor, however, is that Verhagen sits forward in his chair with his head tilted downward. It is possible that one could see contact between the grievant's hand and the patient's neck under these circumstances, but it is unlikely. Wawerka herself testified that Verhagen was about half obscured from her vision. The Panel's view of the premises did nothing to convince it that there was great likelihood that such a slap could be seen with certainty.

In saying this the Panel is not challenging Wawerka's credibility. She was a credible witness and may in her own mind be certain of what she saw. The Panel is less certain.

By Wawerka's own testimony Verhagen did not react to the alleged slap. Wawerka did not examine Verhagen and assumed that because his neck tends to be red that no marks would have appeared from the slap. The Panel is not convinced that such an assumption was warranted. The fact that Verhagen was agitated, according to Wawerka, does not convince the Panel that Verhagen was slapped. Who would not be agitated given the shouting and commotion going on at the time? That Verhagen may have had a hand on his neck and was pointing at the grievant or the bathroom does not mean to the Panel that Verhagen was saying to Wawerka, "E— hit me!"

This case is troublesome also because the Panel is not convinced of the grievant's credibility. It is persuaded, however, that her story is true with regard to Verhagen's persistence in returning his chair to the bathroom entrance and hitting O'Bern's legs. It is persuaded that Verhagen may indeed have made it most difficult for the grievant to move his chair. Thus, the grievant apparently felt that Verhagen's provocative behavior made it necessary for her to handle him more roughly than would otherwise have been the case.

The Panel credits Wawerka's testimony over the grievant's regarding where the latter was standing. The Panel does not credit the grievant's testimony that she did not hear what was going on at the time because of an ear infection. No proof was offered with regard to an ear infection and apparently the grievant was having no difficulty carrying out her duties on November 3. Also there is no evidence that the grievant had any hearing problem at the meeting in the Administrator's office the following day.

Doubts about the grievant's credibility arise also regarding the substance of the meeting at the Administrator's office on November 4. The Panel credits the testimony of Administrator Lucia and his Assistant, De Prey, that the grievant neither denied nor admitted striking Verhagen. The testimony supporting the grievant offered by Union President Sandoval was rather vague and does not convince the Panel that the grievant did in fact deny striking Verhagen.

The Panel has concluded that the evidence is not sufficient to prove that the grievant struck Verhagen although it is apparent that she did not properly control the situation in which she and Verhagen were involved. Thus, the Panel must resolve its doubts in favor of the grievant. However, the Panel is not willing to conclude that nothing happened on November 3 and that full reinstatement of E— is therefore warranted.

During the incident in question E— was apparently shouting at the patient, and as Wawerka testified, was not in control of the situation. E— acknowledges that she gave Verhagen's chair a hard push into the alcove, and Wawerka's testimony indicates that E— treated the patient with more force than the situation required.

Employees in hospital situations are expected to cope with provocation by patients and deal with it in ways which do not cause them to be unnecessarily rough either physically or verbally. The Panel feels very strongly that patients should not be struck by employees and should be handled with a minimum of force.

The Panel also expects a hospital to have rules and give employees thorough training relating to the handling of patients so that there can be no doubt on the part of the employees as to proper methods as to handling patients. No evidence regarding rules or training was brought out at the hearing. However, in answer to the question, "Does the County Hospital have any rules concerning striking patients by staff members?", Wawerka's rather unsatisfactory answer was, "As far as I know it's a no-no, you don't ever strike a patient for any reason at all." Rules regarding patient care should be clearly stated by a hospital and should be made clear to all employees.

The Panel does not feel that Article I of the labor agreement requires it to impose no penalty on an employee where a discharge has been made without proper cause and where, as here, some discipline is found to be warranted. The Panel interprets Article I to require that the employee be made whole for the period during which the employer's action was not justified.

The discipline given herein is felt by the Panel to reflect both the seriousness of an offense involving rough treatment of patients and the fact that this is apparently the first instance of conduct involving the grievant over a five-year period which has been deemed serious enough to warrant discipline greater than a verbal warning.

AWARD

The grievant, E—, was improperly discharged but is hereby given a suspension of five working days. The Employer is ordered to reinstate E— to her former position with full seniority and make her whole for the period from the date of discharge to the date of this Award, less five days of pay and less any interim earnings which she had between the termination date of the five-day suspension and the date of this Award.

Case No. 12

*Was there just cause for discharging a nurses aide
who had violated a rule against personal contact with
tuberculin patients and for other unsatisfactory
performance, which had been noted in previous
evaluations?*

**Middle River Sanitorium and General Hospital (Douglas County, Wis.)
and
American Federation of State, County and Municipal
Employees, Local 1146**

Arbitrator: Donald B. Lee
Date of Award: Not dated
Citation: LAIG 16

Pertinent Contract Language

ARTICLE III — *Probationary Period*

Section 2 — All new employees shall serve a probationary period of six
months duration to determine whether or not they are suited or qualified
for the job. If during that time they do not perform their duties
satisfactorily, they may be discharged without recourse through the
Union. Thereafter they may be discharged for just cause only.

ARTICLE VI — *Grievance Procedure*

Section 1 — Both parties to this agreement agree that the prompt and just
settlement of grievances is of mutual concern. Should differences arise
between the Employer and the Union as to meaning in application of the
provisions of this agreement or as to any question relating to wages, hours

or other conditions of employment, an earnest effort shall be made to settle them promptly under the provisions of this article. Should an employee feel that his rights and privileges according to this agreement have been violated, he shall first submit the grievance in writing to the Grievance Committee. If it is determined by the Committee after investigation that a grievance does exist, it shall be processed in the following manner:

1. Between the aggrieved employee and/or Union Representative and the department head.

2. If not settled in step "1," then the aggrieved employee, the Union Grievance Committee, and/or their Union Representative shall submit the grievance in writing to the Superintendent.

3. If not settled as a result of step "2," then the grievance shall be presented in writing to the Board of Trustees.

4. If not settled as a result of step "3," the grievance shall be submitted to Mediation by the W.E.R.C.

5. If not settled by Mediation, the dispute shall be submitted to Arbitration.

(a) The Arbitration Board shall consist of three members, one member to be chosen by the Employer, one member to be chosen by the Union and the third member, who shall act as chairman of the Arbitration Board, shall be chosen by the two members already chosen.

(b) The results of the Arbitration proceedings shall be final and binding on both parties to this Agreement.

(c) Costs incurred through Arbitration shall be shared equally by both parties.

ARTICLE VII — *Disciplinary Procedures*

Section 1 — The following disciplinary procedure is intended as a legitimate device to inform employees of work habits, violations or policies, etc. that are not consistent with the aims and policies of the Hospital in carrying out its responsibilities to the patients and the public, and thereby to correct those deficiencies.

Section 2 — Employees will be given warning orally by the supervisor that may or may not be accompanied or followed by a written warning notice if an employee fails to adhere to hospital policies, working regulations, or fails to carry out his duties at an acceptable performance level. Frequency of warning notices may bring on a written notice of reprimand that can result in the following:

1. Official reprimand with serious warning.
2. Suspension.
3. Demotion.
4. Discharge.

Section 3 — The warning procedure of Section 2 may be by-passed by the Employer in cases of serious violation, as set forth in Hospital policy "Causes for Discharge," and could result in a reprimand notice with recommended disciplinary action.

The following violations can result in a reprimand notice with immediate discharge:

1. Theft of patient or employee personal property or public property.

2. Violation or conviction of state or federal laws.

3. Molesting, rough treatment or striking patients or other employees.

4. Coming on duty under the influence of liquor or drinking on duty.

5. Gross negligence in care of patients.

Section 4 — A copy of all warning notices and reprimands and discharges, will be given the Employee and the Union. If a notice of warning or reprimand was given unjustly, in the opinion of an employee, he may appeal through the regular grievance procedure.

Background

The Municipal Employer operates both an extended care facility and a tuberculosis sanatorium at the Middle River site. On November 5, 1967, the Grievant, at that time a high school junior, aged 18, was employed as a nurses' aide in the extended care facility. She lived on the premises during the period of her employment, the reason being that her parents were separated and she had no other place to stay. She completed her high school education while working at the facility prior to her discharge on April 29, 1969. Since July 2, 1969, at least until the date of hearing she has been employed as psychiatric technician by the State of Minnesota in its facility at Cambridge, Minnesota, a position she obtained after passing a civil service examination following some months of formal training obtained at the Cambridge Hospital.

Three of the Grievant's supervisors testified that her work habits were "inconsistent" and that she had a penchant for wasting time. While these traits were apparent from the outset of her employment, she, nevertheless, was retained after the expiration of the six-month probationary period.

On or about March 1, 1969, the Municipal Employer launched an Employer Evaluation Program in order to satisfy certain hospital accreditation conditions. The form shown below was developed.[1] Employee attitude and performance was measured accordingly. Apparently corrective counseling followed where indicated. Two of the Grievant's supervisors on March 19,

[1] *See page 94.*

1969, rated her as punctual but inconsistent in performance, requiring close supervision and of limited adaptability. Both stated that she willingly accepted her assignments, however one said she wasted time while the other stated that she rarely volunteered and that she commited many errors. The Nurse Supervisor reviewed with the Grievant her evaluations. In addition, she admonished her concerning her contact with a male tuberculosis patient who purportedly was to help her learn to play a guitar. It was uncontroverted that employees of the Institution who are under 21 years of age are not to have contact with T.B. patients and that by word of mouth at least the Grievant was aware of the rule, however, there is controversy concerning the application of the rule to all persons on the Institution's grounds under the age of 21.

On April 25, 1970, at 7:25 P.M., the Grievant, off duty at the time, was observed by a supervisor from a distance of approximately one-half (½) a

---

1

NAME   DATE

Dependability
    Punctual
    Steady attendance
    Consistent performance
    Always meets deadlines
    Frequently late
    Frequently absent
    Inconsistent performance
    Seldom meets deadlines
Quality
    Few errors — very little waster
    Many errors
Attitudes
    Volunteers
    Accepts assignments willingly
    Works overtime willingly
    Rarely volunteers
    Does not pitch in
    Argues about assignments
    Refuses to work overtime
Job Knowledge
    Works independently
    Requires close supervision
Job Skills
    Ability to do any job in department
    Limited adaptability

block, wrestling on the lawn with a T.B. patient, the same person involved in the guitar-playing incident. This patient (E) and another (S), although inmates of the Sanatorium, were apparently convalescing from tuberculosis. It was uncontroverted that they were allowed to roam about the grounds, mingle with other persons, visit the neighborhood tavern and receive week-end passes from the facility. (S) and the Grievant were returned to the hospital from a nearby tavern on one occasion. The action described by the supervisor as "wrestling" was confirmed by the Grievant as a "birthday spanking." The incident was written up by the supervisor and in turn passed along by the head nurse to the administrator. Incidentally, the 18-year-old son of the head nurse was in the vicinity of the Grievant and the other T.B. patient. The Grievant's testimony to this effect was not challenged.

The Administrator testified that he had earlier reviewed the aforementioned rating sheets of the Grievant with the head nurse and that he was aware of her warnings with respect to "mingling" with T.B. patients. As a result of the ratings which he would characterize as both complimentary and admonitory — depending upon the trait evaluated — and the incident described above, he decided for the good of the facility to discharge the Grievant on April 29, 1970.

Position of the Municipal Employer

The Employer contends that the discharge of the Grievant was for cause per the prescription of the collective bargaining agreement at Article III, Probationary Period, Section 1, inasmuch as she had been warned about her inadequacies as an employee via the aforementioned performance ratings. Furthermore, she was aware of the rules concerning mingling and association with the T.B. patients, a rule which she violated when she went into the hobby shop, which is located in a building separate and apart from the place of her employment to obtain instruction on guitar playing from a patient, and again when she became involved with the same patient in a rather unceremonial laying-on of hands on April 25, 1970.

The Employer submits that the Grievant's shortcomings and general personal conduct left him no alternative but to discharge her for the good of the institution. Employer requests that the discharge be upheld.

Position of the Union

The Union contends that there was no just cause for discharging the Grievant inasmuch as the totality of her alleged inadequacies and other actions do not meet the test. The Union argues that the Grievant, as admitted by the Employer, was untrained and without experience when initially employed, and further that her supervisors testified that the progress shown by the Grievant or any new employee depended in no small measure on her exposure to all the activities encountered on the job. In other words she was not expected to show over-night competency. In this regard the Union rejects the Employer's contention that the newly required work evaluation reports should be permitted to serve as serious warnings or official reprimand, especially in the absence of any declaration of his intent to use the reports in such fashion.

The Union further contends, albeit admitting that the Grievant knew the rule concerning association with tuberculosis patients, that said rule is seemingly more honored in the breach than in the keeping, pointing out that the Grievant's associate had extra-facility privileges which could lead one to believe that his malady was arrested and further that persons other than employees under the age of 21 also associated with this person and another similarly afflicted.

The Union further points out that the collective bargaining agreement at Article VII, Disciplinary Procedures, Section 2, strongly implies that the theory of progressive discipline is embraced by the parties and that in its application a penalty short of the ultimate, i.e., discharge, is proper in view of the total circumstances.

As to the remedy, the Union requests that the Grievant be awarded a sum equal to earnings lost during the period between April 29, 1969, and July 2, 1969.

Discussion and Findings

The facts are not seriously disputed. The Grievant was employed to learn to become a nurses aide. She had no previous experience. She completed her probationary period in the early part of April 1968. Nearly a year later, March 19 and 20, 1969, she received two (2) almost identical work evaluation ratings praising her punctuality, courtesy, attendance and willingness to accept assignments and at the same time criticizing her lack of consistency, adaptability, ability to function without close supervision and her propensity to err and waste time. There is nothing in the record to indicate that these shortcomings emerged only after the probationary period had passed, or immediately prior to April 19, 1970. To the contrary, the testimony of her supervisors indicated that the Grievant's work habits had changed but little during her entire period of employment. There is no testimony to the effect that she was formally reprimanded or warned about her work habits during the year following the completion of her probationary period.

She learned via word of mouth sometime prior to March 19, 1969, that she was not to associate — "mingle" — with T.B. patients. She did however become involved in the incident which led to her discharge after she was warned to cease such association.

Turning first to the incident that triggered her discharge, it is the opinion of the panel that the facts in the record are unable to support a finding that the Grievant's conduct bordered on immorality. The supervisor who observed the incident testified that she was approximately one-half (½) a city block — some three hundred yards — away from the involved individuals; that at least one other patient was in close proximity to the parties described. Grievant testified that the son of the Supervising Nurse was also present during the incident. This statement was not disputed.

With regard to the incident itself, Supervisor (N) on cross-examination testified as follows:

Q: Mrs. (N), how long did you witness this alleged wrestling incident?

A: Oh, just a minute or two. Just as soon as I saw them, I called to them: and, at first, they didn't answer and I went a little closer and called "(S)," because he was sitting there and he turned, and I just motioned them to come, and I pointed to my watch.

They both [patients] came very promptly and I told them that if they didn't get there in time, they wouldn't get their snacks, that they weren't going to get anything to eat, I mean, and I walked away. I didn't pay attention to where [Grievant] went, or I didn't notice if anyone else was there or not. Of course, the garage kind of blocks the way a little. I couldn't see the whole lawn.

Q: Mrs. N, as an R.N., this is the afternoon shift, was it not?

A: Yes.

In view of the foregoing the panel is not persuaded that the Municipal Employer has established just cause for discharge growing out of the wrestling–spanking incident regardless of the innuendos surrounding it. The quantum of proof to sustain a discharge for such conduct is patently lacking.[2]

Returning again to the objectionable work habits of the Grievant, while it may very well be true that her effort and input left much to be desired, it is likewise true that the Employer had every opportunity to correct her faults or if unable to do so to discharge her during her probationary period. Instead he chose to retain her. Also, as noted above, the record is devoid of any criticism directed toward her other than that routinely administered to all learners, during the period forward from April 8, 1968, until March 19, 1969. In view of this situation it is difficult indeed, at this point in time to find that her work,

[2]For some observations concerning quantum of proof in discharges of this nature see Hawthorn–Mellody Farms, Inc., 68-2-ARB-8432 (Lee).

acceptable at least up until March 19, 1969, became intolerable thereafter. For these reasons we are unable to find that the Employer can now consider the Grievant's hitherto acceptable work habits as grounds or just cause for discharge.

The fact that the Grievant knew she was not to associate with the T.B. patients has been established. Furthermore, the incident of April 25, 1970, occurred after she was told to cease such association. In view of these circumstances and in light of the language in the collective bargaining agreement, Article VII Disciplinary Procedures, Section 2, which strongly implies, as the Union urges, that progressive disciplinary measures were within the contemplation of the parties, we have concluded that a disciplinary suspension for a period of two (2) weeks would have been appropriate penalty had the Grievant remained in a position to accept reinstatement.

AWARD

That the Grievant be granted a sum equal to what she would have received for her services as a Nurses Aide during the period between April 29, 1969, and July 2, 1969, less an amount equivalent to her earnings for two (2) weeks during said period.

Case No. 13

Was there just cause to discharge a security officer who attempted to steal several hypodermic needles from a doctor's supply cart? Was the value of the needles (negligible, in this instance) relevant? Was the offense to be judged in the light of the Hospital's responsibility toward patients?

The New York City Health and Hospitals Corporation
and
Individual Grievant

Arbitrator: Jesse Simons
Date of Award: September 10, 1971
Citation: LAIG 294

This is an appeal to the Personnel Review Board by Morris Waleck, Esq., in behalf of Appellant B—, Special Officer, who was dismissed from Bronx Municipal Hospital Center on July 23, 1971, by decision of James A. Roan, Acting Senior Vice President for Personnel and Labor Relations of the Health & Hospitals Corporation, which decision was communicated to Mr. B— via Certified Mail.

Mr. Roan's decision was based on a written report containing findings that Appellant was guilty of misconduct and recommending his termination, which findings and recommendations were made by Hearing Officer Herbert Lefkowitz, who was authorized, pursuant to Section 75 of the Civil Service Law, to preside at and conduct a discipline hearing of the charges against Mr. B—.

The Personnel Review Board is duly constituted pursuant to Chapter 1016 of the Unconsolidated Laws of 1969, the New York City Health &

Hospitals Corporation Act, and it possesses authority under the Act to hear appeals of aggrieved employees, and to review actions of the Corporation pursuant to the terms of the Act, and it is the "Commission" to which "appeals from determinations in disciplinary proceedings" are to be made, pursuant to Section 76 of the Civil Service Law and its decisions possess the conclusiveness and finality provided for in Article 5, Section 76, subdivision 3 of said Civil Service Law.

The Board finds that all provisions of Article 5, Section 76, of the Civil Service Law have been met, to wit: that Appellant was provided with a written copy of charges preferred against him; that a hearing of those charges was held on June 4, 1971, with due notice provided; that Appellant was present and represented by counsel; that a transcript of these hearings was made and was supplied to the Health & Hospitals Corporation, the Personnel Review Board and Counsel for Appellant; that a written statement of the Hearing Examiner was prepared on July 9, 1971, containing findings and recommendations, and was submitted to the Health & Hospitals Corporation Vice President in Charge of Personnel, and a copy was supplied to the Personnel Review Board, the Appellant and his Counsel.

With due notice to Counsel for Appellant and to the Health & Hospitals Corporation, a hearing of the Personnel Review Board was scheduled for September 2, 1971, to hear the appeal of Mr. B—.

On September 2, 1971, the Board convened with all members present. Also present were Counsel for the Corporation, namely Steven J. Goldsmith, Esq., and Counsel in behalf of Appellant, namely Morris Waleck, Esq. The Personnel Review Board had before it Hearing Examiner Lefkowitz's "Report and Recommendations" which contained the following:

> From the evidence before me, I find that on April 27, 1971, at about 4:30 A.M., [B—] removed three or four hypodermic needles from the doctors' supply cart in the Emergency Room, illegally and without authorization.

> Recommendation: [B—] should be found guilty of illegally and without authorization removing three or four hypodermic needles from the doctors' supply cart in the Emergency Room on April 21, 1971 at about 4:30 A.M. His services should be terminated for this misconduct.

The Personnel Review Board also had a copy of the transcript of the hearing conducted by Hearing Examiner Lefkowitz in re Appellant.

Both parties were accorded full opportunity to present evidence and argument to the Personnel Review Board with respect to the appeal of Appellant from his dismissal, and a transcript of the Personnel Review Board's hearing was prepared and is on file in the Board's office.

After careful and detailed review of the transcript of the disciplinary hearings, and after review of the Hearing Examiner's Report and Recommendations, and after consideration and review of argument presented at the Board's hearing of September 2, 1971, the Board makes the following findings:

1.   That Mr. B— was a Health & Hospitals Corporation employee, employed pursuant to Section 5, subdivision 12 of the Health & Hospitals Corporation Act in a competitive title, and that as such, his appeal is properly before the Personnel Review Board.

2.   That Appellant has been accorded all rights pursuant to Sections 75 and 76 of the Civil Service Law.

3.   That formulation, execution and transmittal of dismissal of Mr. B— were performed pursuant to Sections 75 and 76 of the Civil Service Law.

4.   That the Personnel Review Board is the proper and legal forum to hear the Appellant's appeal from dismissal, pursuant to Sections 75 and 76 of the Civil Service Law.

5.   That the Health & Hospitals Corporation had just and sufficient cause to discipline Appellant B— for his misconduct, and that such finding is supported by the evidence and testimony in the disciplinary hearing.

That there are solid grounds for concluding that dismissal from the Civil Service is an appropriate act of discipline of Appellant for his misconduct for the following reasons:

(a)   That theft or attempted theft by an employee on hospital premises is misconduct.

(b)   That in the instant case, though the hypodermic needles that were almost appropriated, were of negligible value, and even though the Appellant did not benefit from said effort to appropriate, these needles are much sought after for a variety of purposes, causes the Board to regard this attempted theft as gross misconduct.

(c)   That a hospital is virtually a warehouse of such objects (needles, hypodermics, drugs, etc.) and, therefore, at all times vigilance of the hospital and the hospital employees is essential in securing them and apprehending those who attempt to appropriate them, and that disciplinary action by the Hospital of employees who steal such items or attempt to steal such items or any other medical equipment or supplies is appropriate, not only in order to remove from service employees who use their employment to traffic in such matters (either for themselves, friends or personal gain), but also to insure that all other employees are aware that theft is prohibited and will bring as a consequence grave penalties.

(d)   That in the current environment pilferage is a common and vexing problem to all employers; however, appropriation of medical supplies and equipment can be distinguished from common industrial pilferage, in that medical equipment and supplies are vital to the performance of medical services for injured and sick patients, and that the absence of said supplies at a critical juncture may have a harmful or possibly lethal effect on patients, and, therefore, greater vigilance and stronger measures are warranted than generally are followed in the employer–employee relationship, both private and public.

(e)   That the attempted theft was committed by a Special Officer, is a factor which weighed heavily with the Board because the Board views Special Officers as having greater responsibility to conform their conduct in all respects to the requirements of the Corporation than other hospital employees, and that as such, their conduct is to be measured by a higher standard than applied to others, and that the Corporation had a right to expect such a higher level of responsibility from, and to apply such a higher standard to Appellant, all in the Board's view lends further justification for sustaining the Corporation's decision to discharge the Appellant.

AWARD

In view of all the findings and conclusions set forth above, the Personnel Review Board concludes and decides that the appeal of Mr. B— from his dismissal by the Corporation is denied.

Case No. 14

Was a five-day suspension justified in the case of an
X-ray technician who hit a malfunctioning
machine with force sufficient to break a glass
panel and jam an indicator needle?

Flint Osteopathic Hospital (Flint, Mich.)
and
American Federation of State, County and Municipal
Employees, Local 1850

Arbitrator: George T. Roumell, Jr.
Date of Award: July 9, 1971
Citation: LAIG 265

Mr. R— is employed as a staff technician at the Flint Osteopathic Hospital. His job consists of working with X-ray equipment.

On February 23, 1971, a Doctor Derderian was performing a Diagnostic operation on a patient. As part of his operative procedure, Dr. Derderian desired to perform an operative cholangiogram, which involved the use of X-ray equipment.

Because of this, Mr. R— was asked to bring a portable X-ray machine to the operating room. Mr. R— did bring the portable X-ray machine to the operating room at about 10:00 a.m.

The machine is bulky, and must be wheeled in. It contains an instrument panel. On the instrument panel there is a rectangular meter box, which is half plastic and half glass. The glass part contains a face with numbers and a needle going from one side to the other. This box is called a kilovolt meter. It is designed to register the functioning of the X-ray machine.

In addition, there are two buttons on the bottom of the panel. These buttons are marked A.M., one referring to a hundred A.M.'s, the other to 30. One or the other button must be pushed in before the machine may be operated and the meter, described above, will register showing that the machine is operating.

Mr. R— testified that after he wheeled the X-ray machine into the operating room, he plugged it in and noticed that the meter was not registering. With the palm of his hand, he hit the plastic part below the glass of the meter. The glass broke. Some of the glass fell down behind the plastic bottom of the meter. The meter did not respond. Thereupon, R— removed the X-ray machine from the operating room.

He asked Dr. Derderian if he wished him, Mr. R— to get the other portable X-ray machine that was available at the hospital. Dr. Derderian advised him that he did not wish the second machine. Doctor Derderian did not proceed with the cholangiogram. There was testimony that the cholangiogram was not always used in the operative procedures being then employed by Dr. Derderian and that it was an optional procedure.

Mr. R— then took the X-ray machine back to Room 3 in the X-ray department. He obtained the other X-ray machine and placed it outside the operating room, so, as he explains, that there would be an option for Dr. Derderian to use the machine if he so desired.

Mr. R— then returned to Room 3. He then went to Room 4 of the X-ray department where his supervisor, Mr. Frank Stoll, was and told him what had happened. Mr. Stoll went to Room 3 following Mr. R—.

Mr. Stoll testified that he saw the X-ray machine with the glass broken in the meter. He also testified that the meter's registering needle was lodged in the face of the gauge and to one side. Mr. Stoll testified that when Mr. R— first came to him, R— had a screwdriver in his hand.

Also present in Room 4 with Mr. Stoll at the time Mr. R— came in was Clyde Striler, a maintenance supervisor. Mr. Striler also went to Room 3 to see the broken X-ray machine. He gave the same description of its condition as did Mr. Stoll. Striler testified that he tried to dislodge the needle in the gauge and in so doing, broke the needle off.

Mr. Striler testified that R— had told him that he (R—) had broken the glass with a screwdriver. Mr. R— denied this and stated that he had used the screwdriver after he brought the machine back to attempt to dislodge the glass in the bottom part of the meter.

The Arbitrator finds that the glass was broken under the circumstances related by Mr. R—. The statement related by Mr. Striler was made in Room 3 where there is little question that R— was using the screwdriver to apparently clean out the glass. It is quite obvious that he had no screwdriver in the operating room, for clearly in such an antiseptic setting, a screwdriver would not be permitted.

After Dr. Stoll had seen the machine, he reported the situation to Dr. E. Edward Kani, Chairman of the Hospital's Department of Radiology. Dr. Kani, James King, the Hospital's Assistant Administrator, and Robert Brown, the Hospital's Personnel Director, later consulted and decided to suspend Mr. R— for five days for abuse of equipment.

Mr. Stoll advised Mr. R— of this decision on the afternoon of February 23, 1971. R—'s suspension covered February 24, 25, 26, and March 1st and 2nd, 1971. He returned to work on Wednesday, March 3, 1971.

The following written grievance was appealed by the Union on behalf of Mr. R—.

I.   Appeal Suspension of Mr. R— dated February 23, 1971.

II.   In the past few weeks, several employees of the X-ray Department have had trouble with the K.V. sticking on the portable used in surgery. Mr. R— assumed the meter was stuck and he tried to jar it loose, so the surgery case could be completed. The breaking of the glass and damage caused to the meter was purely accidental and was done without malice on the part of Mr. R—.

III.   *Decision Reached:* We feel that the decision reached by Mr. Stoll was much too harsh, considering the above-mentioned facts, and we feel the decision is improper and should be appealed.

The Hospital takes the position that by virtue of Article II, Management Rights, of the contract, it had the right "to suspend, discipline and discharge employees for just cause and otherwise to maintain an orderly, effective and efficient operation." The Hospital, relying on this provision, states that its paramount concern is patient care; that it is essential that its equipment not be abused so as to make said equipment inoperative for patient care; that when it suspended Mr. R— for five days, it was using reasonable judgment; that the Arbitrator should not disturb this judgment because of the paramount concern to patient care, and Mr. R—'s activities were such as to affect this care.

Furthermore, the Hospital argues, based upon the above-quoted appeal, that the Union is not questioning the wrong-doing of Mr. R— but only questioning the penalty. Therefore, according to the Hospital, the Arbitrator should limit himself to the question of the penalty.

The Union has responded by questioning both the alleged wrong-doing finding and the penalty.

The Union points out that though patient care is paramount, the employees of the Hospital do have a collective bargaining contract and are entitled to the rights of that contract; that a Hospital is no different than any other employer in this respect.

There is no question that the Hospital is concerned about employee abuse of equipment. Approximately, six (6) months previous to the above incident, Mr. R— was orally reprimanded by his supervisor, Mr. Stoll, for attempting to force open one end of a dark room pass box which was not supposed to be opened. Mr. R— acknowledged this reprimand. Mr. R— also acknowledged, as did another employee, Mr. Michael O'Driscol, that there had also been a meeting about six (6) months ago called by Mr. Stoll where he asked the employees to avoid abusing equipment.

The basic contention of the Union is that when Mr. R— did hit the meter box, he was following standard procedures. On cross-examination the Union brought forth an admission by Mr. Stoll that sometimes when a meter did not respond upon the X-ray machine being turned on, "a gentle tap on the meter" gets a response. Stoll referred to the "gentle tap" as being necessary occasionally. Another Hospital witness, Mr. Robert Brown, who is the Personnel Director, but for some 16 years was the supervisor in the X-ray Department, also stated that a "very light tap" was sometimes called for if the meter indicator did not initially respond. The purpose of the tap would be to dislodge the needle. However, Mr. Brown stated that when he referred to a tap he meant a "very light tap." Mr. Brown not only stated this in testimony, but he stated it at Step 4 of the grievance procedure in discussing Mr. R—'s grievance.

The Stoll–Brown testimony on this point was substantiated by the testimony of three other staff technicians. The first staff technician, Jane Barham, testified that she had been employed in the X-ray Department for two (2) years. She stated that one usually turns the machine on, checks the A.M. buttons and then taps the meter lightly if it doesn't register. She then proceeded to say that if the light tap brought no response, she would hit the meter with the side of her clenched fist. Mrs. Barham demonstrated the type of light tap plus a hard hit with her fist. Interestingly enough, in her demonstration, she hit the meter's glass shield each time.

Philipp Hunt, a Staff Technician for eight (8) years, testified that his procedure was to first turn the machine on, then press the appropriate A.M. button in. If at this point the meter would not respond, he would hit it with his knuckles. He referred to his hitting as "thumping it with my knuckles." His physical demonstration before this Arbitrator showed that his thump was lighter than Mrs. Barham's hitting with the side of her fist. Nevertheless, Mr. Hunt in the demonstration, also thumped the glass, rather than the meter's plastic bottom.

Michael O'Driscol, also a staff technician stated that he would turn on the machine, check the A.M. buttons to be sure they were engaged, and then if the meter did not work, he would hit the glass on the meter with the back of his knuckles. Again, his demonstration established a hitting of the glass, which hitting was much lighter than Mrs. Barham's clenched side of her fist. O'Driscol indicated that this was done quite frequently.

Thus, both management witness and witnesses of the Union verify, as the Union claims, that hitting the meter was not an uncommon practice when it did not initially register.

There was also testimony that about six months previously on another type of X-ray machine an employee broke the glass of the meter involved. He was not disciplined. However, Mr. Stoll pointed out it was known that the machine was in disrepair awaiting repair. Therefore, the employee was excused from his actions.

It is also further noted that Mr. Stoll or Dr. Kani had not received in recent times any reports that the portable X-ray machine was not properly functioning. There was no other testimony indicating that there was any evidence that it was known that the machine was not functioning properly. The only evidence on the point of machine malfunctioning was that frequently the machine's K.V. meter did need some encouragement to get it to respond.

Though it is clear on this record that the meters are sometimes hit as a matter of practice, Mr. R— cannot rely on this to say that he was free of wrong-doing. He had been warned about abuse of equipment, not only individually, but in a group meeting. He did hit the machine with the force of the palm of his hand, rather than with a tap of a knuckle or the side of a woman's clenched fist. The force of his hitting was such that not only did the glass break, but the needle was pressed against the face of the dial and to the side. We admit that Mr. R—, unlike the others, may have used the precaution of hitting the plastic covering the meter rather than the glass. However, it is obvious that he used greater force than the testimony of both the Hospital and Union witnesses indicated should be used. How else can it be explained that not only did the glass break, but the needle was jammed against the dial face?

It should also be noted that both the Hospital's witnesses and the three staff technicians, Mrs. Barham, Mr. Hunt and Mr. O'Driscol testified that the first thing one must do when the needle is not registering is to check to make sure that the A.M. button is engaged (pushed-in) for the machine will not operate and therefore the meter will not register unless this is done. There is testimony on this record that Mr. R— did not do this. His own testimony, unlike the other technicians' testimony, does not reveal that when he was in the operating room he checked the A.M. button or attempted to engage them. Mr. Stoll testified that when he saw the portable X-ray machine in Room 3, both the A.M. buttons were out or disengaged. The Union's counsel attempted to suggest that the buttons could be disengaged by a bumping of the knee such as pushing the machine through the hallway. The Arbitrator was not convinced that this was the fact. It could easily be inferred from this record that Mr. R—'s basic problem with the K.V. meter was his failure to engage the proper A.M. button.

Nevertheless, it is recognized that he was using a somewhat standard, though not necessarily common procedure. He was not attempting to be destructive of equipment. What happened is that he used indiscretion in the amount of force and perhaps was negligent in failing to engage the A.M. button. He was aware that he had a responsibility not to abuse equipment or be negligent. The equipment had to be kept in good repair at all times because of its need particularly in possible life or death situations.

We find therefore, abuse of the x-ray equipment as well as negligence, by Mr. R—. The question then becomes whether or not the penalty assessed by the administration of the Hospital in suspending Mr. R— for five days should be sustained.

Before discussing the specific facts of this case, it will aid clarity to set forth the standards by which the Arbitrator believes this case should be analyzed.

Some arbitrators believe that the proper standard is one in which the arbitrator does not disturb the decision of management with regard to discipline unless there has been a clear abuse of management discretion. Under this theory of arbitrable restraint, the arbitrator examines the penalty only in terms of whether or not it was outside what any reasonable management could do, and if it is not, he then does not disturb it. If he finds he must disturb it, he disturbs only so much as is necessary to place it within the necessity of reason under which management must operate. [See, *e.g.*, opinions of Arbitrator Whitley P. McCoy in *In Re Stockham Pipe Fittings Co.* 1 LA 160 (1945) and *Chattanooga Box Lumber Co.* 10 LA 260 (1948).]

Other arbitrators, such as the well-known Harry Platt, believe, absent restrictive contract language to the contrary, that it is the arbitrator's job to examine the entire situation *de novo*, considering all of the circumstances, practices and equities of the parties in determining whether or not the penalty was suitable for the offense found to have been committed. See, *e.g.*, Mr. Platt's decision in *Michigan Steel Casting Co.* 6 LA 678 (1948); Platt, "The Arbitration Process in the Settlement of Labor Disputes" 31 J.A.M. Jud. 50C., 54, 58; Opinion of Arbitrator Adolph Koven in *Kaiser Sand and Gravel*, 49 LA 190 (1967).

It is the opinion of this Arbitrator that either standard or indeed some combination of the two, may be proper depending upon the contract language of the parties. This Arbitrator believes that his first and foremost duty is to preserve and enforce the bargain which the parties have made. Therefore, in determining what standard should be used in evaluating a disciplinary penalty, the arbitrator should carefully analyze the contract to determine if the parties have, as a part of their bargain, included some guidance as to what such a standard should be.

In examining the agreement between the parties we do find some guidance. In the "management rights" clause Article II, found on page 1 of the agreement, one of the specifically enumerated rights of management is:

> the right to determine the qualifications of employees, and to suspend, discipline and discharge employees for just cause and otherwise to maintain an orderly effective and efficient operation.

Let alone, this language would lead us to the inference that the parties had bargained for a standard under which the right of management to discipline would not be disturbed unless there was an unreasonable breach of discretion.

However, in Article II, Paragraph C, entitled "Appeal of Discharge or Discipline," the parties agreed to the following language which, to some extent, modified the statement of intent contained in the above-quoted Article II:

> Should the discharged or disciplined employee or the steward consider the discharge *to be improper*, a complaint shall be presented in writing through the steward to the employer within five (5) calendar days of the discharge or discipline. The employer will review the discharge or discipline and give its answer within five (5) calendar days after receiving the complaint. If the decision is not satisfactory to the union, the matter shall be referred to the grievance procedure at Step No. 4.

In Section 3 of Article X, dealing specifically with arbitration, the parties indicated by the following language that there has been contemplation by these parties of the possibility of modification of penalties by the arbitrator.

> Except as otherwise provided and limited by this agreement no grievants claiming back wages shall exceed the amount of wages the employee otherwise would have earned plus any remuneration or payments he may have received during his period of suspension from employment with the hospital.

We believe that from the language just cited above, an inference is properly drawn that it was the intent of the parties that the Arbitrator in examining a penalty for employee wrong-doing, not limit himself to the question of whether or not the penalty was not grossly beyond the realm of reasonable management discretion. The term "just cause" is limited by reference to "proper" discipline and discharge. Provision is made for access to the grievance procedure in the event that the steward or the employee feels his discharge is improper, without any statement that in order to obtain relief the discharge must be completely beyond the realm of possible management discretion. Furthermore, the contract contemplates the possibility of amendment or modification of management's disciplinary decision by the arbitrator in that there is language which limits such discretion to time actually lost due to discipline. The Arbitrator therefore finds that the proper standard to use in this case, under the above language, is the standard of review of management's decision in light of the surrounding circumstances, practices of the parties and the equities of the situation.

This interpretation of the contract's language, is not unique to this Arbitrator for well-known Michigan Arbitrator, Russell A. Smith, reached the same result in interpreting similar contract language in a disciplinary dispute, in *McInerney Spring and Wire Co.*, 21 LA 80 (1953).

The Hospital has met the burden of proof of establishing that Mr. R— was guilty of some wrong-doing. In some circumstances, some arbitrators would then hold that the burden of proof now shifts to the Union, to establish that the penalty should be reduced as being unreasonable. See, *Linear Inc.*, 48 LA 319 (1966, Frey). But whether the Platt view or Frey view is followed here, the results are the same.

The Union has established quite clearly that Mr. R— was acting in good faith, when he broke the glass on the meter, for he was attempting to do what other staff technicians do with the approval of management, namely, to "tap," "thump" or "hit" the meter. In Mr. R—'s case he used more force than should have been applied.

Perhaps the analysis of the actual situation in regard to the penalty here can be aided by the language used by well-known West Coast Arbitrator Paul Prasow in *General Telephone Co. of California*, 44 LA 669 (1965), where Professor Prasow refused to sustain a two day disciplinary suspension for violation of safety rules after two employees drove a truck off a road into a sand bank and had to be towed out. In making this refusal, Professor Prasow said at 671:

> Negligence is willful misconduct, often resulting in reprimand, suspension, or discharge. Incompetence, on the other hand arises from misunderstanding, lack of knowledge, or inability to meet the requirements of the job, and usually results in retraining, transfer, demotion, or termination. Disciplinary penalties, such as suspensions are inappropriate in cases of true incompetence, because they are punitive, rather than corrective in purpose.
>
> The line that separates incompetence from negligence is often a fine one. The two sometimes merge or overlap. Because of the understandable confusion between the two terms, it is essential that the

circumstances surrounding an employee's alleged misconduct be carefully evaluated in order to deal with the problem appropriately.

Discipline is imposed for the purpose of changing an employee's behavior so that in the future he will do what is expected of him. It is assumed that he can and will change his conduct. However, when an employee is deficient in his job, or is incapable of performing the work safely, or cannot keep up with the standard of performance, then some kind of warning notice, transfer, demotion, or termination, depending on the employee's past record, length of service, and other mitigating circumstances, are suitable responses because they are related to the employee's competence or qualifications, and not to his willful misconduct. Where negligence is involved, some form of corrective discipline is naturally appropriate rather than transfer or demotion which are not properly used for punitive disciplinary purposes.

. . . In short, there are errors which are the result of willfulness, and errors which are the result of faulty judgment exercised in good faith by the employee.

The Company may certainly take appropriate measures to protect itself from an employee who, with the best of intent, is unable to meet the requirements of a specific situation. In such cases, management often resorts to transfers, demotions, or even separation from the job if there is no work available for which the employee is qualified. However, in the Arbitrator's opinion, it is improper to lump together the two kinds of lapses in performance (error in judgment and willful dereliction) and impose punitive measures in the first category as well as in the second. In cases involving errors of judgment, where the good faith of the employee is not in question, correction, yes — but punishment, no! The distinction is often a fine one, ut it bears repeating.

A suspension is punitive in nature unlike a written warning, for example, which may have for its purpose notifying the employee of an inadequacy not necessarily due to willfulness. A warning, oral or written, serves this purpose but a suspension goes beyond this purpose. It serves notice punitively by depriving the employees of work days, which in the opinion of the Arbitrator is inappropriate where there has been a good faith lapse in performance.

Management is under no obligation to carry indefinitely an incompetent employee. If rehabilitative measures do not succeed, the Company may have no alternative but to terminate the employee. It would be improper, however, to treat his inadequacies as willful so long as he endeavors to improve, but is simply unable to meet the requirements of the job.

This is the point here. Mr. R— was not so much guilty of negligence as he was perhaps of incompetence. He acted in good faith, but apparently exercised "faulty judgment." If this was all there was to the case, then quite clearly, using the Prasow approach, as just mentioned, a suspension, punitive in nature, is not called for. But rather a warning, corrective in nature, is appropriate. Under these circumstances where there is an accepted practice of hitting, to some extent, a non-working meter, only a warning would be appropriate.

However, on this record there was evidence that Mr. R—, to some extent, had crossed the line that separates incompetence from negligence, in that, he failed to check the A. M. buttons. The other X-ray technicians in their testimony before this Arbitrator stated clearly that they had to check the buttons before they could expect the meter to register. R— in his own testimony gave no indication he did this. The machine when seen by Supervisor Stoll showed that the buttons were not engaged.

For this reason, the analysis in the *General Telephone Co. of California* is not completely applicable, though applicable to a point because of these unusual circumstances.

Using the Platt standards in this case, this Arbitrator believes that the suspension should be reduced to one day. He based this on the practice of the parties and the equities of the situation. The hitting of the meter was not unusual. Another employee, six months previously had done the same and broken the glass but was not disciplined, though the Hospital maintains the reason for the failure to discipline was that machine's need of repair.

On the other hand, Mr. R— was warned individually about the abuse of equipment and he was warned in a group about same. And he did more than the usual custom, he apparently failed to check the A.M. buttons.

In its opening statement, the Hospital indicated that Mr. R—'s activities were responsible for cancelling operative procedure involved. If this was the case, this Arbitrator would not disturb the penalty.

But there was no proof of this. In fact, the procedure involved was optional. The inference can be made that the operating doctor exercised his options. This particularly follows when technician R— stated he would obtain the other portable X-ray machine and, in fact, did bring it to a position right outside the operating room on his own motion.

Considering all the factors and the equities, the Arbitrator will order the suspension reduced to one day, because there is more than just a corrective situation involved, although, as already indicated here, negligence and incompetence has to some extent been merged. We further point out that in such situations it is not uncommon for arbitrators to reduce penalties. See *General Telephone Co. of California, supra; Carr Adams and Collier Co.*, 27 LA 656 (Graff, 1956); *New York Ship Building Corporation*, 47 LA 1184 (Crawford, 1966).

We further concede that in cases of negligence, five day suspensions have been sustained, but only where there was a past record of several occasions of carelessness in operating machines, a general uncooperative attitude in using the proper cutting tools and apparently written notice as well as being placed on probation for lack of cooperation as in *Dowingtown Iron Works, Inc.* 18 LA 680 (1952, Riddle).

Here we not only do not have such a situation, but we have Mr. R— doing what other employees normally did in such circumstances with the apparent consent of management, and his attempt to remedy (by making the other portable X-ray machine available) any incompetence or negligence on his part. It is these equities that pursuade the Arbitrator to reduce the penalty.

AWARD

The grievance is granted in part and denied in part. The suspension of Mr. R— is reduced from five (5) days to one (1) day and he is to be paid for the four (4) days lost without interest less any amounts he may have earned elsewhere during said four (4) day period.

Case No. 15

*Was a regulation requiring all beards to be closely
cropped and neatly trimmed reasonably related to
proper exercise of functions of the Hospital in
treatment and care of its patients so as to justify the
discharge of a psychiatric technician for
noncompliance?*

**St. Mary's Hospital and Medical Center (San Francisco, Calif.)
and
Hospital and Institutional Workers Union, Local 250**

**Arbitrator: David Karasick
Date of Award: June 28, 1973
Citation: 60 LA 1141**

The Issue

Whether R— was discharged for just cause.

Relevant Provision of the Contract

ARTICLE X — *Grievance Procedure*

Section 1 — Employee Grievances:

If any employee or the Union has a grievance or complaint
concerning the interpretation or application of the terms of this
Agreement, including a discharge case, it shall be taken up in this
manner:

(a) STEP 1.   The employee may first confer with the department
head or with such other person as the Employer may designate and
attempt to settle the matter.

(b) STEP 2.   If the grievance or complaint is not thus settled, the authorized representative of the Union shall confer with the Administrator of the hospital, or his designated representative, and attempt to settle the matter.

Section 2 — Employer Grievances — STEP 2:

If the Employer has a grievance or a complaint concerning the interpretation or application of the terms of this Agreement, the Administrator of the hospital, or his designated representative, shall confer with the authorized representative of the Union and attempt to settle the matter.

Section 3 — Written Notification — STEP 3:

If any such grievance or complaint is not settled by the procedure above described, it shall be fully, but informally, set forth in writing by the Union or the Affiliation, as the case may be, and submitted to the other. Thereafter, there shall be a meeting between designated representatives of the Union and the Affiliation with respect to the grievance or complaint and an attempt made by these representatives to settle the matter.

Section 4 — Arbitration — STEP 4:

If any such grievance or complaint has not been settled by any of the procedures described, the question may, at the request of either party, be submitted to arbitration by an arbitrator to be selected by the representatives of the Affiliation and the Union. The award of the arbitrator shall be final and binding on all concerned. The arbitrator may award damages for any breach of this contract; but no such award of damages shall be made for any period earlier than the date when the grievance or complaint was first presented. The Affiliation and the Union shall each pay one-half (½) of the costs of arbitration including the fees of the arbitrator and other expenses of the arbitral proceeding, but not including compensation of costs of representation, advocacy or witnesses for either party.

Section 5 — Time Limit:

No grievance or complaint shall be considered unless it has been first presented within thirty (30) days of the alleged occurrence thereof.

If a grievance is not settled at Step 1, Step 2 or Step 3 within fifteen (15) days of presentation in such step, the grievant may take such grievance to the next step.

Section 6 — Power of Arbitrator:

The Arbitrator shall have no power to add to, to subtract from or to change any of the terms or provisions of this Agreement. His jurisdiction shall extend solely to claims of violation of specific written provisions of the Agreement and involve only the interpretation and application of such Agreement.

The award shall be based upon the joint submission agreement of the parties, or in the absence thereof, the questions raised by the parties in respect to the specific interpretation and application of the Agreement. Without limitation upon the foregoing, if either party shall give notice of a desire to modify this Agreement as provided in Article XI, the arbitrator shall have no power to determine what modifications or changes, if any, should be made in the Agreement or otherwise to decide any question with respect thereto, other than the sufficiency and effect of the notice itself . . .

The Facts

R—, the grievant in this case, was employed as a psychiatric technician at St. Mary's Hospital for approximately three years prior to his discharge on August 7, 1972. R— was discharged for refusing to trim his beard in accordance with regulations adopted by the hospital. At the time R— was first employed, beards were not allowed. Similarly prohibited were mustaches that extended below the corner of the mouth. There were no written regulations to that effect, but the policy was enforced by members of the supervisory staff. A change in policy which permitted beards and longer hair styles of male employees occurred approximately in June, 1971, but no written regulations announcing the change were issued. R— testified that he first noticed the change in the appearance of the interns in the hospital. At about that time, R— and two other employees who were in the department began to grow beards.

On June 15, 1972, a bulletin dealing with appearance and dress standards was posted in various departments of the hospital, including the department in which R— worked. The bulletin, in relevant part, stated as follows:

1. *POLICY* —

Cleanliness and appropriate personal appearance are vital considerations in patient care. The patients and public have every right to expect a standard of appearance and personal grooming that promotes an image of neatness, cleanliness and professionalism.

We serve the patient care needs of all segments of our community. It is important for our patients to have confidence in our ability to take care of their needs. Since a "positive" personal appearance can significantly promote confidence, St. Mary's Hospital and Medical Center will encourage appearance and dress standards that reflect an image of professionalism and good taste.

A. *Male Hair Styles and Facial Adornments*

Length of hair to collar only and to the level of the ears only is acceptable. It must be neatly groomed or styled. Sideburns are permissible to the lower earlobe. Full beards are not permitted. Mustaches are acceptable if kept neatly trimmed. Van Dyke beards, if neatly trimmed, are also acceptable.

Following issuance of the bulletin on June 15, R— filed a complaint with the Equal Employment Opportunity Commission. In addition, after protests had been received from several male employees, including R—, the Union wrote to the Hospital on June 20, 1972, stating that the proposed appearance and dress standards were vague, discriminatory, and an infringement upon personal freedoms. The letter suggested that the standards be clarified and that a meeting be held to discuss the matter. No conclusive result, however, was reached.

On July 11, 1972, R— and his immediate supervisor met and discussed the dress standards which had been promulgated by the Hospital. He and a number of other male employees in his department expressed a desire to be permitted to wear full beards, rather than Van Dyke beards as the bulletin required.

The protest of R— and other employees was brought to the attention of the administrators of the hospital. On July 14, 1972, the following bulletin was posted as an amendment to the one which had been issued on June 15, 1972 regarding appearance and dress standards:

The Policy and Procedure Bulletin on Appearance and Dress Standards (PPB A-20) is intended to insure that all hospital employees are presentable and professional in appearance. In order that this policy may be correctly and uniformly applied, I would like to classify the standards set forth and establish a timetable for enforcement as follows:

Standards

Hairstyles: both men and women should avoid extremes. In patient contact areas, men and women with long hair should keep it "neatly contained and generally off the collar." This may be accomplished in several ways; for example, by pulling the hair back in a bun or pony tail, or wearing a wig which is short in length. In any event, the desired result is that hair should be kept, for the most part, off the face, neck and shoulders and should be clean and neatly groomed at all times.

Facial Hair: beards are permitted as long as they are closely cropped and neatly trimmed. Sideburns should not extend below the lower earlobe, and mustaches are to be kept neat and well trimmed.

Enforcement

Verbal counseling — should take place no later than today, July 14,

1972. Notation of such must be made in writing and sent to the Personnel office.

Written warning — should take place one week subsequent to verbal counseling and no later than Friday, July 21, 1972, in the event of continued noncompliance. The warning letter to be used will be provided by the Personnel Department.

Suspension — will begin one week following the written warning, and no later than Friday, July 28, 1972, if compliance is not met. The employee may return to work as soon as he complies any time within the week.

Discharge — will be immediate if the employee fails to comply with the policy within the week of suspension, and should occur no later than Friday, August 4, 1972. The supervisor must notify the employee of discharge in writing and make the necessary recommendation and comments with the Personnel Department. The discharge letter to be used will also be provided by the Personnel office.

If there are any further questions or problems, contact the Personnel office.

On July 19, 1972, a discussion was held between R— and his supervisor regarding the requirements of the July 14th bulletin. On that occasion, R— was told by his supervisor that an interpretation of the original policy had been made and, as a result, full beards would be permitted. R—'s hair, which at that time was past shoulder length, was no longer an issue since he wore it back of his ears in a pony-tail style secured either by a rubber band or bobby pins, which thus conformed to the requirements of the newly-revised standards. There was a difference of opinion among the witnesses at the hearing as to whether R—'s beard was longer at the time he was discharged than at the time of the hearing in this case. I do not believe it is necessary to resolve that conflict. Whatever the exact dimensions may have been it is clear that his beard, neither then nor at the time of the hearing in this case, was closely cropped or neatly trimmed. At the meeting on July 19 R— was requested to shorten and trim his beard in compliance with the amended standards. At the conclusion of the meeting R—'s supervisor gave him a letter advising him that his failure to comply with the appearance and dress standards would subject him "to further disciplinary action, including, but not limited to, suspension and/or discharge." The letter further stated that he would be expected to comply by July 26, 1972.

Thereafter, R—'s beard remained unchanged and on July 31, 1972, another meeting was held between R— and his supervisor. R— still refused to comply and at the conclusion of the meeting his supervisor gave him a letter which stated that as of the close of work on that date R— would be suspended for one week without pay. The letter further stated that, if he did not report for work by August 7, 1972, it would be assumed that he did not intend to comply and therefore his employment with the hospital would be terminated. R— failed to report for work on August 7 and his employment was terminated as of that date.

Position of the Employer

1. The grievant had no constitutional right to wear his beard in a manner which failed to comply with the dress and appearance standards of the Hospital.

2. R— was discharged for just cause since (a) he had notice of the appearance and dress standards and was given ample opportunity to comply; (b) the appearance and dress standards relate to the orderly and efficient operation of the Hospital, are reasonable and enforceable as applied in the instant case, and are not ambiguous; and (c) the appearance and dress standards were not applied in a discriminatory fashion.

3. The penalty imposed was reasonably related to the seriousness of the offense.

Position of the Union

1. The appearance and dress standards adopted by the Hospital are vague.

2. The length of the grievant's beard and appearance were not reasonably related to his "professional appearance."

3. R—'s appearance neither affected nor hindered the performance of his duties.

Summary and Conclusion

At the outset, it must be observed that both parties in this case acted in the utmost good faith and on what each regarded as the highest principles. The grievant entertained a sincere belief in his right as an individual to wear the sort of facial adornment which was most pleasing to him and most suitable to his personality as he saw it. The Hospital, on its part, was also concerned with its personality as reflected in the community by the appearance of its employees. Both views are understandable and equally are entitled to respect.

Having said this is but to pose the problem. An employer is entitled to prescribe reasonable rules governing the conduct of its employees. Similarly, the employees are entitled to freedom of expression in their adornment and personal appearance. The problem is, how are these equally important rights to be reconciled when they come into conflict? If they are to be balanced, one against the other, and, in the final assessment, one must give way, which should it be? As one court which has dealt with the matter of hair styles has observed, state and federal decisions dealing with the question "have reached sharply divergent viewpoints." *(Kirk v. California Unemployment Insurance Appeals Board,* 25 C.A.3d 199, 205) The same may be said of those cases which have gone to arbitration. In their briefs, the parties have cited a large number of decisions. Out of these cases, as the Hospital points out in its brief, the following standards have evolved for determining whether the discipline imposed in this case was warranted: (1) whether the employee either knew or should have known the rules; (2) whether the rule had a reasonable relationship to the orderly and efficient operation of the Employer's business; (3) whether it was reasonably related to the offense. The Union's position does not place it in disagreement with these criteria, although it would arrive at a different result from their application than that urged by the Hospital. Before examining the foregoing standards in light of the facts of this case, it may be noted that only the question of the grievant's beard, and not his hair style or the length of his hair otherwise, became an issue between the parties.

The Union argues that the regulations in question are vague and the directions the grievant was given to bring himself in compliance were also vague. This argument brings into question both the matter of knowledge on the part of the employee and the reasonableness of the rule itself. It is apparently the Union's view that the statement in the appearance and dress standards Bulletin of July 14, 1972, to the effect that it was "intended to insure that all hospital employees are presentable and professional in appearance" is to be regarded as one of the criteria or standards which were being imposed upon the employees. I would regard the word "professionalism" as it appears in the Bulletin to be a statement of the purpose for the rule or the aim which the hospital hoped to achieve by adopting it. But the standards are, as the bulletin itself shows and to the extent applicable in this case, beards which are "closely cropped and neatly trimmed." Perhaps that is not as precise as a linear definition might be, though one could foresee that even such a definition might be difficult to apply and similarly open to attack. See, for example, *United Parcel Service, Inc. 52 LA 1068.* The requirement that a beard be "closely cropped and neatly trimmed" is not so vague as to be unreasonable. While the terms so used are general, it is true they nevertheless provide a reasonable basis for compliance, even though R— was not told by his supervisor exactly how long his beard could be or how much should be trimmed from it. (Compare, *Western Airlines Inc., 60 LA 546; Allied Employers, Inc., 55 LA 1021; Washington Gas Light Company, 57 LA 453.*) A beard is a matter of personal adornment and not of mathematical precision, and while opinions might differ as to whether an individual beard was closely cropped or neatly trimmed, such questions could be decided on an individual basis as they arose. On the state of this record, it cannot be said that the rule in this case was vague or ambiguous. Moreover, the evidence is undisputed that R— was aware of the regulations regarding appearance and dress which had been issued by the Hospital and that his failure to abide by them was not based upon a lack of knowledge as to their existence or their application to him.

The question which now presents itself is whether the appearance and dress standards in question were reasonably related to the necessities of the business enterprise and the duties which the employee in question was expected to perform. As a psychiatric technician, R—'s duties included establishing human contact with patients; engaging them in activities; discussing their problems; orienting them towards reality; and escorting patients to and from areas of the hospital, other than the psychiatric unit, for tests and examinations.

The regulations in question here were the subject of discussion and consideration by the administration of the hospital for a period of two years or more prior to their adoption. According to the undisputed testimony, complaints had been received from patients, doctors and from the general public concerning the appearance of some of the employees of the hospital. During this period of time, the hospital attempted to solve the problem in general terms by providing, among other things, that "employees should be neat." This provided, as the hospital itself recognized, no standard whatsoever and considerable disagreement existed among those in administrative authority as to the policy which should be adopted. About a year before the regulations were issued, it was decided that a single policy equally applicable to house staff employees and full time physicians should be adopted. A number of meetings were held to develop such a policy; copies of policies followed by a number of nonprofit and profit organizations also were secured and studied and the then assistant administrator of the Hospital testified that the purpose sought was as follows:

> What we were attempting to do was to develop a policy that would project the kind of professional image that St. Mary's wanted to project but yet would recognize and allow for the individual rights and freedoms of our employees to dress within a broad range as they desire. So that we were conscious throughout this time of the need for protection of individual rights, and we did not want to arbitrarily or capriciously develop a policy that would infringe upon the rights of the employees.
>
> We also felt a strong obligation to our patients, in that patients, unlike employees, once they are admitted to the hospital, have no real choice about who takes care of them. And they may be reluctant to complain while they're a patient because the people who are providing

the care have some subtle ways of effecting influence on them at times. So that in terms of the individual private practitioner of medicine, or physician, he has the right to dress and look as he desires and the patient has freedom of choice. But once that patient is admitted to the hospital he does not have freedom of choice in terms of who takes care of him.

This testimony does not, of course, constitute proof that the appearance and dress standards in question in this case accomplished the effect which the witness testified was to be desired, but it does show that the Hospital expended a considerable amount of time and effort in working out what it regarded as a justified and reasonable policy.

R— testified, as the Union points out, that many patients especially those of the "hippie" type, related well to him because of his beard and that most other people either tolerated, did not notice, or did not care. If R—'s duties confined him solely to the psychiatric department, one might seriously question whether a reasonable relationship existed between the performance of his duties and the neat appearance of his beard. But, as the record shows, the grievant on occasions, although not frequently, was required to attend or accompany patients to parts of the hospital other than the psychiatric department. The Union argues that the Hospital has many paintings and statues of both religious and historical figures who are fully bearded. While that may be so, members of the public would not regard such figures in the same category as employees of the hospital staff upon whom they must rely for receiving medical care and service. It may be observed in this connection also that the amended regulation did not prohibit beards — it merely required they be closely cropped and neatly trimmed.

One may argue that the standards of medical care delivered by employees of a hospital have nothing to do with the presence of beards, whether well trimmed or not. The record here shows, however, the Hospital believed, on the basis of complaints it had received, that some of its patients felt otherwise. Whether or not one would agree with that assumption if called upon to make it in the first instance, it cannot be said that it was without some rational basis. Nor can it be said that adoption of the rule requiring that beards be closely cropped and neatly trimmed was not reasonably related to the proper exercise of the functions of the hospital in the treatment and care of its patients.

This brings us then to the question whether the rule was equably enforced. In the minutes of a special meeting held on June 15, 1972 by department heads and supervisors of the Hospital, the following statements appear:

> The hospital realizes that in the past it has not been entirely consistent, that generally each department set its own rules, however, it is a form of discrimination to have different sets of standards for different

departments. We feel we have reached a reasonable compromise and which [sic] is equitable.

The Hospital argues in support of its position that the regulations it adopted were reasonable; that, of approximately 1300 employees, R— was the only one who refused to conform and was the only one who was discharged for that reason. Whether that is a legitimate factor for consideration need not be determined under the circumstances of this case. Nor need it be determined whether the assumption is correct that "different sets of standards for different departments" would constitute discrimination. The record shows that the grievant's duties regularly brought him into contact with patients in the psychiatric department of the Hospital and at times with patients in other parts of the hospital as well. It is apparent, therefore, that the rule was not applied to the grievant in a discriminatory manner.

In its brief, the Union cites *Forstner v. City and County of San Francisco*, 243 C.A.2d 625; *Finot v. Pasadena City Board of Education*, 250 C.A.2d 189; and *King v. California Unemployment Insurance Appeals Board*, 25 C.A.3d 199. Each of these decisions is distinguishable from the present case on its facts. In each, the requirement, resisted by the employee was that he entirely remove his beard. Here, the grievant was permitted to retain his beard. The only requirement was that it be closely cropped and neatly trimmed. In this connection, the court in the *Forstner* case (at page 634) declared:

> The subject of neatness enters here. An unkempt beard, like uncut hair, would offend against the neatness which is expected of public officers. The evidence is that the respondent's beard has always been well trimmed . . .

Likewise in *Finot*, supra, the court in its opinion states that:

> The cleanliness and neatness of appellant's beard has never been an issue in this proceeding.

In addition, the first two cases cited involved workers in public employment whose right to wear a beard was regarded as a matter of personal freedom entitled to constitutional protection against unreasonable action by the state.

While the third case cited by the Union was concerned with an employee in private industry who had been discharged for growing a beard contrary to his employer's policy, the issue was whether the state was justified in denying unemployment compensation benefits to the employee. The court held that it was not on the ground that growing a beard was symbolic conduct which was entitled to constitutional protection. The decision expressly limited its application, however, to the right of the state to deny payment of benefits and refrained from passing upon the question on the employer's right in having terminated the employee because he had grown a beard, as the following language from the court's opinion at page 206 shows:

> Our decision goes no further than to acknowledge that the state is constitutionally inhibited from denying unemployment compensation benefits to an applicant who has been discharged from employment because of personal action which is constitutionally protected; we neither hold nor suggest that a bearded person has a constitutional right to a job, and we do not reach or affect a private employer's right to manage its own business.

The recent decision of *Thornton v. Department of Human Resources Development*, 32 C.A.3d 180, to which the Union has called my attention, falls within the principle enunciated in the *King* case, supra. In addition, the court, at page 183 of the reported decision in that case, distinguished, as the court had also done in *Finot*, supra, between constitutional protections which would inhibit the state in depriving an employee of unemployment compensation benefits and the right of a private employer to discharge that employee.

The final question remaining is whether imposition of the penalty of discharge was justified. The termination of an employee under any circumstances is the most severe penalty which can be visited upon him and requires convincing proof of its necessity. In this case, it seems quite clear, however, that the strongly held personal beliefs of both the Employer and the grievant placed them upon a collision course which could only end as it did. It is undisputed that the matter of trimming his beard to conform to the standards adopted by the Hospital was discussed with R— by his supervisor on two occasions, the first time after the bulletin of June 15th was posted and the second time following the amended standards posted on July 14; that on the latter occasion which occurred on July 19, R refused to comply and was suspended for one week, with the warning that if he did not comply with the Hospital's standards and report for work by August 7, 1972, his services would be terminated; and that R— thereafter did not again report for work. On such a showing, it cannot be said that the grievant was not given adequate opportunity to comply or that his discharge was unwarranted.

Based on the foregoing facts and the record as whole, it is concluded that the discharge of R— was for just cause. The grievance, accordingly, is denied.

AWARD

The discharge of R— on August 7, 1972, was for just cause and did not violate the collective bargaining agreement between the parties.

Case No. 16

*What was the proper penalty to be imposed on a
Psychiatric Nursing Assistant who took no action
when an unauthorized, intoxicated acquaintance
entered her ward and talked to the patients? Was
the Assistant guilty of improper patient contact when
she talked to a patient who was troubled about the
unauthorized visit of the grievant's acquaintance?*

Johns Hopkins Hospital (Baltimore, Md.)
and
National Union of Hospital and Nursing Home Employees, Local 1199E

Arbitrator: Peter Florey
Date of Award: January 25, 1972
Citation: Previously unreported

Grievant was employed by the Henry Phipps Psychiatric Clinic of the
Hospital on February 2, 1970. She received the customary training in patient
care, including specific instructions not to discuss personal problems with
patients. Grievant was assigned to Ward East Four. Although the Head Nurse
seemingly was dissatisfied with grievant's performance from "day one,"
grievant's employment was not terminated within the sixty-day probationary
period. On July 13, 1970, the Head Nurse prepared an Anecdotal Report
stating in detail how grievant's "behavior is interfering with therapeutic
nursing care and, also, how her behavior is affecting her relationship with her
co-workers." Specific items related that grievant complained to patients about
the staff and that she seemed to overidentify with patients.

As a result of this report, grievant was transferred to Ward East Three
which, reportedly, has a more structured staff set-up. On April 24, 1971, the
Head Nurse of E-3 started to work on an evaluation report on Grievant. The
report contains the following statement on grievant's health:

I would say her health has been poor before and after her back injury (and her poor health before and after back injury has been due to other types of illness). This definitely interferes with staffing.

While the evaluation was in progress, grievant's supervisor issued three warnings on April 29, 1971, relating to three different absenteeism problems. The evaluation was completed on May 10, 1971, and was discussed with grievant. It shows the Head Nurse's conclusion that grievant was not suited for her job and contains the following comment concerning grievant's present placement and advancement: "She has not been successful in this work setting and it would be my suggestion she be transferred to another work area." Three reasons are given for grievant's unsuitability in her job:

1. Interferes with therapeutic plans set up by staff for patients.

2. Her persistent habit of dumping her problems on patients.

3. She seems unable to deal with constructive criticism and learn from it.

(Grievant was aware that supervision was concerned about these shortcomings, but did not expect that they would subject her to discipline.)
Under the heading of "Handling of Personal Stress," the Head Nurse commented:

It is difficult to know how she really feels. At times she is very hyper-active which tends to make them (patients and staff) anxious. She still insists on talking with patients about staff problems (particularly involving her instead of doing it at a staff meeting). Patients find this disturbing and generally prefer not being put in this position.

For reasons not further explained at the hearing, the recommendation of the Head Nurse to transfer grievant from the psychiatric clinic was not followed up.
Grievant's "chronic and habitual absenteeism" problem persisted after the evaluation, and she was suspended for three days in July, 1971. No grievance was filed.
The events which gave rise to grievant's discharge occurred on August 20, 1971. An initial two-day suspension (subject to discharge) was based on an alleged violation of Disciplinary Rule Number One: "Deliberate inattention to patient care." The events covered by this charge are set forth in a Stipulation of Fact:

1. A personal acquaintance of grievant entered the Ward without authorization and talked to patients.

2.   Grievant noticed the visitor, but failed to ask him to leave the Ward or to step outside with him.

3.   Grievant failed to notify supervisors or security about the visitor's presence.

4.   The visitor was removed by supervisors who happened to come on the scene.

After a review of grievant's case, Management decided to discharge her, and she was handed the following note when she reported to work after her initial suspension:

> Violation of Hospital Disciplinary Rule #1 (Deliberate inattention to patient care) resulted in suspension pending discharge, effective 8/24/71 through 8/25/71, while investigation of the cited violation was conducted.
>
> Investigation established that, in addition to the violation cited, violation also occurred of Hospital Disciplinary Rule #4 (Failure to fulfill the responsibilities of the job to an extent that might or does cause injury to a patient.)
>
> Therefore, it is the judgment that disciplinary action taken include discharge from employment, effective Thursday, August 26, 1971, at 8:30 a.m.

It developed that, after the visitor had been removed from the Ward, a schizophrenic patient talked to a nursing assistant and expressed some concern about the incident, mixed with the fear that the visitor might harm grievant. The aide, hired in May of 1971, was not quite sure about her success in resolving the patient's problems and talked to the Licensed Practical Nurse on duty who recommended that grievant talk to the patient. This suggestion was relayed to grievant by the aide. Grievant confronted the patient but, according to grievant's testimony, the patient avoided a discussion with the explanation that she had already covered the subject with the aide. Thereupon, the grievant summoned the aide, and they sat down with the patient for another attempt to clear the air. Grievant said something to the patient to the effect that grievant understood grievant's visitor had reminded the patient of the patient's father and assured the patient that she had known the man long enough to know that he would not harm her.

However, the patient seemingly discussed the incident with her doctor (a Junior Assistant Resident who had come to E-3 in July of 1971) who issued an order restricting contact between grievant and his patient. In addition, he filed the following Anecdotal Report:

On Friday evening an incident occurred involving one of my patients, Miss [S —] and her boyfriend. While it may seem unreasonable to hold the staff member responsible for the drunken actions of her boyfriend already reported, not only is it reasonable but mandatory that staff members be able to control their own contribution to the delicate boundary between private and professional lives — in words of one syllable they have to have the ego strength to deal with the problems of others as well as their own. What happened after the reported incident was the opposite. Miss [S —] went to my patient and began to tell her about all of her *own* problems obviously asking for help and understanding. The patient, who is little able to handle her own problems, was quite distressed by all this remembering arguments between her mother and father with her in the middle — precisely the problem that resulted in her psychotic breakdown and then hospitalization. While the patient did remarkably well throughout this episode — she could have completely decompensated. It should be pointed out that we have maintained a strict restriction on parent visits to avoid precisely this sort of experience.

It seems quite clear to me that all this is grounds for dismissal. It would seem that the Union as well has an obligation to the patients (as well as the staff) which can be discharged in only this fashion.

The Hospital argues that it can impose on a Psychiatric Nursing Assistant far different standards than those required of the ordinary nurses aide, because the former are given a *three*-week training period during which they are instructed as to the handling of patients and the proper method of dealing with problems arising out of the actions of mentally ill patients. (However, the record shows that "ordinary" nurses aides receive a *five*-week training period.) According to the Hospital, the incidents of August 20, 1971, made it apparent that grievant was either unable to cope with the requirements of her job or was so irresponsible that she completely ignored her duties and subjected her patients to possible harm from the traumatic effect of the presence of an outsider in the ward. Moreover, the Hospital charges, it should have been obvious, even to an untrained layman, that one would not bring up a mental patient's father if the patient's mental illness was caused by her relationship with the father. Grievant allegedly was showing in her handling of this situation that she was not able to absorb the training to which she had been exposed during her employment at the Hospital. Finally, the Hospital states that a transfer to a different area of the Hospital was not warranted on the basis of grievant's qualifications and in light of her prior poor work record.

The Union takes the position that some discipline might have been warranted but that discharge was too severe because the Hospital retained grievant in an employment situation for which she obviously, and by prior, unheeded statements of the Hospital staff, was not qualified.

Findings

Considering the added charge of improper patient contact first, it cannot reasonably be found on the basis of this record that grievant violated Rule of Conduct Number Four by talking to the patient. The Rule provides:

The following will make employees subject to disciplinary action, up to and including discharge:

1. Deliberate inattention to patient care.

2. Divulging confidential information concerning patients or their care.

3. Refusal to carry out orders or instructions.

4. Failure to fulfill the responsibilities of the job to an extent that might or does cause injury to a patient or any other person or damage to, waste or loss of material, supplies, equipment facilities or other property.

The patient's doctor assumed that grievant initiated the discussion with the patient and came to the patient for help with her own problems. The testimony given at the arbitration hearing does not support the doctor's baseless accusation. The Hospital's own witnesses made it quite clear that the patient discussed the disturbance on the floor with an aide other than the grievant, and that this employee turned to grievant for assistance at the suggestion of the Licensed Practical Nurse on duty. When grievant was unable to get to the root of the patient's concern, she called on the aide to join the conversation. It is at this stage that grievant, allegedly, made an interpretative statement on which the charge of violating Rule Number Four rests. A careful review of the account given by the Hospital's own witness leads to the conclusion that grievant did precisely what the Licensed Practical Nurse had asked grievant to do: she allayed the patient's fear that the visitor might harm her. It is doubtful that she undertook that assignment with the skill of a certified psychiatrist, at the same time, it would not be reasonable to rely on the judgment of another aide who had been on the job for a mere three months for an evaluation whether grievant's explanation to the patient was interpretative or not.

Turning to the Hospital's charge that grievant violated Rule Number One by deliberate inattention to patient care, the stipulation of fact discloses gross dereliction of duty as a *Psychiatric* Nursing Assistant on part of grievant when the unauthorized visitor appeared on the floor. While it may have not been reasonable to expect grievant either to remove the man herself or to step outside the Ward with him alone, she should at least have alerted hospital personnel to his presence. This finding raises the question whether discharge was the proper discipline under the circumstances. The incident took place almost four months after the Head Nurse of E-3 had found grievant unfit for her job in a psychiatric ward and had recommended her transfer. Nursing assignments cannot reasonably be treated in the same manner as industrial jobs, and grievant's failure to handle the situation properly may justify her immediate removal from the psychiatric ward and may even be proper cause for a mild form of discipline, but it does not support the type of discharge for misconduct which would deprive grievant of Unemployment Compensation which is now payable to hospital employees in Maryland.

For this reason, the discharge is converted to a thirty-day suspension and to a disqualification from further assignment as Psychiatric Nursing Assistant. Grievant shall be paid full back pay from September 20, 1971 to January 31, 1972, and the Hospital shall consider reassignment of the grievant to another position. This ruling does not wipe out grievant's record of absenteeism, and the Hospital will be able to take further disciplinary measures should grievant fail to improve her attendance record. To assure reasonable compliance with this award, this arbitrator will retain jurisdiction until the question of grievant's status is resolved by the parties. To save the parties further expense, any problems can be initially discussed by the attorneys and the arbitrator by long-distance conference call.

AWARD

The grievance is sustained in part and denied in part as set forth in this decision.

Part III

Work Schedules
and Working
Conditions

Case No. 17

When the Hospital experienced an unusually low patient census, could it, in the absence of a share-the-work provision, institute a general reduction in the work schedule? Or was it required to lay off employees according to seniority?

Community General Hospital (Sterling, Ill.)
and
Nurses Staff Association

Arbitrator: Alex Elson
Date of Award: February 1, 1973
Citation: LAIG 766

Grievants, members of the nursing staff at Sterling Community Hospital, claim that the Hospital violated its contract with the Union by unilaterally instituting a hospital-wide reduction of hours from 40 to 32 hours per week between August 14 and August 22, 1972. The facts are not in dispute.

As a result of an unusually low patient census at the Hospital during the first two weeks of August, 1972, Hospital Administrator, John Berhow, determined that it would be necessary to reduce wage expenses by effectuating a reduction of 20% in the number of hours worked by employees (R. 19). He therefore posted a notice to all employees as follows:

> During the past week we have been plagued with an extremely low census, consequently, effective immediately, each and every employee, except for Supervisory Personnel, will be scheduled to work one day a week less than the normal work schedule.

* * * * *

This policy will in no way affect the continuance of employee benefits and seniority. (Jt. Ex. 2)

The reduction in work force remained in effect until August 22, 1972, at which time all employees were returned to the work schedules which had applied prior to August 14 (R. 15).

On the day after Berhow posted the notice mentioned above, the grievants initiated grievance procedures. The grievance is as follows:

The Community General Hospital Nursing Staff Association hereby files its grievance pursuant to Article XXI of the Contract between the Board of Community General Hospital, Sterling, Illinois, and the Association, contesting the unilateral action of John Burhow, Administrator, in arbitrarily reducing the regularly scheduled work week for all employees.

On August 14, 1972, members of the Association were given copies of a certain memorandum over the signature of the Administrator stating, in substance, that beginning August 14, 1972, certain employees would be required to work a reduced week. The reduction indicated was 8 hours per week for all full-time and part-time employees below the level of supervisor.

Article VII B of the Contract defines a regular work week as follows:

B.   The regularly scheduled work week of a full-time employee shall be five eight-hour days, totaling forty (40) hours in any one period of seven consecutive days.

Article IX of the Contract defines a part-time employee as:

A part-time employee is one who is regularly scheduled to work less than forty hours per week.

*   *   *   *   *

The Association further requests that all employees affected by this arbitrary reduction in the work week be immediately restored to their normal work week and compensated in full for all time lost as a result of this action. (Jt. Ex. 3)

At both the first and second Step grievance proceedings, the Hospital denied the grievance (Jt. Ex. 4, 6). The Personnel Committee of the Hospital Board of Directors denied grievants' second appeal on the basis the complained of action was authorized by Article III of the Management Rights Clause of the Agreement (Jt. Ex. 8). The grievants thereupon demanded arbitration (Jt. Ex. 9).

The Association asserted a second ground for their complaint at the hearing of this arbitration. It contended that the reduction in hours effectuated by Berhow was, in fact, a layoff in violation of Article VIII D of the contract (Jt. Ex. 1). That provision entitled "Seniority and Promotion," provides that "In case of layoff from the hospital, the employee with least seniority in the classification subject to the layoff shall be laid off first and recalled in reverse order" (Jt. Ex. 1). As the "layoff" affected all employees equally, the Association contends it did not comply with the requirement that layoffs be made in ascending order of seniority and consequently was a violation of the agreement.

The only testimony presented at the hearing was on behalf of the Hospital. This testimony was unrefuted and will be referred to in considering the parties' contentions. The Association contends that the reduction in hours effectuated by Berhow on August 14 has obliterated the distinction made in the contract between full-time and part-time employees. It argues (1) that certain benefits, particularly those relating to vacations, holidays, sick leave and insurance are governed by the distinction between full-time and part-time employees; and (2) Articles VII B and IX state that "the regularly scheduled work week of a full-time employee shall be five eight-hour days, totaling forty (40) hours in any one period of seven consecutive days," (Art. VII B, Jt. Ex. 1) and "A part-time employee is one who is regularly scheduled to work less than forty hours per week" (Art IX, Jt. Ex. 1).

Concerning the rationale of Berhow's decision to effectuate a reduction in work force in the manner he chose and the testimony in support thereof, grievants take the position that regardless of the wisdom or rationality of that decision, the contract explicitly prohibits an across-the-board reduction in hours. The contract, grievants argue, requires that if a layoff is to occur, it must be accomplished in ascending order of seniority. A temporary reduction in work force was accomplished through a reduction in the working hours of each employee rather than by way of a reduction in the number of employees at the Hospital. Nonetheless, the purpose, cause and monetary result of the Hospital's action were identical to those which result in layoffs.

Accordingly, the Hospital's characterization of its action as a "reduction of the work week" does not alter its essential nature as a layoff and cannot be justified under plain wording of the contract. Whether or not the action was based on a sound and rational interpretation of the circumstances in which it was made, the contract forbids such action and the parties are bound by the contract.

The Hospital's response is twofold. First, it contends that there is in fact and effect a difference between a reduction in work week pursuant to a "work-sharing program" and a layoff. In this case, the Hospital contends, a reduction in work week was effected. Second, the action taken by Berhow was not arbitrary, but rather, was the most appropriate means of effectuating a reduction in work force which was required by the low patient census which existed prior to August 14.

In support of its first contention the Hospital argues that Article III of the contract governs the issues presented. That article provides in relevant part:

ARTICLE III — *Management Rights*

The management of the Hospital and its operation, the direction of the work force, including the right . . . to assign . . . transfer, promote, . . . maintain discipline and efficiency, determine standards of care of patients, and to exercise normal functions of management, subject to the express provisions of this agreement, are vested exclusively in the Hospital; provided that the exercise of such rights in the area of terms and conditions of employment shall be subject to Article XXI. (Jt. Ex. 1) [Art. XXI — Adjustment of Grievances.]

As the contract does not explicitly deny the Hospital the right to institute "work sharing" programs, that right the Hospital argues is conferred upon it by virtue of its power to "maintain . . . efficiency . . . and to exercise normal functions of management."

Consequently, it is not compelled to guarantee all full-time employees a 40-hour week or to elect between providing all employees with a full work schedule or selectively laying some employees off in order of seniority. Rather, the Hospital contends, it may elect an intermediate position in which the available work is shared equally by all employees. In the current case such work sharing was accomplished by Berhow's directive of August 14.

In support of its position that a layoff did not occur the Hospital asserts that a layoff involves a "loss of an employee's status as such," (Hosp. Brief at 5) and that the status with which seniority provisions are concerned is the "employee's status as a permanent incumbent of a job" (Hosp. Brief at 6). As no employee lost her status as an incumbent of the job she held prior to August 14, and as no employee was deprived of any of the benefits dependent on her status as a full-time employee or as a member of the seniority roster, no layoff occurred. Accordingly, if the Hospital was not arbitrary in the exercise of its right to maintain efficiency, grievants have no basis for their complaint, and the grievance must be denied.

The Hospital's second contention is that its decision to effectuate a work-sharing program was justified and reasonable. The evidence presented by the Hospital with regard to this issue was not disputed in any respect by grievants.

Hospital Administrator, John Berhow, testified as follows: Upon his assumption of his position as Administrator on July 10, 1972, he determined that the Hospital was over-staffed (R. 12). This determination was based upon his discovery that during the month of July the Hospital employed an average of 3.09 persons per occupied bed per day (R. 14). In contrast the normal employee to patient ratio in most hospitals is 2.5 (R. 13). While there are usually fewer patients in hospitals during the summer months than in the remainder of the year (R. 14), occupancy in the Hospital during the first two weeks in August was substantially below that which Berhow would normally have expected (R. 14). As a result, the employee-patient ratio at the Hospital between August 1 and August 14 climbed to 3.25 (R. 14). Berhow, therefore, determined that a 20% reduction in employee hours worked was necessary (R. 17).

Upon further study, Berhow determined that a layoff in ascending order of seniority would cause severe problems in certain specialized units of the hospital and that if such a layoff were effectuated, the standards of patient care in the Intensive Care and Coronary Units would decline inordinately (R. 15). Because most of the employees in those two units were some of the most recently hired by the Hospital, they would be among the first employees laid off (R. 15-18). For example 50% of the Registered Nurses employed in the Intensive Care Unit would have been laid off while none of the Registered Nurses in Pediatrics would have been laid off (Hosp. Ex. 1). Because the Intensive Care and Coronary Units are specialized units requiring constant attention, Berhow determined that a layoff would not be appropriate. As he understood the contract to give him the right to adjust work schedules, Berhow issued the directive of August 14 (R. 21).

The day after Berhow's directive was issued, a number of nurses from the Obstetrics Department met with him to discuss the problem (R. 21). Berhow testified, without contradiction from grievants, that after the nurses expressed their concern with the effect the reduction in hours would have on their department, he explained the situation to them. The nurses conceded that the reduction was necessary and did not further discuss the problem with Berhow (R. 21-22).

Finally, Berhow testified that although the contract permits layoffs within a classification of employees without regard to the seniority of those employees over employees in other departments, the classification established under the contract is based upon job title rather than by department (R 26, 27, 30). There are 12 such classifications, including among others, "Registered Staff Nurses," "Licensed Practical Nurses," and "Aides" (Jt. Ex. 1). A 20% reduction in employees, by full-time layoff of the least senior personnel would have removed from the Hospital a substantial number of full-time employees in the Coronary and Intensive Care Units and would not have accomplished the purpose for which it would have been ordered without drastically affecting the standards of patient care desired by the Hospital (Jt. Ex. 1).

The Hospital's second witness, Director of Nursing Services, Rosemary Beran, testified that a layoff by seniority would have "wiped out" two shifts of employees in the Coronary Care Unit and would have left patients in that unit without adequate medical attention (R. 39). A similar, but less drastic result would also have occurred in the Emergency Room (R. 42-3). As both the Intensive Care and Coronary Care Units had opened during the 2½ years before August 14, most of the nurses in those sections had low seniority (R. 34).

Both units involve the use of sophisticated equipment and require nurses with specialized training and experience (R. 35, 39). Nurses from other departments could not have been transferred to the Intensive Care or Coronary Units and operate effectively in those areas (R. 40, 46). Furthermore, the other nurses had demonstrated their unwillingness to serve in those areas when they failed to bid for positions when the two units opened (R. 41). Hence, if layoff had occurred on the basis of seniority, it would not have been possible to staff the Intensive Care or Coronary Units separately or to staff a combined Intensive–Coronary Care Unit (R. 46). During the period in question, it was necessary to combine the two units to maintain adequate coverage (Tr. 45).

The Hospital also relies on the "Hospital Handbook," issued prior to the collective agreement and which the Hospital claims is still in force. It provides:

> The hospital reserves the right to change the work schedule of any employee when it is considered to be in the best interest of the hospital. (Hosp. Ex. 2, p. 7.)

Discussion

The issue in this case is one of contract interpretation. Put in simplest terms, the question to be resolved is whether the provisions of the collective agreement specifying 40 hours a week as the regularly scheduled workweek or the requirement that layoffs be in the order of seniority bars the Hospital from temporarily reducing the workweek from 40 to 32 hours as was done in this case for a period of eight days, August 14 through August 22, 1972.

The Hospital relies on the management clause and specifically the language which gives it the right to "the management of the hospital and its operation, the direction of the work force including the right to assign, . . . maintain discipline and efficiency, . . . determine standards of care of patients, and to exercise the normal functions of management . . ." As is true of most collective agreements, the management clause is made subject to the express provisions of the agreement.

The management clause further provides that the exercise of management functions shall be subject to the grievance procedure of the contract, thereby affording employees the right to challenge the exercise of management rights on the basis that the exercise is arbitrary or discriminatory.

There is no dispute in this case that there was a rational basis for the Hospital's action. There was an excess of personnel during a period of slack. The reduced workweek was chosen as a device for cutting back on excess personnel because this would be least disruptive of the needs of the Hospital and patients. It appears that a layoff in the order of seniority would make it impossible to staff the Coronary Care Unit and Intensive Care Unit and would also affect the emergency room. The Intensive Care and Coronary Units had been in existence for only about 2½ years and most of the nurses in these sections had low seniority.

The Association did not offer any evidence to rebut the case made by the Hospital that layoffs might have seriously impaired the operation of the above specialized units. It takes the position that even if the management function was exercised, as it must concede was done in this case in good faith and for sound reasons of efficiency, the provisions of the agreement relating to seniority in the event of layoff and the specified workweek do not permit the Hospital to reduce the work week temporarily. The Arbitrator agrees with the fundamental proposition that if, in fact, the proper construction of the provisions of the Agreement referred to by the Association bar the use of the reduced workweek as a temporary measure, the Hospital could not use this procedure. This is implicit in the management right's clause which recognizes that rights therein given are subject to other provisions of the Agreement. Accordingly, if the Arbitrator were to conclude that the provisions of the Agreement relied upon by the Union did in fact bar the action taken by the Hospital in this case, the Arbitrator would have no choice except to sustain the grievance. The Arbitrator does not have authority to ignore the provisions of the Agreement because of the overriding necessity urged by the Hospital in this case, to assign personnel in such a way as to maximize patient care. The Arbitrator's role is limited to interpreting the Agreement. We come then to a consideration of the several provisions of the Agreement relied upon by the Association.

First, the Association argues that the provisions of Article VIIB, providing that the regularly scheduled workweek for a full-time employee should be five eight-hour days totalling 40 hours, and Article IX, defining a part-time employee as one who is regularly scheduled to work less than 40 hours per week, bars the Hospital from reducing the workweek as it did in this case from 40 hours to 32 hours for the period here involved, some 8 days. There is no language in Article VIIB or Article IX or any other provisions of the Agreement which guarantees to an employee 40 hours of work per week. The key words are "regularly scheduled." These words relate both to full-time employees and part-time employees. The provisions bar the Hospital from establishing as a regular schedule hours of work less than 40 hours per week, for full-time employees. The establishment of a regularly scheduled workweek of less than 40 hours would change full-time employees to part-time employees. The contract draws various distinctions between full-time employees and part-time employees with reference specifically to vacation pay, holiday pay, sick leave pay and insurance benefits. The impact of part-time work is to reduce all of such fringe benefits.

The use of the term "regularly scheduled" contemplates that there may be irregular or unusual scheduling which affects full-time employees. In the case of such irregular or unusual scheduling the other provisions of the Agreement relating to meal and rest periods, vacation pay, holiday pay, sick leave pay and insurance benefits would continue to be applied as though the employees were on a full time basis. It is to be noted that those benefits are not dependent upon the number of hours worked insofar as full-time employees are concerned. In the case of part-time employees, the benefits made available to full-time employees are allowed on a prorata basis. For example, an employee who is regularly scheduled for 4 days a week receives 80% of full-time vacation and 80% of full-time holiday pay. The same is true with reference to sick leave and insurance benefits.

The reduction in work force in this case was accompanied by a statement: "This policy will in no way affect the continuance of employee benefits and seniority," indicating that the employees would be regarded as full-time employees under the Agreement even though the workweek was being temporarily reduced.

The reduction in the work schedule was kept in force for only eight days. As stated above, the term "regularly" implied that there can be an "irregular" scheduling for brief periods of time. If a reduction in the workweek would be kept in force for a substantial period of time, as was the case in the *Aro Corporation* case discussed below, it could be argued that the regularly scheduled workweek has in fact been reduced in violation of the Agreement. Under the circumstances of this case and within its particular context, the Arbitrator is satisfied that the reduction in hours for the period in question was not in fact an establishment of a regularly scheduled workweek in violation of the Agreement.

We turn next to the contention that the reduction in workweek amounts to a layoff in violation of seniority. There is no question but the Hospital had a choice of alternatives. It could have reduced the work force by 20% by laying off 20% of the work force having least seniority, or it could accomplish the objective herein involved by reducing the workweek. But it doesn't follow from this fact that a reduction in the workweek is in fact a layoff. A layoff involves a change in the employee's status as an employee. Under Article

VIID seniority applies where there is a "reduction to the number of positions in any classification." The reduction in the hours from 40 to 32 cannot be said to be a reduction in the number of positions. As a result of the reduction in hours, no employee lost his status as a permanent incumbent in his job. The status of the employees, as employees, was not affected by the reduction from 40 to 32 hours. There was no reduction in work force, no loss of status and accordingly the seniority provisions were not applicable.

The Union's argument that in effect the reduction in hours was a substitute for the layoff and had the same effect is logically sound. In this case, however, the action taken was not designed to affect the status of the employees as full-time employees under the Agreement. The notice which accompanied the reduction of hours specifically stated that the reduction would "in no way affect the continuance of employee benefits and seniority." This was another way of saying that the employees would be regarded as full-time employees even though the workweek was reduced. The benefits which the employees had as full-time employees continued during the period of a temporary reduction in hours. The status of the employees as full-time employees was in no way affected. The only change was in the loss of one day's work during each of two workweeks. Under such circumstances the reduction in hours involved in this case cannot be regarded as a layoff, and accordingly, the seniority provisions applicable to layoff were not violated by the reduction in hours. This is not to say that the employees have no rights with reference to the scheduled workweek. On the contrary, as above stated, they have a right to a regularly scheduled workweek of 40 hours.

The citations referred to by the Association do not support its position. The case of *In re Aro Corporation and International Association of Machinists and Aerospace Workers, Lodge 1349,* 55 LA 859, involved contract terms substantially different than the contract terms here involved. The contract in that case contained a specific provision which authorized reduction of hours only by mutual agreement. The Company was held to violate the agreement when the Union refused to agree to a reduction in workweek and the Company nevertheless reduced the workweek. The provision for a reduction in workweek specifically respected the seniority principle by providing for layoff procedures according to seniority to go into effect after a reduction to 32 hours. With this type of contract plan, the Arbitrator in that case was in a position to treat the reduction in hours as a layoff, in violation of the layoff provisions. The other cases cited are clearly inapplicable to the instant dispute.

AWARD

The grievance is denied.

Case No. 18

*After deciding that a night shift nurse needed more
supervision of the kind that was available only on the
day shift, did a VA Hospital have the right to effect
that transfer and replace her with a day shift nurse
who preferred not to go on the night shift? Did the
need for the original transfer constitute an
emergency, justifying the disregard of procedures
that would otherwise apply in inter-shift transfers?*

Veterans Administration Hospital (Pittsburgh, Pa.)
and
American Federation of Government Employees, Local 2028

Arbitrator: Ralph D. Tive
Date of Award: January 24, 1975
Citation: 74-2 ARB ¶8611

Although the parties did not submit an agreed upon statement of the
issues for submission to Arbitration, they seemed to be in substantial
agreement as to what the issues are. In his opening statement, the Counsel for
the Grievant indicated the following three issues:

1. That the change in the Grievant's tour of duty was improper under
the terms of the collective bargaining agreement.

2. That arising out of the first issue above, her reassignment from the
Coronary Care Unit was a form of punishment as a result of her complaint
and for asserting her rights under the collective bargaining agreement.

3. In relation to step three of the grievance procedure, the hospital
officials refusal to recognize [T—], the Elected Chief Steward, as her
representative in the grievance procedure was improper.

The hospital submitted suggested issues to be considered by the Arbitrator and they were as follows:

1.   Did management violate Article VI, Section 1 and Article XII, Section 3 of the negotiated agreement when it changed the tour of duty for Miss [S—] on February 12, 13 and 14, 1974?

2.   Can an employee, other than a professional nurse, act as a steward or chief steward for the PSNU?

3.   Is the reassignment of Miss S— from the Coronary Care Unit grievable or arbitrable? If so, was it carried out for good reason?

4.   Was the reprimand given Miss [S—] proper for her deliberate refusal to report for duty, as scheduled on February 13 and 14, 1974.

As indicated above, the Union and the Hospital are in substantial agreement as to the issues with the exception that the Hospital has raised the question as to the propriety of the reprimand given to the Grievant for not reporting to duty on February 13 and 14, 1974. Therefore, these issues will be accepted and considered as the matters to be decided in this case.

History of the Case

On February 10, 1974, the Grievant was employed by the hospital at its Oakland facility as a nurse performing the duties of a staff nurse in the Coronary Care Unit. She had been so employed from September of 1970, which according to testimony was about the time this specific unit was instituted at the hospital.

The Grievant was on vacation prior to February 12, 1974, and was called at her home and was informed that she would be transferred to the evening shift although when she was to return on February 12, 1974, it was to the "day shift." There was apparently a problem with another nurse who was proving unreliable on the late evening shift and a decision had been made to transfer the other nurse to the day shift where she could be given more adequate supervision.

The Grievant accepted the change in shift from 7:30 to 4:00 to 3:30 to 12:00 on February 13, and 14, 1974, apparently, because she thought that it was because of the illness of the other nurse in question. However, when the Grievant discovered that the other nurse was not ill, but had replaced the Grievant on the 7:30 to 4:00 P.M. tour on the dates in question, [Grievant] stated that she did not feel that she should be required to work the late shift for the other nurse because of that person's problems. She requested a meeting with Miss M—, Chief Nurse, relative to this matter and had an appointment for 2:30 P.M. on the 13th of February, 1974. The Chief Nurse, unfortunately, happened to be busy at that time and she met with the Assistant Chief Nurse. She indicated that she was not satisfied with the explanation given her for the change in tour of duty and protested the reasoning for it. She is, according to certain testimony, alleged to have stated that she would report for day duty on the 14th, but that she would not report for the night duty, as instructed. At the time of the meeting with the Assistant Chief Nurse, the Grievant did report in uniform and, to all intents and purposes, appeared ready to go to work after the meeting was concluded.

The Grievant did not report for duty on the 13th and 14th; she did, however, report for her usual tour as scheduled on the 3:30 to 12:00 P.M. shift on Friday, the 15th. She was told by one of the supervisory personnel of her transfer out of the Coronary Care Unit to the Ward 4 West Urological Section and also that she would receive a notice of intent to reprimand for being AWOL because she did not work on February 13th and 14th, 1974.

In accordance with the provisions in the collective bargaining agreement, the Grievant instituted grievance procedures and although the question of her representation in step three of the grievance procedure is one of the issues to be decided and further, although it is not clear that the grievance procedure was ever completed through the various steps as set forth in the collective bargaining agreement, apparently the parties agreed to Arbitration and the matter was submitted to the Arbitrator, as indicated above.

Hospital's Position

The position of the Hospital is clearly delineated in the submission of the issues before the Arbitrator and was also set forth in the testimony of its witnesses. Briefly stated, the Hospital attempted to prove by oral testimony, that it was the intention of both parties in negotiating the collective bargaining agreement that "nurses should be represented by nurses." This related to the appearance of the Chief Steward, Mr. T—, on behalf of the Grievant at the third step of the grievance procedure.

The Hospital, also, by the testimony of various levels of supervisory nurses, including the Chief Nurse, took the position that the first duty of a nurse is the care of patients and that the action of the Grievant in refusing to work the evening shift on the days in question and, in fact, her nonappearance was a dereliction of duty of such magnitude as to justify, perhaps, even stronger sanctions than were taken and certainly justified the reprimand. The transfer of the Grievant from the Cardiac Care Unit to another, less critical, unit, was in the Hospital's opinion, justified by her action in not reporting for work, as evidence of her dissatisfaction with the change in working arrangements.

Position of the Union

The position of the Union clearly is that the actions and the sanctions taken, relative to this particular Grievant, were because she chose to exercise her rights under the various provisions of the collective bargaining agreement and it constitutes a violation of the agreement and of fair labor practices.

Findings and Opinion

The Arbitrator has, in the process of determining this issue, reviewed his notes carefully, and has also carefully reviewed the numerous exhibits presented by both sides and the able arguments presented by the representatives of both the Hospital and the Union.

Under the terms of the collective bargaining agreement, Article XXV, Section 3 the decision of the Arbitrator is binding on both parties.

In making a decision in a case of this matter, the Arbitrator is faced with the necessity of delicately and fairly balancing important equities as between the parties to the arbitration.

Not the least of these rights and equities, which are specifically recognized in the collective bargaining agreement is what is known, generally, as "management rights." These are explicitly recognized in the collective bargaining agreement and in Article II, Section 2, it states that, "Nothing in this agreement shall restrict the VA in exercising the right, in accordance with applicable law and regulation, to: direct employees of the VA; hire, promote, transfer, assign and retain employees in positions within the VA, and to suspend, demote, discharge or take other disciplinary actions against employees . . ." At the hearing it was obviously the tenor of the Hospital's position that the action taken in this instant case is in full and fair exercise of this right which has been recognized by the Union.

On the other hand, the existence of a collective bargaining agreement, which included as an integral part thereof a grievance procedure culminating in arbitration, evidences, the desire and intention of both parties that employees, generally, and any individual employee has a right to protection against arbitrary action on the part of the employer.

Disciplinary actions taken by an employer can have serious effects, although in this case the most severe sanction, i.e., dismissal was not resorted to. Nevertheless, the action of the employer in issuing a reprimand and in transfer has an effect on the morale of the employee and may have a deleterious effect on future employment prospects of the employee. This is particularly true, in the case of a professional person who has been reprimanded for being absent without leave and therefore by implication for neglect of duty.

A review of the testimony and the statements by the representatives of both parties to this matter would indicate that there was no dispute as to the potential seriousness of a nurse not covering her assignment as this relates to patient care. An institution, such as the Veteran's Administration Hospital, in Oakland, exists for the purpose of healing the sick, and the first duty of a hospital and of its employees, professional or nonprofessional, is to provide the highest quality continuous care to the patients of that hospital. It is even more true that in a Unit such as the Coronary Care Unit, in which the Grievant was at that time employed, constant supervision and monitoring of the patients is of the utmost importance. One cannot lightly dismiss the statement of the Chief Nurse when she indicated at the hearing that this very important and very professional attitude must obtain if a hospital is to function properly.

Having said this, it is also incumbent upon the Arbitrator in a situation such as this to determine whether both parties acted reasonably and whether the sanctions that were imposed were reasonable under the circumstances.

It seems clear that the decision to transfer the Grievant from her regular shift upon return from her vacation to the evening shift was made by the nursing supervisory staff in order to accommodate a situation involving another nurse. There seems to be evidence that at the time the Grievant was notified that she would go on the evening shift there was no full explanation for the reason for it and, although it is not clear that she was specifically told that the person she was replacing was ill, there does not seem to have been any attempt to explain the exact situation. Therefore, as testified by several witnesses, both for the Hospital and by the Grievant herself, it appears that when the Grievant discovered that the reason she was shifted was, at least in her mind, to accommodate the other nurse who did present a problem and against whom, at least as of that time, no sanctions were imposed she became disturbed and requested the interview. It might have been better, and it might have resolved the problems all around, if a full explanation had been given to the Grievant in the first instance, rather than to let her discover for herself why she had been transferred from the day shift to the evening shift.

We will now proceed to a discussion of the specific issues involved in this case.

First, it was asked, "Did management violate Article VI, Section 1 and Article XII, Section 3 of the negotiated agreement when it changed the tour of duty for the Grievant on February 12, 13 and 14, 1974?" This involves a reading of the specific sections and there was much testimony as to what is meant by an emergency and whether this declaration of an emergency was within the purview of the head of the nursing service or was only reserved to the director and whether an emergency meant a general hospital-wide emergency as opposed to a situation where there was a shortage of personnel on a particular shift or in a particular unit and who had the power to declare such an emergency.

Article VI, Section 1, which has been cited, indicates that if there is an emergency declared by the director (of the Hospital) then the Hospital has a right to take all actions deemed by it to be necessary in such situations notwithstanding any of the provisions of the collective bargaining agreement. Article XII, Section 3, is concerned with hours of duty and it indicates that schedules for nurses are posted in two-week segments and the schedule would be posted two weeks in advance, it then goes on to say, "time schedules will not be changed, except in time of emergencies."

It is apparent that in view of the Hospital, this was an "emergency" which could be in effect determined by the chief of the nursing staff and therefore, the time schedule of the Grievant could have been, and in fact was, changed so that she would work the evening shift. The Grievant's case largely rested on the fact that this did not constitute the kind of emergency which is contemplated in Article VI, Section 1 and, in fact, was not an emergency since the other nurse involved had missed her turn on some other occasions and no emergency was declared and it was possible to adjust the workings of the Coronary Care Unit without the action that was taken in the instant case. These sections, specifically Article XII, Section 3, are somewhat vague in their language and leave much to interpretation and therefore, unfortunately, bring about situations where controversy such as the instant case can arise. It is not clear to this Arbitrator, exactly what is intended by Article XII, Section 3, beyond the fact that the management has the right to fix working schedules.

Article XII, Section 3 also states as follows: "Any nurse that believes she is not being scheduled fairly, may question her immediate supervisor regarding her schedule." In this instance the Grievant upon belatedly discovering the true reason for the rescheduling did request an interview and did question the rescheduling. She was given an explanation, which she didn't agree with or like and therefore, took the action which resulted in further disciplinary action.

It seems to this Arbitrator, that the question posed above is in the negative and that management did not violate these sections by rescheduling the Grievant.

The second question posed is, "Can an employee, other than a professional nurse act as a steward or chief steward for PSNU?" It was strongly urged by the Hospital and there were witnesses that testified that the intention of the parties negotiating the collective bargaining agreement was that, "nurses would represent nurses and that under these circumstances the chief steward, if he or she was not a nurse, would not be eligible or permitted to represent a nurse at any step of the grievance procedure." The Union argues that the contract clearly states that at step three of the grievance procedure the chief steward should be involved and is the only one that can be involved under the terms of the contract and argues that the Hospital was in error in not negotiating with Mr. T—, who was the Elected Chief Steward. A careful reading of the two sections would seem to bear out the contention of the Union and the Grievant. Article VIII, Section 1, clearly states that the Union agrees that stewards will be representative of their unit and therefore must be professional nurses. The word steward in this instance, in the opinion of this Arbitrator, is a word of art and refers to the unit stewards, the stewards at the immediate level of operation and it is clear that by this language such stewards must be professional nurses, it says, in fact, that they will be designated by ward areas at Oakland and Aspinwall.

However, when one reads the grievance procedure Section 3, Step 3, it clearly states that, "if not satisfied with the decision in Step 2, the *employee through the Chief Steward* may, within five working days . . ." It further states, "that at this point the employee, the chief steward and the service chief will meet as soon as possible to attempt resolutions of this matter."

This Arbitrator is fully aware of the testimony of the various witnesses who indicated that it was the intention of the parties that only nurses should represent nurses and that it was not intended that a non-nurse should be involved in these proceedings. Nevertheless, it seems to this Arbitrator that the clear language indicates that it is *the* Chief Steward, who represents members at this point in the grievance procedure and it is clear from the testimony and this Arbitrator's understanding of the testimony that there is an elected Chief Steward, that there is only one elected Chief Steward and that person was Mr. T—. Therefore, it is the decision with regard to this issue that the Hospital was incorrect in refusing to negotiate step 3 procedure with Mr. T— and this should have been done and therefore the question Number 2 as posed above is answered in the affirmative.

It may be that the parties, now that this matter has come to light, wish to rewrite the contract, but, of course, the Arbitrator in this instance is limited to the contract as it exists.

A third issue was, "Was the reprimand given Miss S— proper for her deliberate refusal to report for duty as scheduled on February 13 and 14, 1974?" There seems to be no question as to the facts, which relate to this particular question. There is no dispute as to these facts, that the Grievant was informed that she would be shifted to a later shift and whether explicitly or not she got the impression that it was because one of her co-workers was ill. She discovered, in fact, that the reason for the shift is because the co-worker was considered unreliable and required further supervision and, therefore, was put on the day shift. It was for this reason that the Grievant was moved to the evening shift for the days in question. She asked for a meeting with her superiors and was granted one, at which time she refused to accept the explanation and said that she would not report to work on the evening shift on the days indicated, but would report for work on the 15th of February on the regular shift to which she had been previously assigned. The Hospital then instituted action to reprimand her through the regular procedure of giving her a notice of reprimand and then an official reprimand, which is on her record.

The answer to this question must be based, in the opinion of this Arbitrator, on the ethics, mores and tradition of the profession of nursing. This Arbitrator was much impressed by the testimony of Miss M—, the Chief of Nursing Services, and her discussion of the matter of the duties and responsibilities and traditions of nursing and the absolute necessity that patients, generally and particularly patients in a Coronary Care Unit, be constantly under surveillance. There can be no lapse in the high degree of care required of professionals in the health area.

This is not to say that the Arbitrator agrees with the Hospital's handling of this matter. In this Arbitrator's opinion, the Grievant was not fairly dealt with. There was lack of candor and no explanation as to the reason for the shift in tour of duty. The Grievant has been performing efficiently and loyally for several years. This has been recognized by her ratings. She deserved to be told exactly why she was being shifted.

It is this Arbitrator's opinion that a reprimand for the Grievant was "proper" in general, under the circumstances. It is further this Arbitrator's opinion, that the length in which the reprimand will remain in the Grievant's record is inordinately severe, in relation to her past service and to the fact that the situation which brought about the reprimand is not entirely her fault, if that term can be used. It is strongly recommended that the Hospital, if consonant with other rules and regulations governing personnel in the agency, now remove the reprimand from the Grievant's file jacket since she has suffered the disadvantage of the reprimand for almost a year.

Lastly, the question was asked, whether the reassignment of the Grievant from the Coronary Care Unit is grievable or arbitrable? If so, was it carried out for good reason? It is obvious and requires very little discussion that in the opinion of this Arbitrator, the transfer is grievable and arbitrable. The burden of the following discussion is whether it was carried out for good reason. The Union and the Grievant assert strenuously and repeatedly that the only reason for the transfer was "punishment" of the Grievant for the assertion of her rights under the collective bargaining agreement and that it had nothing to do with "emergency" or had nothing to do, really, with the question of her dependability. The Hospital, in direct argument and through witnesses, indicated that this was not the case but that they felt that because of the seriousness of the Grievant absenting herself from this unit for the two days involved that she should be placed in a less critical area.

The Arbitrator is struck by the fact that in all of the personnel service ratings prior to 1974, which was clouded by this unfortunate incident, the Grievant was considered to be an above average employee, that she took responsibility and it was indicated that she had leadership potential and could develop into a leader, that she had taken courses and was continuing to take courses relative to the Coronary Care Unit and that this Grievant was a credit to the Hospital and credit to the Unit, and a needed functionary within that Unit, which is such an important and critical area.

It is unfortunate that the incident occurred, and it is unfortunate that the Grievant may have allowed her emotions on this occasion to overcome reason. On the surface it might be considered to be a good idea to transfer her to another unit.

Nevertheless, the patients in a critical area, such as the Coronary Care Unit, should not be deprived of the Grievant's expertise and the good care which the Grievant rendered to these patients. It is also, in the opinion of this Arbitrator, unfortunate that the Hospital and the service should be deprived of the training and experience which this Grievant has acquired over the years since 1970 in this particular specialty and further that the Hospital and the service should be deprived of the potential leadership ability which has been attested to in the proficiency ratings which the Grievant received.

Although it was vigorously denied, it appears to this Arbitrator that there was an element of punishment in the transfer of the Grievant to another less critical unit. Therefore, the answer to this last question is that this reassignment is grievable and arbitrable, and that it was not for a good reason, in that it deprived a trained nurse of her specialty and deprived the Veteran's Administration and the Nursing Service and the Cardiac Unit of a valuable employee, who could in the future render even better service to those critically ill patients.

AWARD

Therefore, in view of the above the Arbitrator orders and awards as follows:

1. That the change in tour of duty for the Grievant on February 12, 13 and 14, 1974 was not in violation of the collective bargaining agreement.

2. That the Grievant was properly represented by [T—], the only Elected Chief Steward for the Union, as defined in the collective bargaining agreement.

3. That the reprimand given to the Grievant was proper in view of the high standards required in the nursing profession, coupled with this is a recommendation that the period the reprimand remain in the Grievant's file be limited to one year.

4. That the reassignment of the Grievant from the Coronary Care Unit was not proper and that the Grievant should be returned to the Coronary

Care Unit where her training and experience is more valuable than in the unit to which she is now assigned.

5.   Whatever loss of pay has been assessed is permitted to stand and the Grievant's request that this pay be returned to her is herewith denied.

The grievance is therefore affirmed in part and dismissed in part, as indicated above.

Case No. 19

*Where the contract contained a
maintenance-of-standards provision, could the
Hospital unilaterally change the method of
scheduling weekends off for nurses? Was the
Hospital relieved of a duty to bargain by the fact
that it was contractually obligated to evenly
distribute weekend time off?*

**Marinette General Hospital (Marinette County, Wis.)
and
Marinette General Hospital Employees Union, AFSCME, Local 1752**

Arbitrator: Douglas V. Knudson
Date of Award: February 19, 1974
Citation: LAIG 1023

Issue

The parties stipulated the following issue:

Did the Employer violate the terms and provisions of the contract when
it unilaterally changed the method of scheduling weekends off in the
Nursing Services Department? If so, what is the appropriate remedy?

Pertinent Contractual Provisions

ARTICLE VI — *Working Hours, Shift Premiums and Overtime*

6.01   The Hospital operates twenty-four (24) hours a day, seven (7) days
a week. This means that many employees must work on weekends and on

holidays and on different shifts. The Hospital will attempt to distribute the weekend time off evenly in each job classification. The usual pattern is five (5) eight-hour shifts a week for full-time employees. Employees who work beyond 5:00 p.m. will receive an additional $1.00.

ARTICLE XV — *Management*

The Hospital has the sole and exclusive right to determine the number of employees to be employed, the duties of each and the nature and place of their work, whether or not any of the work will be contracted out and all other matters pertaining to the management and operation of the Hospital. This clause will not be used for the purpose of destroying the bargaining unit.

ARTICLE XVIII — *Existing Practices*

All existing practices pertaining to working conditions not specifically mentioned herein shall continue in force as at present until they are adjusted by mutual agreement between the Hospital and the Union. Nothing shall be construed as a practice unless it meets each of the following tests: It must be (a) long continued; (b) certain and uniform; (c) consistently followed; (d) generally known by the parties hereto; and (e) must not be in opposition to the terms and conditions of this Agreement.

Facts

On or about April 24, 1973, the Union filed a grievance over the Employer's decision to alter the scheduling of weekends for the Nursing Services Department. For several years prior to that time the employees had worked every other weekend and had been off duty on the alternate weekends. The Employer implemented a new program in May, 1973, based on four-week periods. During each four-week period, an employee would work two weekends, be off duty one full weekend and work either a Saturday or a Sunday on the remaining weekend. Sometime during June, 1973, the method of scheduling weekends to be worked was again altered so that in each four-week period an employee would work two weekends and be off duty two weekends. However, the off duty weekends would not necessarily be alternate weekends as had been the case prior to May, 1973. On or about September 16, 1973, the Employer again revised the scheduling of weekends for the Nursing Services Department. Subsequent to September 15, 1973, in each four-week period, the employees were off duty on one full weekend, worked two full weekends and worked either a Saturday or a Sunday on the remaining weekend.

Position of the Union

The Union argues that the contract is silent with respect to the scheduling of off duty weekends except for Article 6 which requires an even distribution of weekend work. The Union relies on Article 18 to support its position that the Employer may not alter the scheduling of weekends off duty absent the mutual consent of the Union. The practice of alternate weekends off duty is well established. Said practice had been in effect for at least 10 years prior to the Employer's attempt to alter that method in May, 1973. The Employer's job postings and the memos to all Hospital employees posted by the Employer show that the practice has been consistently followed. There is absolutely no doubt that both the Employer and the Union were in full knowledge of said practice for scheduling weekends off duty. The practice is not in opposition to any contractual clause. The Employer did not seek a change in the scheduling procedure during the negotiations culminating in the contract which took effect on July 1, 1973. Inasmuch as the method of receiving every other weekend off duty has been an established practice and that the Employer did not attempt to alter said practice through negotiations with the Union, therefore, the Union requests that the Employer be directed to return to its previous practice of scheduling every other weekend off duty.

Position of the Employer

The Employer contends that Article 18 refers to "conditions not specifically mentioned," and that Article 6 does, in fact, mention the specific condition of working on weekends. Therefore, Article 18 does not control the instant dispute. The only requirement found in Article 6 is that weekend time off be distributed equally within each classification. The specific method of scheduling weekend time off is reserved to the Employer. The Employer met the requirement in Article 6 and, therefore, did not violate the contract when it altered the method of scheduling weekend time off. The Employer seeks a finding which would deny and dismiss the grievance.

Discussion

Although the record is unclear concerning the details of the various methods for scheduling time off on weekends utilized by the Employer beginning in May, 1973, said lack of clarity is unimportant since the parties agree that the Employer did alter its method of scheduling time off on weekends and the undersigned has been asked to decide whether the

Employer had the right to make such unilateral changes, regardless of what the changes were.

Article 18 of the contract sets forth five tests a practice must meet in order to qualify for the definition of an existing practice which cannot be changed without the mutual agreement of the Employer and the Union. The practice, followed until May, 1973, of scheduling every other weekend as time off meets the first four of those tests. It had been continued over a long period of time, was uniformly applied and was consistently followed during that period of time. The record leaves no doubt that the parties were well aware of said existing practice, since it consistently was stated in job postings and bulletin board memos. The dispute arises over the fifth test, i.e., whether the practice is in opposition to the terms and conditions of the contract, specifically, Article 6, which states "the Hospital will attempt to distribute the weekend time off evenly in each job classification." Contrary to the Employer, the undersigned concludes that by making an equal distribution of weekend time off the Employer is not relieved of its burden to continue scheduling said weekend time off in the same manner as it had done prior to May, 1973, unless and until it and the Union adjusted said method by mutual agreement. Weekend time off is a very important working condition to the employees involved herein. Allowing the method of scheduling weekend time off to be changed only through mutual agreement does not oppose the other terms and conditions of the contract, but rather, supplements the contractual language, found in Article 6. If Article 18 did not apply, the Employer could schedule weekend time off in such a manner that no employee would have a full weekend off, but would have to work a Saturday or Sunday in each weekend. The undersigned does not believe that such a broad change was contemplated in the language of Article 6. Article 6 requires that regardless of the method utilized in scheduling weekend time off, the result must be an equal distribution of such weekend time off within each job classification. The method of scheduling the weekend time off does meet the criteria of an established practice and consequently cannot be altered unilaterally by the Employer. There is no evidence in the record to indicate that the Employer attempted to revise the language of either Article 6 or Article 18 during the negotiations which culminated in the current contract. Said contract took effect on July 1, 1973, a date subsequent to the filing of the initial grievance by the Union. Accordingly, said language continued in effect and protected the method of scheduling time off as it had existed prior to May 1, 1973, when the Employer first attempted to alter the existing practice of scheduling weekend time off. Based on the foregoing and the record as a whole, the undersigned enters the following:

AWARD

That the Employer did violate the terms and provisions of the contract when it unilaterally changed the method of scheduling weekends off in the Nursing Services Department; and that the Employer return to the previous method of scheduling weekend time off, i.e., alternate weekends, as was in existence prior to May, 1973.

Case No. 20

*Did a shortage of full-time nurses during the
summer months constitute justification for a
Hospital's requirement that part-time nurses agree
to work two weekends in four under a collective
agreement that did not require them to work
weekends? Did full-time nurses have the right to
change their status to part-timers for the summer
months, the object being to avoid weekend work?*

Hurley Hospital (Flint, Mich.)
and
Hurley Hospital Registered Nurses Organization

Arbitrator: Leon J. Herman
Date of Award: October 9, 1972
Citation: LAIG 702

Hurley Hospital and the Organization are parties to a collective
bargaining agreement for the term July 1, 1971, through April 30, 1973,
covering registered nurses employed by the Hospital. Article XII divides the
nurses into three categories:

A. *Full-time Employees* — Full-time employees are those who are
regularly scheduled to work eighty (80) hours in a fourteen (14) day
period.

B. *Part-time Employees* — Registered Professional Nurses who work at
the Hospital, but for less than full-time, shall be classified as part-time
employees.

(1) Except as specifically provided in this section, part-time
employees shall not receive benefit provisions of this contract.

(2) Part-time employees shall advance through the steps of the
compensation schedule in accordance with their accrued hours.

(3)   Those part-time employees who work one hundred (100) hours per four (4) week schedule and who work two (2) weekends in each four (4) week schedule shall receive benefits provided in the following sections of this contract:

> Holiday Premium (when worked)
> Regular Holidays (when worked)
> Sick Leave (on pro-rata basis)
> Maternity Leave
> Liability Insurance
> Hospitalization Insurance
> Medical Services
> Retirement
> PR&R Representation
> Overtime Payments
> Shift Differential
> Injury Compensation
> Military Leave
> Jury Duty
> Court Time
> Bereavement

(4)   Those part-time employees who work a schedule less than that provided in (3) above shall receive only the following benefit provisions of this contract:

> Holiday Premium (when worked)
> Maternity Leave
> Liability Insurance
> Medical Service
> PR&R Representation
> Overtime Payments
> Shift Differential
> Injury Compensation
> Military Leave
> Retirement (must work 80 hours per month)

For purposes of simplified reference in this opinion I have entitled these groups of employees as full-time nurses, 100-hour nurses and part-time nurses.

It has been the practice that full-time nurses shall work two weekends in every four-week schedule. The 100-hour nurses, by contract, are required to work two weekends in every four-week schedule. The contract makes no specific reference to weekend work for part-time employees. It is the claim of the Organization and the aggrieved employees that part-time nurses may be required to work only one weekend in every four-week schedule.

In May, 1972, Mrs. Hinkle and Mrs. Lanford, 100-hour nurses, requested transfers to part-time employment. Mrs. Long, a full-time nurse, also asked that she be reassigned to part-time work. Each was asked by the Nursing Service to sign a waiver in substantially the following form:

HURLEY HOSPITAL

Department Nursing Service

EMPLOYMENT WAIVER

Recognizing the need for continuing patient care requirements and needed relief for full time nurses, I, _____, will work two (2) weekends per schedule with my part-time schedule.

I also agree that I will work Memorial Day *or* the 4th of July, Labor Day *or* Thanksgiving and Christmas *or* New Years.

These terms are effective until I am promoted to full-time employment.

_____   _____

DATE   Signed

_____

WITNESS

All three nurses refused to sign the waiver. On May 16, Mrs. Hinkle filed a grievance alleging that "there is a violation of contract in areas of purpose and intent, Article I-A and Article V." Mrs. Scott, Director of Nursing, answered at the second step:

> Nursing Service denies this grievance in that it is against H.H.R.N.O. Contract. This case was discussed on two occasions at the conference table: see minutes for March 16, 1972, and April 10, 1972. We feel that sufficient explanation has been given and know that this was written with the prime purpose of sending it to third step.

Mrs. Long and Mrs. Lanford filed grievances on May 26, alleging that the Hospital discriminated against them because of their request for part-time work. Mrs. Long's grievance is substantially representative of both:

> I must go on Part-time because of personal reasons. I hired in as a part-time employee and worked one weekend out of four. I have been working full-time and now have gone back on part-time, and before when I worked part-time it was one weekend out of four.
>
> I do believe that you are discriminating against part-time RN's in the fact that you are trying to force two weekends out of four on to me. I do

not reap the benefits of full time help while on part-time and therefore I do not feel the necessity of two out of four weekends, and I feel that the duress that you are trying to apply is not necessary or called for. Signing a waiver is setting a new precedent for part time and is discriminatory.

Disposition: Reconsideration of my original request to be put back on part-time and work one weekend in four week schedule. (Since a precedent has already been established thru years of practice.)

Mrs. Scott answered both grievances in the same language:

Nursing Service will reconsider the original request of Mrs. E. Long to permit part-time work, but we retain management rights according to Article IV ". . . to hire, lay-off, assign and direct . . ." To provide necessary staffing for patient care and relief for full-time staff, it is essential that we maintain sufficient weekend coverage. Therefore, we shall expect Mrs. Long to work two (2) weekends per schedule.

On June 14, the Organization filed three policy grievances alleging (1) discrimination and intimidation of employees who refused to sign waivers; (2) that the Hospital failed to give 14 days notice prior to institution of a change in the rules and regulations with respect to waivers and to working more than one weekend in four; and (3) that a practice had been established whereby part-time employees are required to work only one weekend in a four-week schedule.

These policy grievances followed by one day the service of a summons and complaint against the Hospital in an action in Circuit Court for the County of Genesee, wherein the Organization charged the Hospital with discrimination against part-time employees and the threat of disciplinary action. The complaint alleged that certain hospital employees had invoked the grievance procedure provided for in the collective bargaining agreement, but that the Hospital had refused to discontinue its attempt to impose a new condition of employment pending the determination of the grievances. A temporary injunction was requested of the Court.

Circuit Judge John W. Baker issued the following order:

DEFENDANT IS HEREBY ENJOINED, pending the outcome of binding arbitration, from requiring any part-time registered nurse employees to work more than one weekend in any four-week period and from subjecting any such employee to discipline or discharge for failure to do so, except those employees who volunteer in accordance with the following paragraph and who do not appear without reasonable excuse.

This injunctive Order is granted upon the condition that within one week from the date hereof, Plaintiffs supply a list of part-time nurses willing to volunteer to work additional weekends, to cover for the weekends lost by these nurses who have switched or are switching to part-time status from full-time or 100-hour part-time status.

The matter was thereupon processed to arbitration.

At the hearing Patricia Smith, an Assistant Head Nurse and Chairman of the Organization for the past four years, testified that a substantial number of nurses transfer from full-time to part-time during the summer months because of family obligations. To ease the strain upon the Hospital scheduling caused by these summer transfers, the Hospital proposed in negotiations leading up to the present contract that it make weekend work more attractive by introducing a new classification of 100-hour employees, who would be given extra benefits with the understanding that they were to accept two weekends of work in a four-week schedule. The Union concurred and the proposal was incorporated into the contract.

In the negotiations nothing was said about weekend work for part-time employees. In the ten years that Mrs. Smith has been employed at Hurley Hospital part-time employees have been required to work only one weekend in four. There is no restriction upon a part-time nurse working extra weekends if she so desired. It has been the practice to require that a part-time nurse working extra weekends sign a waiver of overtime pay. No other waiver has ever been required of these employees until the past May.

Mrs. Smith went on to say that she, as Chairman of the Organization, had never received a formal notice from the Hospital that any change in policy had occurred nor was she notified of the Hospital's plan to obtain waivers from the part-time employees. She had never been asked to discuss the matter with the administration. At a special meeting between the employer and the Union held on June 2, the Hospital proposed a modification of the collective bargaining agreement:

> It is agreed between the parties that on and after this date all new-hire part-time Registered Nurses shall work not less than two weekends in each four-week scheduling period. It is further agreed that present part-time nurses who work only one weekend may, with their consent, be scheduled to work not less than two weekends in each four-week scheduling period. And it is further agreed that any Registered Nurse who requests a reduced work schedule will be granted the request provided the nurse agrees to work not less than two weekends in each four-week scheduling period.

The Union committee rejected the proposal. The Union filed its policy grievances after receiving several complaints from nurses other than the individual grievants. When the Hospital threatened to continue its demand for waivers the Union went to Court in order to retain the status quo until a decision was had in arbitration.

Mrs. Smith emphasized that under the prior contract, when there was only one class of part-time employees, they were required to work only one weekend in four, although some voluntarily worked weekends exclusively.

Loretta Lanford testified that she had been working as a 100-hour nurse on a four-day week. When school was about to let out she requested that her hours be cut to two days per week as a part-time employee because she needed time to take care of her children. She had made the same requests on other occasions and they had been granted. This time Mr. Viele, Nursing Staff Coordinator, presented her with a waiver and told her what it contained. As she recollected the conversation, the language was similar to that in the waiver quoted hereinabove. She refused to sign it. He told her that if she did not sign he or she would have to report the matter to Mrs. Scott.

Mrs. Lanford testified that she understood that part timers were only to work one weekend in a month and that this had been true for the past five to six years or more. She learned of the Hospital change of policy in this respect only when she was presented with the waiver. It has been her practice to transfer back and forth, at her own option, some two or three times a year, from 100-hour work to part-time work. In the summer she could only handle part-time work because of her family needs. Nonetheless, in August she volunteered for an additional weekend.

In early May, 1972, Ethel Long, an Assistant Head Nurse for approximately seven years, with eight years of service at this Hospital, requested a transfer from full-time to part-time work. The Head Nurse told her to see Viele for a definite answer. Viele asked that she sign a waiver agreeing to work two weekends out of four and three holidays a year. She refused, whereupon he told her that she would be disciplined and might even lose her job.

She declared that the policy in the Hospital for the past eight years had been that part timers work one weekend in four weeks. She had hired in as a part-time employee and was then informed that this was her schedule. Over the years she has switched back and forth from full-time to part-time and in every case of part-time employment worked one weekend in four weeks. She now wished to work ten days in a four-week schedule.

Lenie R. Perry, a Head Nurse, has been employed at Hurley Hospital on and off since 1955 and continuously for the past seven years. As Head Nurse it was her duty to make up schedules for the nurses and turn them into the Staffing Coordinator of Nursing Services. She always scheduled part-time employees for one weekend in a four-week schedule. She stated that she had never been officially informed that part-time employees were to work two weekends, although she had heard rumors to that effect. As far as she was aware, part-time employees had been working one weekend in a four-week schedule ever since she came to the hospital in 1955.

The Hospital offered no testimony at the hearing, relying instead upon the contract and upon written summation.

The parties referred to specific portions of the collective bargaining agreement as primarily applicable to the determination of these grievances:

ARTICLE IV

The Hospital retains the sole right to manage its business, including but not limited to the rights to decide the number and location of its buildings and the services to be rendered and the equipment and supplies to be purchased; to maintain order and efficiency in all of its operations, to hire, lay-off, assign and direct, transfer and promote employees and to determine starting and quitting times and the number of hours to be worked; and all other rights and prerogatives, including those normally exercised in the past, subject only to such regulations and restrictions governing the exercise of these rights as are expressly provided in this Agreement.

The Hospital retains the sole right to discipline and discharge employees for cause, provided that in the exercise of this right it will not act in violation of this Agreement. Complaints that the Hospital has violated this paragraph may be taken up through the grievance procedure.

The right of the Hospital to make such reasonable rules and regulations, not in conflict with this Agreement, as it may from time to time deem best for the purposes of maintaining order, safety and/or effective operations, and after fourteen (14) days advance notice to the Organization, to require compliance therewith by employees, is recognized. The Organization reserves the right to question the reasonableness of the Hospital's rules and regulations through the grievance procedure, and may request a joint conference meeting during the fourteen (14) day period mentioned above and before such rules and regulations are to become effective.

All pertinent provisions of the Charter of the City of Flint are made a part of this contract.

ARTICLE X

E. Changes or additions to existing work rules and/or Hospital Guidelines for the conduct of Registered Professional Nurses, when drafted by the Hospital, shall be presented to and reviewed by the Organization fourteen (14) days prior to their being placed in effect. If the

Organization disagrees with the proposed rules, they shall be proper subjects for discussion under the provisions of Article VIII, Special Conferences, prior to their becoming appropriate subjects for the grievance procedure.

ARTICLE XI

A.   The City, in providing a Hospital to serve the community, and the Registered Professional Nurses, as a professional group, share the common goal and the common responsibility of providing to the citizens who require it, nursing care which is both safe and adequate and to define and recognize the proper role of the Registered Professional Nurse in the operation of the Hospital.

E.   The parties further agree that it is the Hospital's responsibility to provide adequate nursing and auxiliary personnel on all shifts seven (7) days a week except on those shifts when auxiliary personnel are not regularly scheduled to work and to fill vacancies as soon as possible in order to provide safe and adequate nursing care and to make maximum utilization of the training and competencies of all nursing personnel.

ARTICLE XXVII

Except for specific provisions made elsewhere in this Agreement, all privileges and benefits will be maintained during the term of this Agreement at not less than the current minimum standard in effect.

The Union contends that the Hospital has violated the Agreement with respect to part-time nurses in failing to give 14-days advance notice to the Organization of a unilateral change in the rules and regulations covering part-time nurses (Article IV). The Hospital violated Article XII B(3) by requiring part-time nurses to work more than one weekend in a four-week schedule and violated Section D(3) of the same Article by failing to notify all nurses in writing in advance of the change in schedule of part-time nurses for weekend duty. The Hospital violated Article V by discriminating against part-time nurses transferring from full-time to part-time and by employment of threats and coercion. Article VII was also violated in that the Hospital unilaterally changed the working conditions of part-time nurses without the knowledge or approval of the Organization.

The Union also contends that it is unreasonable to expect part-time employees to work a weekend schedule equivalent to that of full-time nurses. Furthermore, the contract as to part-time employees is permissive and not compulsory. There is nothing in the contract which requires that part-time employees work weekends. The Hospital has imposed a change in working conditions which it had no right to do without bargaining with the

Organization and obtaining its consent. The grievances should therefore be sustained.

The Hospital stated that it offered no oral testimony, since there is no factual dispute involved in these issues. The grievances present only the matter of contract interpretation. As the Hospital recites the facts:

> In past summers, a problem has existed concerning scheduling of the work of Registered Nurses in Hurley Hospital. Prior to the contract now in effect, there were only two job classifications of Registered Nurses within the Hospital — full-time and part-time. The distinctions between these two classifications were several. Full-time employees, for example, received more fringe benefits than part-time employees. Part-time employees were not required to work two weekends out of every scheduling period of four weeks. Part-time employees did not work as many hours as full-time employees. As a result of this, some part-time employees worked one weekend per four-week schedule, some worked two weekends within a four-week schedule, and some worked three weekends within a four-week schedule. These records, together with a synopsis of these records appear in Appendix 1.

> In the summer months many of the Registered Nurses, especially those with school age children, requested a transfer from full-time employment to part-time employment. Since these requests were never predictable, they created acute work scheduling problems, especially on the weekends. These scheduling difficulties were remedied on an ad hoc basis by last-minute work requests, often of full-time employees, often across department lines. This method of curing the acute scheduling problems resulted in payment of significant amounts of overtime to full-time employees, inefficiency in the operation of several of the departments, together with general depreciation of nursing standards where nurses were required to work in an area which was not their field of expertise.

The Hospital then quoted the current contract terms and went on to say:

> In spite of these contract provisions providing for a new classification of part-time employment, scheduling problems again cropped up in the summer of 1972. In addition to the problems created by summer vacation scheduling, and the requests of full-time employees to be transferred to part-time employment, some other complicating factors occurred. For example, other specialized units have either been opened or expanded. To the extent that these new units are specialized, the Registered Nurses serving these units are not fully interchangeable over departmental lines.

> This acute scheduling problem was presented to and discussed with the Registered Nurses Organization at one of the regular union-management meetings. (See minutes, Appendix #2). In addition,

a proposal was made to the nurses organization proposing to clear up the problem. (See Appendix #3). Management then made the policy decision to require regular part-time Registered Nurses who were formerly full-time Registered Nurses to continue to commit themselves to two weekends of service out of every four-week schedule.

Article XII, "Employee Definition" does not specifically outline which employees are required to work weekends. As a matter of practice, full-time employees are required to work two weekends out of every four-week schedule and yet the definition of full-time employees contained in Article XII makes no such mention. The description of "100 Hour" employees makes specific reference to weekend work and also to hours worked. It provides:

> "Those part-time employees who work one hundred (100) hours per four (4) week schedule and who work two (2) weekends in each four (4) week schedule shall receive benefits provided in the following sections . . ."

Regular part-time employees are described as:

> "Those part-time employees who shall work a schedule less than that provided in (3) above (the definition of 100 hour part-time employees)."

It is management's position with regard to these definitions that a part-time employee is limited only in that she must work less than either 100 hours per four-week schedule or less than two weekends in each four-week schedule. Thus, the definition of regular part-time employees fails to resolve the issue before the arbitrator. Reference must necessarily be made to the more general provisions of the collective bargaining agreement.

Authority for these actions can be found in Article IV "Management Rights and Responsibility" which provides:

> "The Hospital retains the sole right to manage its business, including but not limited to the rights to decide the number and location of its buildings and the services to be rendered and the equipment and supplies to be purchased; to maintain order and efficiency in all of its operations, to hire, lay-off, assign and direct, transfer and promote employees and to determine starting and quitting times and the number of hours to be worked; and all other rights and prerogatives, including those normally exercised in the past, subject only to such regulations and restrictions governing the exercise of these rights as are expressly provided in this Agreement."

Thus, management retains the exclusive right to regulate the management of its business, including the exclusive right to assign and schedule work for its employees.

The only specific regulation of scheduling is contained in Article XXII of which in no way restricts management's right to schedule weekend work as the need provides.

The issue, as stated by the Hospital, is whether the management decision to require two weekends of service in every four-week schedule as a prerequisite for registered nurses transferring to regular part-time work for the summer months is permissible under the bargaining agreement. Except for the limitation to the summer months the Union's statement of issue is substantially in accord.

In support of its position the Hospital points out that Article XII "Employee Definition" does not specifically state which employees are required to work weekends. As a matter of practice, full-time employees work two weekends out of every four-week schedule. One hundred-hour employees are specifically directed to work two weekends in each four-week schedule. There is no such description included in the part-time employee definition.

As the Hospital sees it, "a part-time employee is limited only in that she must work less than either 100 hours per four-week schedule *or* less than two weekends in each four-week schedule." It therefore contends that the definition of regular part-time employees fails to resolve the issue presented herein.

The Hospital then turns to the management clause (Article IV) wherein it is provided that the right to assign and direct employees and determine the number of hours to be worked is a management prerogative. While regulation of scheduling is contained in Article XXII of the Agreement, nothing in that article restricts management's right to schedule weekend work.

Of paramount importance, in the eye of the Hospital, are Sections A and E of Article XI which declare that the Hospital and the Organization share a common goal and responsibility in providing health care to the citizens who require it, and further agree that it is the Hospital's responsibility to provide adequate nursing care on all shifts seven days a week.

Basically, says the Hospital, the scheduling of employees is a management prerogative which it may modify or amend at any time as it sees fit in order to maintain adequate hospital service to the public.

I concur with the Hospital that scheduling of employees is a management prerogative and that the Hospital has retained scheduling authority under its contract with the Organization. Nor do I question that the Hospital, like similar institutions throughout the country, is suffering from the current shortage of qualified registered nurses, and must do everything it can to relieve that need by the most efficient scheduling possible. It is also understandable that weekends and holidays present a particularly difficult scheduling problem, in that these are the days that nurses, like employees in any other field, are most anxious to devote to personal accommodation. Nor can it be disputed that a hospital is a necessary public service which must be maintained day and night throughout the year, weekends and holidays to the contrary notwithstanding.

Nonetheless, it is outside my authority as arbitrator to predicate the determination of this issue on the basic fundament of public service. I am restrained by the agreement to restrict my conclusions to the terms of the contract itself, and pursuant to those terms to determine whether a firm established practice exists to which both parties are bound. The Organization witnesses insist, and the Hospital has conceded in its summation, that "part-time employees were not required to work two weekends out of every scheduling period of four weeks" prior to the inception of the current contract. It would appear, therefore, that a practice had been established which had been recognized over the years by both parties, and which must therefore be continued in existence pursuant to the maintenance of benefits requirements of Article XXVII, which directs that "all privileges and benefits will be maintained during the term of this agreement at not less than the current minimum standard in effect." An established practice must be deemed as inviolable as the written agreement as long as it falls within contractual limits. It cannot be disputed, therefore, and must be accepted as fact, that part-time employees, by established practice, may be required to work no more than one weekend in every four scheduled weeks.

I disagree with the Hospital's conclusion that part-time employees must work either less than 100 hours in a four-week schedule or less than two weekends in a four-week schedule. I take this to mean that a part-time nurse must work either on the 100-hour schedule or must work at least two weekends in a four-week schedule. There is nothing in the wording of Article XII which indicates an attempt to adopt the disjunctive syntax. Employees who work 100 hours in a four-week schedule and who work two weekends in four weeks are entitled to certain benefits. Part-time employees who work a schedule less than that of the 100-hour employees receive less liberal benefits. There is no intimation that a part-time employee must work either a schedule of less than 100 hours *or* at least two weekends in every four weeks. To insert the particle "or" is a distortion of the language employed, not warranted by anything contained in the section. Since the definition of a part-time employee makes no allusion to weekend work, reference can only be had to the established practice, which, both parties agree, directs that part-time employees need only work one weekend in four scheduled weeks.

This is not to say that the Hospital may not make reasonable rules and regulations for the direction of its employees, or that it may not schedule employees as it deems proper, but in such scheduling the Hospital must conform to the agreement and to such past practices as by custom are inferentially included in the agreement. In executing a collective bargaining contract with a labor organization, the employer agrees to abide by the terms of that contract, even to the extent of waiving a management right which it formerly held. There is no question that here the employer has waived any right to compel part-time employees to work more often than one weekend in four weeks. This waiver cannot be cured by the imposition of amended rules and regulations nor by the establishment of new policies. It can be corrected only by negotiation and agreement with the Organization.

It follows that the Hospital did not violate Article X(E) by failing to give the Organization fourteen days notice of its intent to add to existing work rules and/or guidelines. The Hospital did not add new work rules. What the Hospital attempted to do was to restructure the contract by adding a new condition of employment. This it may not do, with or without notice, unless it has the concurrence of the bargaining unit to the change. The Hospital sought such agreement but failed. It may not subvert the contract by compelling individual nurses to waive their contractual rights. I do not intend by the foregoing to imply that a part-time nurse may not voluntarily work more than one weekend in four. It has been the practice to permit nurses to agree at their option to such additional weekend work. No change is intended in this voluntary arrangement. Conversely, the Hospital may not change the established practice whereby full-time and 100-hour nurses are permitted to change to and from part-time work upon request.

The Organization, in its grievances, has made charges of discrimination against the employer which I do not find to be sustained by the evidence. Article V of the contract prohibits discrimination against any nurse because of "race, color, national origin, religious affiliation, sex, marital status, membership in or activity on behalf of the Organization." None of these factors were in any way involved in the Hospital's attempt to obtain a change in scheduling practice.

Unfortunately, the Hospital's scheduling dilemma will survive this decision and eventually must be resolved. Now that the animosities engendered by this dispute have been dissipated, I urgently recommend that the parties engage in serious discussions to the end that a solution be reached. As tentative suggestion only, perhaps arrangement could be made whereby part-time nurses agree to an extra weekend every six weeks, plus an occasional working holiday. Possibly a *quid pro quo* could be had through reallocation of benefits. Nurses too owe an obligation to the patients they serve. Given an amicable atmosphere, I am sure the parties can come to agreement, with the ultimate benefit accruing to those to whom both parties devote their service — the sick and afflicted. Given good will and good intent, the problem could be resolved.

AWARD

(1)   The Hospital shall continue to recognize the established working condition whereby part-time nurses are required to work no more than one weekend in four scheduled weeks.

(2)   Part-time nurses may, at their option, work more than one weekend in four scheduled weeks.

(3)   The Hospital shall make no change in the established practice whereby nurses, at their option, change their definition to and from full-time nurses, 100-hour nurses and part-time nurses working less than 100 hours, provided the working schedule requested is available.

(4)   The individual grievances and the grievances of the Organization are sustained as above directed.

Case No. 21

In an effort to insure the best possible patient care,
could a VA Hospital assign LPN's to the night shift
against their wishes?

Veterans Administration Hospital (Canandaigua, N.Y.)
and
Service Employees International Union, Local 227

Arbitrator: Robert W. Miller
Date of Award: July 31, 1972
Citation: LAIG 914

The Issue

Did the Employer violate the Agreement dated November 5, 1971, by assigning Paula McDonald, Bernice Hickey and Alberta Peters, Licensed Practical Nurses, with a GS-6 grade and seniority, to the midnight shift against their wishes.

Provisions of the Agreement

The Agreement further provides:

ARTICLE XVII — *Tours of Duty*

Section 4 — Senior employees will be given preference in the selection of shift or tour of duty in all Services and Divisions.

The Agreement further provides:

ARTICLE IV — *Mutual Rights and Obligations*

Section 4 — Nothing in this Agreement shall restrict the VA in exercising the right, in accordance with applicable laws and regulations to: direct employees of the VA; . . . transfer, assign . . . in positions within the VA; . . . maintain the efficiency of the Government operations entrusted to the VA; determine the methods, means and personnel by which such operations are to be conducted . . .

ARTICLE XVII — *Tours of Duty*

Section 5 — A. Establishment of new tours of duty or changes in existing tours of duty will be brought to the attention of the Union in advance and their views considered prior to any action taken or any changes made.

Contentions of the Parties

There are only four GS-6 Licensed Practical Nurses in the Nursing Service. While but three signed the grievance, all four were present at the hearing and all had been assigned to the midnight to 8:00 a.m. shift which action all were protesting. The three grievants were given notice of assignment to the midnight to 8:00 a.m. shift in January, 1973, and the fourth was so assigned within thirty days thereafter. Assignment became effective on or about February 4, 1973.

The fact of such assignments and that such were made after notice to the Union as required by Article XVII, Section 5(A) of the Agreement was stipulated by the parties. The LPN's were advised "to accept reassignment to the 12:00 to 8:00 a.m. shift and retain their grade or be reassigned to the day shift with a down-grading to a GS-5 position."

It should be noted that Licensed Practical Nurses must have completed a one-year approved training course and are licensed to practice as LPN's by a state licensing bureau.

The Union contends that Position-Classification Standards issued June, 1970, by the Civil Service Commission are the only standards used in establishing grades for federal employees and that the same set of standards are had for Nursing Assistants and LPN's within the same grade level. Employer contends such standards apply only to classification and not to the assignment of duties or persons to such classifications. In other words, the Civil Service standards are used to determine classification and grade but, insists Employer, they have nothing to do with the duties which may be assigned.

Employer on February 2, 1973, amended the GS-6 position descriptions made in March 1971, by *deleting* "Incumbent will be assigned to an open psychiatric building, medical, surgical or psychiatric medically infirm ward on the 3:30 to 12 tour of duty." Also *deleted* was assignment of the incumbent (LPN, GS-6) to the 7:30–4:00 tour of duty. In effect, only the midnight to 8 a.m. shift remained open for the LPN's, GS-6.

The reason for this change in job description and assignment of the LPN's, GS-6, to the midnight shift was an "incident" allegedly occurring on the midnight shift. By management decision along with that of the Acting Chief Nurse, professional nurses were used in the buildings on the 3:30 p.m.–12:00 shift. This meant LPN's on such shift were replaced with only the midnight shift available. Employer stated the belief was that LPN's could assume responsibility for certain buildings not declared "open" and where no nurse was stationed, together with an adjacent ward or building staffed with a professional nurse over whom the LPN's would have supervision. Acting Chief Nurse McCarthy stated the "needs of the patients" plus the belief that the LPN's were the most qualified to take charge of the wards or buildings "not open" during the midnight shift was the basis for the change.

Union contends there is no pay differential between Nursing Assistants, GS-6 and LPN's, GS-6, and that they are as capable as the LPN's, GS-6; that for more than forty years since the hospital was built LPN's, GS-6, were never used exclusively on the midnight to 8 a.m. shift; that Nursing Assistants at a GS-6 level and with less seniority were available for assignment to the midnight shift.

Employer contends the LPN's, GS-6, by reason of better training were better qualified to serve in an "in charge" capacity and were needed on the midnight shift to insure the best patient care.

Discussion

On pages 19–20 of the Civil Service Position-Classification Standards of 1970 heavily relied on by Union, appears:

GS-621-6	Nursing Assistant GS-6	GS-621-6
Part II	Licensed Practical Nurse GS-6	Part II

Nature of the assignment

GS-6 employees typically serve in an "in charge" capacity on a ward or other patient unit (usually on the evening or night shift) where the nursing care work requires a level of skills and knowledge equivalent to that described at grade GS-5. Positions at the GS-6 level typically involve responsibility for directing the efforts of nonprofessional nursing care personnel of lower grade level on the ward to insure that all required personal and nursing care is accomplished. This includes responsibility for helping to train these employees during the time that they are assigned to the ward on the shift. The GS-6 employee makes decisions as to modifications in the nursing care plan based on previously outlined instructions of physician or nurse as to what changes in each patient's condition will indicate the need for initiating change in nursing care, and the kind of change to be initiated.

The GS-6 employee is responsible for receiving the nursing report from the earlier shift and for making the report to the later shift in order to assure continuity of nursing care around the clock. The GS-6 "in charge" assignment typically involves responsibility for pouring and administering medications required by patients on the ward during the shift.

"Charge" responsibility is not equivalent to supervisory responsibility. While many of the functions of the charge responsibility may be found in some supervisory positions, the charge nursing assignment does not include the full range of responsibilities that constitute supervision. The charge employee balances the workload among the staff on the ward and sets priorities during the shift. He does not normally approve leave, complete performance rating and recommend promotion, or deal with employee complaints and grievances. Typically, the GS-6 charge employee works with whichever employees are assigned to his unit.

The GS-6 level also applies to comparable assignments other than charge assignments that require the same level of skills, knowledge, and responsibility. For a more complete discussion of assignments other than "charge" responsibility warranting grades above GS-5, see pp. 7 and 8 of the introduction to this standard.

Person-to-Person work relationships

In addition to the close rapport with patients that is required at GS-5 in performing services for them, the GS-6 assignment requires effective work relations with the other personnel assigned to the ward in coordinating work activities to adjust to changes in workload. The GS-6 employee assigns work to other nonprofessional nursing care personnel on the ward during the shift. He also establishes effective working relationships with nurses and physicians elsewhere in the hospital who can be available for consultation and assistance as required.

Supervisory control

Supervision is typically provided by a professional nurse who covers a number of wards in addition to this one, and who holds ultimate nursing care responsibility for all patients on these wards. The registered nurse is, for the most part, remote from the ward of which the GS-6 has charge, and is therefore not easily accessible at every moment. Consequently, the GS-6 nursing care employee has to work quite independently. However, the GS-6 employee contacts the supervisor to keep her informed of critical situations on the ward and to seek assistance with patient care or personnel problems that may arise. The GS-6 employee contacts the supervisor or other medical and nursing personnel for emergency or potential emergency situations arising during the shift.

Three things are noticeable from the above:

1) GS-6's are grouped together and only at the beginning does Nursing Assistant and Licensed Practical Nurse appear (as contended by Union),
2) Assignment of GS-6's to the evening or night shift is usual, and
3) "Charge" responsibility is normal for GS-6's.

Executive Order 11491 as amended provides in part:

Section 11(b) [T]he obligation to meet and confer does not include matters with respect to . . . the numbers, types, and grades or positions of employees assigned to . . . work project or tour of duty; the technology of performing its work . . .

Section 12(b) management officials of the agency retain the right, in accordance with applicable laws and regulations —
1) to direct employees of the agency;
2) to . . . transfer, assign, and retain employees in positions within the agency . . .
3) to maintain efficiency of the Government operations entrusted to them;
4) to determine the methods, means, and personnel by which operations are to be conducted . . .

Employer relies upon the quoted provisions of the Executive Order together with Article IV, Section 4 and Article XVII, Section 5 of the Agreement, previously set forth, as justification for their actions in changing both the shift and tour of duty insofar as LPN's, grade GS-6, are concerned.

A difficult problem for the Arbitrator is thus posed. On the one hand is the desire of Employer to secure the best available patient care and the belief that the Licensed Practical Nurses, GS-6, are the ones best qualified to be in "charge" of those areas not "open." Further, Employer abided by the Agreement insofar as prior notice of the change was concerned and relies upon the rights of management as contained in the Executive Order and the Agreement for its policy change as noted in the amended job descriptions. The Civil Service Position-Classification Standards are viewed as guidelines only and as not controlling the job descriptions or assignment of duties. On the other hand the Union relies upon the GS-6 Position-Classification Description in the Civil Service Regulations whereby Nursing Assistants and Licensed Practical Nurses, whose salary is the same, are treated alike as to duties. Further, the seniority provision of Article XVII, Section 4 of the Agreement is stressed, the argument being that the LPN's have greater seniority than Nursing Assistants who are qualified for taking "charge" on the midnight shift; that the change in job descriptions for LPN's should be a negotiable item with the Union, especially since it effects a change in policy in existence since 1932, when the VA Hospital was erected.

The Arbitrator is further troubled by the fact that all four of the Licensed Practical Nurses, there being no others, having secured a license from the state, completed VA training courses, arrived at a classification of GS-6. Now having top seniority they have but two alternatives, (1) work the midnight–8:00 a.m. undesirable shift, or (2) voluntarily take a reduction to GS-5. If all took the offered reduction, Employer's plan of using the LPN, GS-6, employees on the midnight shift could not presently be effected.

Conclusion

The Arbitrator acknowledges with deep appreciation the Post-Hearing Briefs timely filed by the parties. It was evident that each side believed in its contentions and arguments.

I have read and studied my notes taken at the Hearing, all exhibits which were offered, the Post-Hearing briefs of the parties, the Executive Order, the Civil Service Regulations and the grievance itself.

I have concluded that the grievance of Paula McDonald, Bernice Hickey and Alberta Peters should be sustained. Their seniority rights as provided in Article XVII, Section 4 of the Agreement must be recognized as to shift and tour of duty in the Nursing Services. Others with GS-6 ratings, either Nursing Assistants or newly employed LPN's with lesser seniority, must be considered for the midnight–8:00 a.m. shift before assignment of the grievants to such shift and tour of duty.

AWARD

The grievance filed by Paula McDonald, Bernice Hickey and Alberta Peters is sustained.

Case No. 22

*Did a VA Hospital have the right, in an effort to
increase efficiency, to relocate the office of a ward
clerk (a woman) so as to combine it with the nurses'
station? Did the relocation of the grievant subject
her to undue embarrassment from patient exposure
and increased fear of bodily harm?*

**Veterans Administration Hospital (Murfreesboro, Tenn.)
and
American Federation of Government Employees, Local 1844**

Arbitrator: Walter F. Eigenbrod
Date of Award: August 7, 1972
Citation: LAIG 678

ARTICLE IV — *Purpose of Agreement*

Section 1 — The Employer and the Union representing the eligible
employees of the Employer desire to enter into a Labor–Management
Agreement which will have for its purposes, among others, the following:
(a) to promote fair and reasonable working conditions; (b) to promote
improved programs designed to aid the employees in achieving their
acknowledged and recognized objectives; (c) to promote the highest
degree of morale and responsibility in the Unit; (d) to adjust all
differences arising between them related to matters covered by this
Labor–Management Agreement; (e) to promote systematic employee–
management cooperation between the Employer and its employees; and
(f) to provide a safe and healthful work environment.

Section 2 — "Collective bargaining" for the purpose of contract
negotiation under E.O. 11491 and the terms of this Agreement is defined
as the mutual obligation of the Employer and the Union to meet at
reasonable times and confer and negotiate where appropriate in good

faith with respect to procedures for settlement of grievances, personnel policies and practices, and other matters affecting general working conditions and other conditions of employment of employees in the Unit.

ARTICLE V — *Management Rights*

Nothing in this Agreement shall restrict Management in exercising the right, in accordance with applicable laws and regulations, to: Direct employees of the hospital; hire, promote, transfer, assign, and retain employees in positions within the hospital; and to suspend, demote, discharge, or take other disciplinary action against employees; relieve employees from duties because of lack of work or for other legitimate reasons; maintain the efficiency of the Government operations entrusted to the hospital; determine the methods, means and personnel by which such operations are to be conducted; and take whatever actions may be necessary to carry out the mission of the hospital in situations of emergency.

ARTICLE VIII — *Mutual Rights and Obligations*

Section 3 — Management officials are obligated to confer with Union representatives concerning personnel policies and practices and matters affecting working conditions, as appropriate, subject to law and policy requirements and this Agreement. The Personnel Officer is designated the representative for the Hospital Director in working with the Union on consultations and negotiations.

The Grievant was employed by the Veterans Administration as a Ward Clerk (this title may not be technically correct, but throughout the hearing she was referred to as "Ward Clerk") with principal duties being the providing of clerical assistance to the Ward Nurses and other members of the professional staff. Prior to her Grievance her work area or office was located in approximately the center of the second floor. In both the North and South end there are sleeping areas, Day Rooms and other facilities necessary for patient care, including a nurses' station. The Grievant's place of work or office was moved from the center of the floor to the South end immediately adjacent to the Nurses Station to which she objected. After many conferences between the parties without a solution being arrived at, the following Grievance was filed:

My duty assignment is Ward Typist on 5 B.

My grievance is the re-location of my office on 5 B from a centralized location to behind locked doors. This will affect the efficiency of my work and endanger my own mental and physical well-being.

The corrective action I desire is to remain where I am now located which is a central location.

I have discussed this with Mr. Gaither but not to my satisfaction.

I desire the AFGE Local 1844 to represent me.

Positions of the Parties

The Union

1. That the moving of the Grievant's office put her in a position of possible bodily harm.
2. That the Grievant was subjected to, as a result of the move, embarrassments which other ward clerks were not.
3. That working behind doors affects the Grievant's efficiency both from a work standpoint, as well as from a mental standpoint.
4. That the moving of the Grievant's office violated the purpose of the Agreement, i.e., "to promote fair and reasonable working conditions;" the highest degree of morale and responsibility in the unit and to provide a safe and healthful work environment.
5. That Management's officials are obligated to confer with Union representatives concerning personnel positions and practices and matters and working conditions as provided for by the Agreement between the parties.
6. That "the remedial action we seek is that Mrs. Hadway be returned to her original station prior to move of January 11, 1972, or that she be given a place of work which has an access door to corridor whereby she will not have to walk among patients who can do bodily harm or expose her to acts of indecency. That her work station be in such a place she can serve all requirements of her position — specifically to serve the Nursing Stations on both ends and to work with the doctor who is centrally located."

Management

1. That the moving of the Grievant's work area, i.e, be located as combination Ward Clerk–Nursing Station, had been the goal of Management prior to entering into the Agreement between the parties and the Directive from the appropriate Veterans Administration office and Grievance.
2. That the primary duty of the Ward Clerk is to reduce the clerical work of the ward nurses and the combination was to relieve the ward nurses of their duties enabling more time to be devoted to patient care.
3. That in relocating the Grievant's office, Management merely exercised their rights under the Agreement to promote the efficiency of the

service, which right is given to Management by the Agreement.

4.   The relocating of the Grievant's principal work area did not place the Grievant's life or health in jeopardy, reduce her efficiency or endanger her well-being because her being behind locked doors did not put the Grievant in a position of being subjected to many embarrassments.

5.   That the Grievance be denied.

Discussion

Prior to the taking of the testimony and after a statement of the facts by the parties, an attempt was made by the arbitrator to reduce the issue to writing. Unable to accomplish this, the parties did stipulate that the arbitrator resolve the issue between the parties taking into consideration the Collective Agreement between the parties, the Grievance, all exhibits and the facts as illicited at the hearing.

The Veterans Administration maintains a Neuropsychiatric Hospital at Murfreesboro, Tennessee and its patient care is divided into four categories. The category of patient care, in which we in this matter are interested, is that category described as "Psychiatric Medically Infirm." These neuropsychiatric patients require continued treatment and care. The patients are geriatric and the medical problems are usually more severe than the psychiatric problems. Patients of this type are primarily the elderly (both psychotic and nonpsychotic), stroke victims, the senile with heart or kidney disease, diabetes, arthritis, etc. The Grievant was assigned for duty to those professionals administering to this category and her duties consisted primarily of administering to the professionals, i.e., 90 percent of her work time to clerical work, thus relieving the Ward Nurses of these responsibilities and affording more patient care time to be given to the patients and approximately 10 percent other tasks in assisting the other professionals administering to patients in this category.

On or about the month of May, 1969, the Veterans Administration issued a memorandum directing the hospital to combine the "Nurse–Ward Clerk Stations" in order to provide a more efficient operation. This memo was acted upon by the Hospital Director except in certain cases where funds were needed to renovate or remodel and these funds were requested. It is interesting to note that this facility had already taken steps to so relocate these stations prior to the receipt of the Directive and 11 out of 14 had been so relocated.

The office occupied by the Grievant from which she performed her assigned tasks (prior to her Grievance) was located on the second floor approximately centrally located between the North and South wings. Each wing had a Nurse Station, Day Room and other patient facilities including coffee room, shower room, toilets, sleeping area, etc. Each Nursing Station maintained its own patient files, thus patient files on each wing. In order for the Grievant to go to the Nurses Station she had to go through locked doors, which doors were locked for many reasons. The testimony was to the effect that the doors were locked to keep the patients, because of their mental and physical problems, and not because they were deemed dangerous, from roaming from the area. However, I might add that the testimony as to the patients being dangerous was in direct conflict.

To afford the efficiency and to carry out the Directive of the Administration, the Grievant was relocated from the center of the floor to an office adjacent to the Nurses Station on the South wing, as well as all records from the North wing being transferred to the South wing. To enter the Nurses Station, one had to go through a locked door, through another locked door to the Grievant's office, and the Grievant, to enter the corridor, had to pass through a door which had to be locked. It must be said that to enter either the North or South wing, one had to pass through a door which was locked, and which existed prior to the relocation of the Grievant.

The Grievant testified that she was shocked when told that her office would be relocated and made inquiry as to why, only to learn that the moving of her office had been planned to comply with the theory of efficiency in combining the Ward Clerk and Nurses Stations. She further testified that she had been touched by the patients and is in fear of bodily harm from the patients; that her office faces the showers and toilets and is subjected to many embarrassments resulting from the exposing of themselves by the patients; that there are no curtains on the doors to the showers or toilets; that the language used by the patients is most embarrassing; that in addition to these determents which affect her work, she must tolerate the noise, including the loud talk by the patients and that the fact of the door being locked in such a small area is also a mental determent to her efficiency and health. On cross-examination she admitted to being given an offer to move, i.e., "Float," but would prefer a permanent ward; that the other combination work stations are "behind locked doors to various corridors." She also testified that she had worked in other combination work stations within the facility.

Other witnesses on behalf of the Grievant testified in substance that the patients were dangerous because they are unpredictable. The Ward Physician testified that he did not believe the relocation of the office was a "wise move." Another witness testified that the Grievant could not take a coffee break because the coffee room was across the hall. A Social Worker testified that in her opinion the patients were dangerous; and that the Grievant was exposed to more indecent exposure than before and that other ward clerks are not in closed areas like the Grievant.

Management, in presenting its case, testified that the duties of the Grievant, which summed up, amounted to assisting the professionals by relieving them of clerical work and making for more efficient patient care; that Grievant was given the opportunity "to move" because another ward clerk has asked to move; that Grievant stated she did not want to move but later said she was misunderstood; that the Grievant had worked in a locked ward before and did not object; that when ward clerks are hired they are told and they know where they are going to work but not which particular assignments; that the Grievant had had previous appointments, knew what her appointment would be as she had worked on various wards before; that Grievant is not subjected to more embarrassment than before and no more exposure to Grievant by patients now than before.

There was also testimony by other professionals on behalf of the employer that the patients were not dangerous and a number of the patients were allowed to leave the hospital on occasions; and in their opinions the Grievant was not exposed to more embarrassment or exposure than before and that the patients in the wing where Grievant is now assigned are less disturbed than those where she had previously been assigned.

One of the professionals testifying on behalf of the employer testified that the patients are not potentially dangerous but could be irrational but not dangerous.

The parties introduced an exhibit, attesting to the fact that the Personnel Health Clinic's files did not include anyone being injured due to a patient assault or combativeness on Ward 5 B from December, 1969, to January 25, 1972, which exhibit was offered for the purpose of reputing a statement by a Union witness that he had been severely scratched by a patient.

A study of the evidence reveals many conflicts as to the facts. However, the fact that the combining of the ward clerk's office and the nurses' station to increase efficiency is a positive one. This procedure was deemed advisable in 1969, and the records so indicate. The record also substantiates the fact that the Grievant's relocation was the last unit to be consolidated. As to the relocation of the ward clerk to efficiency operation, the hospital management certainly has that right. Management, under those provisions of the Agreement, has the right to assign its employees to accomplish that end. However, the right to assign, as granted by the Agreement, must be construed along with the provisions of the Agreement, and particularly in view of the type of facility, that provision which the employees and the Union representing the eligible employees' desire to enter into a Labor-Management Agreement which will have as its purpose the promotion of fair and reasonable working conditions.

The right of assignment is vested in Management but the working conditions of those assignments must be considered in the assignment itself. Here we are dealing with a hospital where mental and physical conditions of the patients are not those of a usual hospital. The employees so applying for work in these types of facilities must realize this when making application and as testified to, the Administration makes the applicants aware of this situation. The Grievant was relocated for a valid reason and the reasons for the relocation must be sustained. However, in so relocating and in view of the evidence, this arbitrator does not agree with Management that the Grievant was not, by her relocation, subjected to more embarrassment, increased fear of bodily harm and a diminishing of her efficiency and mental state of being behind all locked doors, even as to access to the corridors. It was interesting to note that the testimony was to the effect that the Grievant's work area was the only one which had locked doors, even to the corridors.

This arbitrator has no authority to relocate the Grievant's work area to her former office in the center of the floor, i.e., a central location, but does have the authority to sustain the Grievance in that the Grievant be provided with a work area which would diminish the embarrassment to her resulting from the alleged profanity, a work area wherein she would be less exposed to the bodily exposure of the patients and possible danger to her health. In making these adjustments, the Employer can do so to maintain the efficiency of the Ward Clerk-Nurses' Station theory.

This arbitrator must also add that the Grievant must also be cognizant of the reason for her employment, i.e., the efficient operation of the facility.

AWARD

The Grievance is sustained only insofar as the remedy sought conforms to this opinion.

Case No. 23

In an interest arbitration, should Hospital social workers be granted the same number of vacation days as all other Hospital workers, or should they be granted two extra vacation days so that their vacation benefits equal those negotiated for social workers in all other area contracts?

St. Luke's Hospital Center (New York, N.Y.)
and
Drug and Hospital Union, Local 1199

Arbitrator: Morris P. Glushien
Date of Award: November 16, 1973
Citation: 63 LA 71

The question submitted is the number of annual vacation days MSW Social Workers shall receive after one year's service. Under the contract, all other workers get 20 vacation days. St. Luke's claims that MSW Social Workers should receive the same number. The Union asserts they should get 22 days.

What we have here is a conflict between the dictates of logic on the one hand, and the actual practice of the unionized industry on the other. Weighing the two, I uphold the Union's position.

St. Luke's makes a forceful presentation that, as an abstract matter, the MSW's are not entitled to more vacation time than any other workers. There are not theoretical considerations calling for more. MSW's are not in short supply in the job market. Their work is not more arduous. With Masters degrees, they are not nearly as well educated as Ph.D's and physicians who get only 20 days. Other employees with Masters degrees, as in Dietary, get the lesser number. Indeed, MSW Social Workers, outside the industry of hospitals and nursing homes, receive no more than 20 days under Local 1199 contracts. Why then should St. Luke's give more?

The answer is that, in all hospitals and nursing homes covered by Local 1199 contracts, MSW Social Workers are uniformly entitled to 22 days of vacation. The major industry agreement is between the League of Voluntary Hospitals & Homes of New York and Local 1199, covering 31 hospitals and nursing homes.[1] In addition, there are some half dozen "independent" agreements which provide the same. There is not a single 1199 hospital and nursing home contract which departs from this pattern.

St. Luke's describes the two extra days given to MSW's as an "aberration" and in a sense it is. It apparently originated more or less through happenstance. The first 1199-hospital contract, years ago, was made with an institution which for some reason had a practice of giving two extra days to MSW Social Workers even before the hospital was organized; and this was carried into the initial Union contract. The Union then used this precedent to demand and obtain the same superior provision in each contract made with another hospital. This continued until, as indicated, the provision covered the entire industry without exception.

At the hearing St. Luke's, in answer to the Arbitrator's query, conceded that its situation did not differ from that of other voluntary hospitals nor call for special treatment. Rather it asserted that the illogic which it perceives in the industry contracts generally should not be carried forward by the Arbitrator to the case of St. Luke's.

This request I cannot grant. I am impelled to this view by several considerations.

The New York Legislature, when it abolished the right to strike in nonprofitmaking hospitals and substituted provisions for binding arbitration, set forth certain standards for arbitrators to consider. See Section 716 of the New York State Labor Relations Act, subdivision 7. Among these is par. (c), dictating a comparison of conditions between the employees involved and those "doing the same, similar or comparable work . . ." I hold that, in the present case, this requires a comparison with the rest of the unionized industry, and this in turn argues strongly for, if it does not demand, two extra days for MSW's.

I would reach the same result apart from the New York statute and the responsibilities of an arbitrator which I discern thereunder. Even on an empty slate, I feel the same conclusion is called for. It is true that, applying the dictates of logic alone, MSW's do not seem to be entitled to more vacation days than other workers. But logic is not the major determinant. Many years

[1]Had St. Luke's too become a member of the League (instead of negotiating an independent agreement) the MSW Social Workers would of course have automatically received the 22 days.

ago the great Oliver Wendell Holmes pointed out that the life of the law is not logic but experience. The same is no less true of industrial relations and collective bargaining.

Here we have an entire industry, almost 40 unionized hospitals and nursing homes, granting 22 days vacation time to MSW's. Altogether some 700 MSW Social Workers have achieved and are now receiving this benefit despite its "illogic." Along comes St. Luke's and seeks to deny it to the relative handful of MSW's in this unionized hospital. From a collective bargaining standpoint, it simply does not add up. Uniformity of working conditions within an industry is the proper goal of every union, and to withhold this benefit from the MSW's in St. Luke's while it is granted everywhere else is likely to be a bridgehead for friction and unrest throughout the unionized industry.

I might state in conclusion that in 1972 Arbitrator George S. Roukis, in a proceeding to settle all the contractual terms for another unionized voluntary hospital, granted the standard 22 vacation days to MSW Social Workers, the same result I reach here.

AWARD

The contract between St. Luke's and the Union shall provide that MSW Social Workers receive 22 annual vacation days after one year's service.

Part IV

Work Stoppages,
Concerted Activities and
Union Business Disruptive
to Patient Care

Case No. 24

Was the Hospital justified in discharging an acting
steward of nurses aides and orderlies who, when
only half the scheduled work force reported for work
on a Sunday, threatened the Hospital with a walkout
unless the remaining employees were paid at a
premium rate not otherwise called for in the
contract?

Lahser Hills Nursing Home (Southfield, Mich.)
and
Service Employees International Union, Local 79

Arbitrator: M. David Keefe
Date of Award: October 8, 1974
Citation: Previously unreported

The prevailing Agreement between the parties dated 3-25-74, (Joint Ex. #1), is their initial contract. The installation has been in operation since early in 1972, but the present ownership only recently took over. The Grievant was hired at the time the facility opened, sometime in April of 1972. Her record is clear of previous disciplinary action. At the time of the incident on Sunday, May 19, 1974, she was Acting Steward. Her discharge was effected on Thursday, May 23, through the following written notice (Jt. Ex. #2):

> After a thorough investigation of the events of Sunday, May 19, 1974, it has been determined by Management through discussion and written statements by employees that you assisted, participated, supported and encouraged threats toward an unauthorized stoppage of work. This action is specifically prohibited by our agreement with the Union and is an extreme violation of this nursing home's policies.

Due to the above mentioned activities on your part, we find it necessary to terminate your employment as of May 23, 1974, and in the future, Mrs. L— is not allowed on the premises without expressed permission of Management.

The Union protested this action on grounds that no cause at all existed to substantiate the severance.

*   *   *   *   *

Positions of the Parties

The Employer asserted that, on Sunday, May 19, 1974, the Grievant and five other Employees in the Nurses Aide and Orderly Division did report at the regular starting time of 7:00 a.m. but that six who were scheduled were absent and could not be replaced, although call-ins were attempted. Sometime around 8:00 a.m., the Grievant came to the Nursing Director and suggested rather bluntly that those who were working short-handed should be paid time-and-one-half for their efforts that day. No threats of possible stoppage were voiced then. The Director promised that she would consult Administrator Fishman to ascertain if this would be granted. The Director, who had covered the night shift, left shortly thereafter with nothing more being said. Before the Director could call the Administrator after reaching her residence, the incident had come to its conclusion.

LPN E. Weiss, in charge during the day-shift on 5-19-74, apparently tried to get the Director on the phone before she got home. In her absence, the LPN in charge did contact the Assistant Director at home. This was about 9:00 a.m. The LPN reported that the facility was short-handed and that those on the job wanted 1.5 time pay or would walk out. The Grievant had made this statement to Mrs. Weiss who attempted to report to the Director but could not reach her. In other phone calls, Mrs. Weiss informed the Assistant Director that some of the staff were proffering excuses to cover their leaving. The Assistant Director talked to the Grievant. She confirmed there would be departures unless the 1.5 time pay was forthcoming. The Assistant Director asked the Grievant to keep them on the job until the answer was forthcoming. The reply was that the Steward would do so if the Administrator gave a favorable response. It was then agreed that the Assistant Director would convey the answer on the time-and-one-half proposition to the Grievant as soon as the Administrator made the decision. Shortly, thereafter, authorization was given (under duress to protect patient-care, the Employer stressed in the hearing), the word was passed to the Grievant who thereupon assured the Management that the affected Employees would continue working.

The Employer concluded the foregoing account by explaining that the institution could not afford to take disciplinary action against all of the Employees involved without risking a crisis of inadequate personnel quotas to carry forward the care of patients and, consequently, narrowed its action to the Grievant who was identified as the most responsible individual about whom the Employer had awareness in the *squeeze play* resorted to so as to force up the pay-rate for the day.

Management asked that its action be sustained.

*   *   *   *   *

The Union asserted that *just cause* for the discharge was lacking. No stoppage occurred. None was threatened. A simple request was tendered to Supervision that, under the adverse working conditions which prevailed on the particular Sunday, equity should be served by payment of time-and-one-half to those loyal Employees who were acting responsibly and were at work, carrying the burden of covering for the absentees. When Management volunteered to extend the premiums, it had seemed to have reacted forthrightly in recognizing the intensified work schedule to which the staff was subjected. Later, the Employer apparently had second thoughts and contrived to reprise against the Grievant as if she had, in fact, acted wrongfully.

The Grievant denied that she ever predicted there would be a work stoppage. She explained that the few who did show up were overburdened with the double work-load facing them. They proposed that their extra output should merit premium pay recognition. The Grievant merely suggested this treatment to the Director of Nursing. Later, after the Director left without giving an answer, the Grievant spoke with Mrs. Weiss, the LPN-in-charge. At that time, another Nurses Assistant, Mrs. Mann came out of the elevator with her coat on and announced that she was leaving because her baby girl was ill. The LPN directed her to reduce the explanation to writing. At that point, the LPN made a phone call to the Assistant Director and asserted that a walkout was shaping up. The Grievant spoke with the Assistant Director who requested her to keep the workers on the job until the Administrator could be contacted for authorization of the 1.5 time pay. The Grievant, herself, called the former Steward (who no longer worked at the facility) and explained that the LPN was making the affair look like a walkout. She was advised to have those who were leaving write out excuses for their departures. Three such memos were obtained (Un. Ex. #2):

1.   I am going home because my Daughter is sick and I have to take her to Doctor.   E. Mann

2.   Have a bad headache. I am going home. Took some aspirin, didn't help. I am sick.   Phylliss Adams

3.   Upset stomach, I am going home because I am sick.   B. Cooper

Mrs. Mann waited. She had no transportation and had to be picked up. Eventually, the Assistant Director informed the LPN that the premium pay would be paid. The Grievant was told by Mrs. Mann to have this put in writing so that it could not be rescinded. The Grievant spoke with the Assistant Director and it was arranged that the LPN and the workers would sign a statement to be pushed under the Assistant Director's door. A document was prepared (Un. Ex. #1) which was written out by the Grievant as follows:

All employees on this date, 5-19-74, will receive time and half for working under-staffed this day.

(for the Employer)	(Affected Employees)
E. Weiss, LPN	B. Cooper
	P. Eisenburg
	L. Sexton
	E. Blotkamp
	E. Mann
	A. Lockett (Steward)

Mrs. Mann then reportedly called her home, discovered her baby was recovered and stayed on the job. So did the others, including the personally-ill Employees. The Grievant asserted that she was in the installation, either working privately with patients or as an Employee of the Home on Monday, Tuesday and Wednesday but had no inkling of Employer intent to discipline her until she received the actual discharge on Thursday.

Mrs. Mann also testified. She related that her husband worked on the night shift at Ford's and was sleeping on the Sunday morning in question. Her older daughter called and reported the baby's indisposition to the mother at about 8:00 a.m. Mrs. Mann resolved to go home and take the child to the family doctor who had Sunday office hours. She didn't talk to her husband nor was he awakened. Nevertheless, when she came down into the lobby, she waited there for him to pick her up . . . although she had told no one at home that she was leaving. After the premium pay was verified, she told the Steward to get it in writing and again called home. She discovered the baby was fortunately recovered. She did not talk to her husband who was still asleep. This witness stated no *walkout* of the Employees impended, that the Grievant had not advised the witness to contrive an excuse to cover her departure. She added that, even after learning that her daughter was better, she stayed possibly because the time-and-one-half was put in writing.

The Union deduced from all this that no stoppage took place nor was one intended. None was threatened. The Grievant was utterly innocent of the charges against her.

Discussion

The evidence in this case clearly supports the conclusion that concert of action to circumvent the Labor Agreement and suborn improper bargaining outside of recognized channels did occur. The testimony of Mrs. Mann was convincingly conclusive that this was so. When she appeared in the lobby wearing her coat, there was not a chance that her husband would appear to take her home. He was still asleep and no one in her residence knew at all that she was leaving. The remarkable coincidence of the baby's recovery as soon as Management capitulated to the extortionist pressures it was subjected to was equalled only by the improbable, coincidental recovery of Nurses Assistant Adams from her debilitating headache and Nurses Assistant Cooper's instant recuperation from her enervating upset stomach. This chain of incredible coincidences all fortuitously transpired as soon as the Grievant reduced to writing the guarantee of the premium pay. Obviously, the overtime rates on straight-time hours was the elixer which cured all of the Employees' hardships and afflictions. The *sickness* which infected or influenced the group was plainly best described as being *sick of work at regular pay*. They wanted out — unless they got their way. This was undertaken on their own — not through the intermediary good offices of the Union. It was concert of action, disguised by self-serving excuses which so thinly veil the underlying motive that it shows clearly through, which repudiated the ordained representation rights of the Union as much as it shredded the terms of the Labor Agreement.

Management demonstrated a laxness in controlling absences which were established to be habitually excessive on Sundays. To this extent, the Employer helped create the crisis situation which arose. However, no single Employee can be expected to do two workers' complete jobs. All that can be demanded is that the active worker perform at a normal pace to accomplish as much as an ordinarily competent Employee could do in a single shift. Perhaps extra recognition could have been fairly contemplated by the Employer in return for the cooperation which would have been contributed. But that could have come about only through Management's spontaneous reaction or the Union's request for consideration. It could not be extorted, in defiance of authorized channels for dealings between the parties, by unilateral, illegal concert among the workers. This last type of action leads to chaos and destroys the vital machinery of collective bargaining. In such an atmosphere, the

Union has no effective life or force and the Employer has no assurance as to the terms under which the workers will perform. Such an aberration on the process, which was created out of the sweat and blood of workers who struggled for decades to gain recognition of bargaining rights for Labor, generally, and which, today, is recognized and protected by virtue of the laws of the land, cannot be tolerated and is most properly eradicated.

AWARD

The Grievance is denied.

Case No. 25

*Could the Hospital discharge an RN with a good
record who actively engaged in picketing for a union
representing nonprofessional hospital employees?
Was it relevant that the Hospital did not discharge
the nurse until more than a month after the strike
ended?*

Assosciation of Hospitals of Santa Clara County (Calif.)
and
California Nurses Association

Arbitrator: Arthur B. Jacobs
Date of Award: March 6, 1974
Citation: 74-1 ARB ¶8004

Whether the discharge of Grievant L— was for just cause and, if not,
what should be the appropriate remedy?

Contract Provisions

ARTICLE III — *Management Rights*

Hospital retains all the rights, powers and authority exercised or had
by it prior to September 15, 1966, except as the same may be affected or
limited by the provisions of this Agreement. Such rights include but are
not limited to the right to hire, fire, transfer, classify, or assign employees
for economic or administrative reasons.

ARTICLE XXV — *Discipline and Discharge*

After the completion of three (3) months employment in the
Hospital, nurses may be dismissed and/or disciplined by the Hospital for

just cause only. In the interpretation of this Section, the parties recognize that it is in their mutual interest that the Hospital be staffed by competent, moral nursing personnel. It is further understood that this Agreement covers a number of Hospitals and the term "just cause" as used herein, shall not be restricted to definitions contained in personnel policy booklets, or other written employee handbooks, or other documents circulated or maintained by any individual Hospital.

ARTICLE XXVII — *No Strike or Lockout*

The parties agree that during the life of the Agreement, there will be no strikes, lockouts, slowdowns, or work stoppages of any kind for any reason.

Facts

The Association consists of five nonproprietary general Hospitals located in Santa Clara County, one of which is San Jose Hospital & Health Center, Inc., hereinafter called "Hospital." The CNA represents the majority of the registered nurses, hereinafter called "RN's," employed at member Hospitals, including some 375 RN's employed by the Hospital.

Grievant was permanently employed by the Hospital as a full-time staff nurse in Pediatrics on the 11:00 p.m. to 7:00 a.m. shift in July, 1972, and she is a member of the CNA. She had previously worked six months at Valley Memorial Hospital where she was a member of the County Employees Association.

Neither during the time of her employment at the Hospital, nor during any other period of her life, had the Grievant been involved in, or been familiar with, Union activities, strikes, walkouts and the like. No evidence was produced at the hearing to indicate anything other than the Grievant's having had an unblemished record during her year of employment at the Hospital. There was no evidence of any previous unauthorized absences nor any other form of problem or dispute with the Hospital regarding her work.

In January or February, 1973, Hospital and Institutional Workers Union, Local 250, AFL-CIO, hereinafter called "Local 250," began an organizing drive among various classifications of unrepresented Hospital employees. At about 6:00 a.m. on Friday, March 9, approximately 375 of the unrepresented employees struck the Hospital for purposes of recognition and a picket line was established outside the Hospital by Local 250. From conversations with other employees, Grievant had advance knowledge of the strike. She crossed the Local 250 picket line to report for her regular shift which began at 11:00 p.m. on the evening of March 9, and worked until 7:00 a.m. the following morning. She has not worked at the Hospital since that date.

At the end of her shift, at 7:00 a.m. on Saturday morning, March 10, Grievant left the Hospital and saw the picket line again. She recognized a business agent of Local 250 who told her he was surprised that she had crossed the picket line and gone to work. She told him that Local 250 knew that the nurses had a no-strike clause in their contract, that there was nothing the CNA or Local 250 could do about it and, therefore, that she understood Local 250 didn't expect the CNA nurses to honor the picket line. The Local 250 business agent then told her that Local 250 had sent a letter to the CNA promising to support any nurses who honored the picket line. She told him she "didn't know that" and left.

She was not asked to do anything during this conversation and the Local 250 business agent did not ask her what she was going to do. At this same time, Grievant saw many of her friends and co-workers actively participating in the strike for Union representation. It was, apparently, a very emotional scene and Grievant was in tears when she left.

At about 2:45 p.m. that afternoon, Grievant returned to the Hospital. She went to Pediatrics, obtained her timecard, and erased the pre-recorded time she had not yet worked. [Employees in Pediatrics regularly recorded their timecards two weeks in advance.] She also told an employee on the Pediatrics floor that she would be back when the strike was over and that the CNA and Local 250 would back up and support any nurse who honored the picket line.

At approximately 5:15 p.m. on the same day, Grievant received a telephone call from the day shift supervisor of the Hospital who inquired as to whether she was going to report for work on Monday, her next-scheduled shift. Grievant replied it would depend on the outcome of a CNA meeting which was to be held on Monday evening.

The CNA meeting was held at 7:30 p.m. on Monday, March 12. Prior to the meeting, Grievant called the Hospital. [The nature of this call is not completely clear in the record.] Approximately 25 to 30 RN's were present at this meeting. The principal CNA spokesman told the nurses they should not do anything other than their own jobs as nurses and should be neutral. At some time during the meeting, Grievant stood up and spoke on behalf of the striking employees and asked what she could and should do. Both at the meeting and in a private conversation thereafter, she was informed by the CNA official that individual nurses' actions would probably not be effective, was against the contract between CNA and the Association which contained a no-strike clause, that they had the right to honor the picket line but cautioned them about walking the picket line. After the meeting, Grievant specifically asked the CNA official whether or not she had the option of honoring the picket line. She was told that she could decide to respect the Local 250 picket line and that either CNA would file a grievance on her behalf or would see to it that she was not punished for this decision. She was also told that it would not be a good idea to carry a picket sign.

Later that night, Grievant called the Nursing Office, spoke to a Mrs. D— and informed her that she would not be coming to work that night, nor in the future until the strike was over. Grievant had participated in picket line activity on March 10, March 11, and prior to the CNA meeting on March 12. Following the meeting on March 12, Grievant actively engaged in picket line activity on behalf of Local 250 and the striking employees, including the carrying of picket signs on several occasions, during the first two weeks of the strike. Thereafter, and until the conclusion of the strike on April 12, Grievant continued to honor the picket line by refusing to return to work and met with friends on the picket line but did not actively engage in picket line activity. Grievant was the only RN represented by CNA and covered by the Collective Bargaining Agreement who honored the picket line and engaged in picketing activity on behalf of Local 250. There was no violence directed at Grievant by the picketers. Her action in honoring the picket line was voluntary. She was aware that she was not included in the group of employees Local 250 was seeking to represent.

The Hospital has a "Standing Order" providing that unauthorized or unexplained absences for a period of three consecutive working days is considered a resignation which becomes effective on the fourth day of the absence. The same "Standing Order" specifies discipline and discharge, *inter alia* for willful neglect of duty and excessive absenteeism. This "Standing Order" was known to Grievant.

At the commencement of the strike the Hospital initiated a procedure of advising all employees who called in to report that they would not be in to work due to the strike that their absence was unauthorized and unexcused. Each day during the strike, Grievant called the Hospital and stated that she would not be in to work because she was honoring the picket line. She was regularly told that her absence was unexcused and/or asked whether or not she realized that the absence was unauthorized. When asked, she replied affirmatively. No mention was made in these conversations of threatened suspension, discharge or any other form of proposed disciplinary action if she did not return to work. On March 28, a letter was sent to Grievant and all other strikers stating that work was available, that the Hospital was hiring to fill vacancies and that it could not assure their continued employment.

The strike ended on April 12. After attending a Local 250 meeting that night at which it was announced the strike was over, Grievant went to the Nursing Office sometime after 9:00 p.m. with a group of employees who had been on strike to indicate that she was ready to return to work. She was told she could not return to work that night and was to wait until she received a call. Grievant replied that she would return the next night and did so. When she returned the next night, she was again sent home and told to wait for a call. On April 12, another RN had been transferred to fill Grievant's position.

By April 18, Grievant learned that her name had been removed from the Pediatrics seniority roster and she called a Hospital supervisor and asked whether she had been terminated. According to her testimony, she was told that she was not terminated and should continue to wait for a call. The "Leafletter" (Hospital's news sheet) for the week of April 23 advertised Grievant's position as an open job opportunity.

On May 5, Grievant directed a letter to the Hospital advising of her availability for work and inquiring about her job status and as to when she could return to work. It would appear this letter was not received by the Hospital until May 10. By letter dated May 25, she was advised that she was terminated for refusing to report to work (unauthorized absenteeism) and violating the no-strike provision of the Collective Bargaining Agreement. Grievant protested her termination by a telephone call on May 30, and by letter dated May 31. Thereafter, CNA submitted the dispute to arbitration.

Union Position

While it is conceded that Grievant's actions were violative of the Collective Bargaining Agreement and there is no disagreement that some disciplinary action should be taken, under all of the facts and circumstances of this case the penalty of discharge was too severe. Thus, under circumstances where the employee has a good work record, neither the employer nor the employee were familiar with collective bargaining agreements or strikes, the employee was never warned that she was liable to disciplinary action (including discharge) after initiating her complained-of action, no preliminary stages of threatened or imposed discipline were ever attempted by the employer prior to discharge, the long and vague period of inaction on employer's part prior to termination without notice and the disparate treatment between the employee and others similarly situated, it may fairly be said that although some discipline may be warranted, just cause is lacking for discharge.

Hospital Position

Both Grievant's unauthorized and excessive absences as well as her participation in picket line activities which constituted participation in a work stoppage or strike in violation of the no-strike provision of the Collective Bargaining Agreement coupled with the fact that she had been forewarned and was aware that her unauthorized absences and activities on behalf of Local

250 subjected her to termination, constituted just cause for discharge.

No discrimination or disparate treatment has been proven and Grievant's employment record and length of service neither mitigates the separate and independent offenses for which she was terminated nor renders the penalty of termination unreasonable.

The Hospital's delay in formally notifying Grievant of her termination was not so unreasonable as to nullify the otherwise proper termination in that it did not justify or excuse her conduct or prejudice her rights in the arbitration proceeding.

Opinion and Decision

While the facts resulting in Grievant's discharge are simple and, realistically speaking, unchallenged the decision is deceptively complex. It is conceded by the Union that Grievant violated the no-strike provision of the Collective Bargaining Agreement. Without comment as to the advice given to her at the CNA meeting, the Arbitrator is satisfied that she was at least made aware of the no-strike provision of the Collective Bargaining Agreement and that if she elected to participate in picketing activities or even to withhold her services by honoring or respecting the picket line, she could have problems. It is unimportant that she was told that if she had problems CNA would back her up. It is equally unimportant that Local 250, of which she is not a member, also told her that she would be backed by that organization if she honored the picket line. It is clear that she not only elected to honor the picket line, but at least during the first two weeks of the strike actually engaged in picketing activity against the Hospital and, more specifically, carried a picket sign and walked the picket line. The Arbitrator is also satisfied that Grievant was aware of the Hospital rule regarding unauthorized or unexcused absences and that she was repeatedly told that her absences were either unauthorized or unexcused.

Inherent in the Arbitrator's authority to determine sufficiency of cause is the authority to determine whether, under all of the facts and circumstances of a given case, the penalty of discharge was too severe. If, under all of the involved facts and circumstances, he determines that the penalty of discharge was too severe then the discharge was not for just cause. Because discharge is the extreme economic penalty of industrial relations and has grave consequences for both employer and employee, enlightened employers utilize this penalty only in compelling situations. It follows, that the question of severity of penalty and the justification thereof must be evaluated in the light of all of the facts and circumstances of each individual case and the reasonableness of the action of the employer in connection therewith.

The complexity of this case arises from the fact that for several reasons the temptation to "look the other way" and find some basis for returning the Grievant to work is substantial. Grievant was simply acting pursuant to sincere personal beliefs. She was supporting her friends and acquaintances as well as Local 250. The Hospital delayed its decision to terminate her for an undue and lengthy period of time following the end of the strike. It is considerations of this kind which render the sustaining of the discharge a difficult task. However, even though one might personally sympathize with a particular Grievant, notwithstanding the fact that her predicament is of her own making and choice, a just cause discharge should not be reversed or mitigated on that basis alone.

Although the Union concedes that Grievant violated the Collective Bargaining Agreement, in an evaluation of the severity of penalty in this case some comment is required both as to the nature of the contractual violation as well as the violation of the involved Hospital rule. Obviously, the Hospital has the right to promulgate reasonable policies and rules necessary for the conduct of its operation as a Hospital. Clearly, the absenteeism rule involving unexcused or unexplained absences is a reasonable one. This is especially true in the case of a hospital where the basic and overriding consideration is that of patient care. The Arbitrator is completely satisfied that Grievant was aware of this rule and of the fact that the Standing Order provided that employees could be disciplined and/or discharged for excessive absenteeism. She was well aware of the fact, and had been repeatedly told, that her absences during the strike were unexcused absences. Absent mitigating circumstances which render the penalty of discharge too severe, the discharge of an employee for deliberate violation of a rule which is known to that employee, and especially when it is known to that employee that violation of such rule may subject him to discharge, is for just cause.

In addition to the violation of a Hospital rule which was known to her, Grievant also knowingly violated a basic provision of the Collective Bargaining Agreement namely, the no-strike provision thereof. It cannot be successfully argued that the no-strike provision does not contain express language prohibiting a refusal to cross the picket line of another union as the evidence clearly establishes that Grievant was fully aware that it carried that meaning. No such specific language is necessary (*National Labor Relations Board v. Rockaway News Supply Company*, 345 U.S. 71, 31 LRRM 2432 [1952]; *News Union of Baltimore v. National Labor Relations Board*, 393 F. 2d 673, 67 LRRM 2487 [D.C. Cir. 1968]). The no-strike clause clearly bars work stoppages of any kind for any reason. This prohibition is both broad and clear. Again, absent mitigating circumstances which would render the penalty of discharge too severe, violation of this no-strike provision of the Collective Bargaining Agreement constitutes just cause for discharge.

Although Grievant's work record was good, she had only been employed for approximately one year prior to the strike. Her good work record during this relatively short period of time is not, standing alone, sufficient to justify a finding by the Arbitrator that the penalty of discharge was too severe in this case. Neither can she successfully claim disparate treatment. Obviously, there was no disparate treatment between that accorded Grievant and other RNs, members of CNA. Grievant was the only member of CNA who elected to honor the picket line of Local 250, all other members of CNA having crossed the picket line and worked throughout the strike. Neither can it be successfully argued that Grievant was accorded disparate treatment because of the fact that certain engineers, members of another union, refused to cross the picket line and were not discharged for their action. These engineers refused to cross the picket line for one or two shifts at the commencement of the strike and, after having been directed to do so by their Union, returned to work and crossed the picket line throughout the balance of the strike. Grievant did not report to work until after the strike ended. The factual situations are in no way comparable and do not justify a finding of disparate treatment.

The Hospital was wrong in not notifying Grievant that she was terminated until May 25. Even with due allowance for the fact that the Hospital was not experienced in matters of this kind and that it was necessary that it contact its attorneys regarding this matter before notifying Grievant of her termination, this was an unduly long period of time and to the detriment of Grievant. The question is, however, whether this constitutes sufficient grounds for setting aside the discharge. The Arbitrator does not believe that it does. The ultimate decision to discharge Grievant was based on her actions during the strike. Those actions constituted just cause for discharge unless, under all of the facts and circumstances of the case, the penalty of discharge was too severe. While the Hospital was wrong in its action in having failed to notify Grievant of the fact that she was terminated prior to May 25, and this action was detrimental to Grievant, it does not go to the question of severity of the penalty. Grievant was deprived of no substantive right under the Collective Bargaining Agreement. The action of the Hospital in no way deprived her of any rights, either substantive or even procedural, under Article XXVI of the Collective Bargaining Agreement and has in no way prejudiced her rights in arbitration. It cannot, therefore, constitute a proper grounds for setting aside the discharge. Grievant was, however, damaged by this action to the extent that not knowing whether she had been terminated she was in no position to seek other employment. Certainly, an employee who has been terminated is entitled to be made aware of that fact and without undue delay. The evidence establishes that on April 18 Grievant was told that she had not been terminated. She was not actually terminated until May 25.

The Arbitrator will make provision in his Award to compensate Grievant for the period between April 18 and May 25.

Based on all of the evidence in the case, the Arbitrator is satisfied that the discharge of Grievant was for just cause and, under all of the facts and circumstances of the case, the penalty of discharge was not too severe. In the final analysis, although the Arbitrator may sympathize with and respect Grievant for having stood upon her principles, a finding by him that the discharge was not for just cause would have the effect of rendering meaningless the no-strike provision of the Collective Bargaining Agreement which is basic and fundamental to the relations between the Association and CNA. He cannot do so.

AWARD

Based on the Collective Bargaining Agreement, the stipulations of the Parties, the evidence and all of the facts and circumstances of this case, the following Award is made:

The grievance is denied.

Grievant is awarded compensation at her regular straight-time rate of pay for the period of April 18, 1973, to May 25, 1973.

The Arbitrator retains jurisdiction over the subject matter of this dispute until the terms of this Award shall have been effectuated.

Case No. 26

*What was the proper discipline to be taken against a
head nurse with 27 years of service who was absent
for two days in protest of her working conditions?
Was it disparity of treatment in that lesser penalties
were given to nonprofessional co-workers who also
withheld their services?*

The New York City Health and Hospitals Corporation
and
Individual Grievant

Arbitrator: Jesse Simons
Date of Award: January 15, 1975
Citation: GERR 599, B-11

This is an Appeal to the Personnel Review Board (hereinafter the
"Board") by Albert Loew, Esq., in behalf of E— (hereinafter "Appellant"),
who was demoted and suspended for thirty (30) days by decision of William C.
Howe, Sr. Vice President for Personnel & Labor Relations of the New York
City Health & Hospitals Corporation (hereinafter "Corporation"), which
decision was communicated via letter to Appellant dated March 12, 1974.

Mr. Howe's decision was based on a written report containing findings
that Appellant had committed the acts of misconduct with which she was
charged, and recommending suspension and demotion, which findings and
recommendations were made by Hearing Officer Charles S. Sobol, who was
authorized, pursuant to Section 75 of the Civil Service Law, to preside at and
conduct disciplinary hearings of the charges against Appellant.

The Board is duly constituted, pursuant to Chapter 1016 of the
Unconsolidated Laws of 1969, the New York City Health & Hospitals

Corporation Act, and it possesses authority under the Act to hear appeals of aggrieved employees, and to review actions of the Corporation pursuant to the terms of the Act, and it is the "Commission" to which "appeals from determinations in disciplinary proceedings" are to be made, pursuant to Section 76 of the Civil Service Law, and its decisions possess the conclusiveness and finality provided for in Article 5, Section 76, Subdivision 3 of said Civil Service Law.

The Board finds that all provisions of Article 5, Section 76 of the Civil Service Law have been met, to wit: that Appellant was provided in timely fashion with a written copy of charges preferred against her dated December 5, 1973; that hearings of those charges were held on January 22, 1974, and February 5, 1974, with due notice provided; that Appellant was present and represented by Counsel; that transcripts of those hearings were made and were supplied to the Corporation, the Board and Counsel for Appellant; that a written statement of the Hearing Officer was prepared, containing his Findings and Recommendations, and was submitted to the Corporation's Vice President in charge of Personnel & Labor Relations, and a copy was supplied to the Board, the Appellant and her Counsel.

With due notice to Counsel for Appellant and to the Corporation, hearings of the Board were scheduled and occurred on June 24, 1974, and July 25, 1974, to hear the instant Appeal.

At the June 24, 1974 hearing, Messrs. Simons and Collins were present; at the July 25, 1974 hearing, all Board members were present. Also present were Counsel in behalf of the Corporation, namely David Lew, Esq., and Counsel in behalf of Appellant, Albert Loew, Esq. Also present were Gloria Cappella, Regional Representative and Richard J. Silber, Esq., both of the New York State Nurses Association. The Board had before it Hearing Officer Sobol's "Report and Recommendations" and copies of the transcripts of the hearings conducted by him.

Both parties were accorded full opportunity to present evidence and argument to the Board with respect to the instant Appeal. Records of the Board's hearings were prepared and are on file in the Board's office.

After careful and detailed review of the transcripts of the disciplinary hearings, and after review of the Hearing Officer's Report and Recommendations, and after consideration and review of the evidence and the argument presented at the Board's hearings, the Board makes the following findings:

1.   That Appellant is a Health & Hospitals Corporation employee, employed pursuant to Section 5, Subdivision 12 of the Health & Hospitals Corporation Act in a noncompetitive title, but is a Veteran and that, as such, was entitled to the rights contained in Section 75 of the Civil Service Law and her Appeal is properly before the Board.

2.   That Appellant has been accorded all rights pursuant to Sections 75 and 76 of the Civil Service Law.

3.   That formulation, execution and transmittal of Notice of Suspension and Demotion of Appellant were performed pursuant to Sections 75 and 76 of the Civil Service Law.

4.   That the Board is the proper and legal forum to hear Appellant on Appeal from suspension and demotion pursuant to Sections 75 and 76 of the Civil Service Law.

5.   That the written charge against the Appellant consisted, in summary form of:

An unlawful job action by failing to report for duty as scheduled on June 2 and 3, 1973, and for subsequent falsifications of the reason for said absence.

6.   That, in summary form, Hearing Officer Sobol found:

1.   That the testimony of the Corporation's witnesses were credible as to Appellant's statements made at a Goldwater Hospital Community Board meeting in October of 1973 to the effect that, she (Appellant) had deliberately and intentionally stayed out of work on June 2 and 3 as a protest of working conditions in the hospital, and that Appellant "engaged in this action to force the hospital administration to acquiesce to her demands," [for changes on the ward of which she was in charge].

2.   That the testimony of Appellant was not credible as to her contention that her absence was due to phlebitis and/or due to her being so "disheartened, disgusted and frustrated and so entirely distressed . . . [that it could not have been possible for Appellant] to function that week either physically or emotionally."

3.   That Appellant's absence on the June 2 and 3 weekend was part of an organized and concerted effort of Appellant to force her views upon the hospital administration, and further that "the evidence was overwhelmingly conclusive that (Appellant) deliberately engaged in a job action that weekend."

7.   That Hearing Officer Sobol, in recommending a penalty appropriate to the above findings, noted that Appellant had been employed at Goldwater Hospital for 27 years, was Head Nurse of the particular ward to which she was assigned for some six years and that Appellant's service record was devoid of any prior disciplinary action, and therefore, recommended a thirty (30) days suspension and demotion of Appellant from position of Head Nurse to Regular Staff Nurse, which recommendation was effectuated by the Corporation.

8.   That the Board, in its entirety, in reviewing the transcripts of the hearings before the Hearing Officer, and the transcripts of the two hearings conducted by the Board of this Appeal, and the written brief filed on behalf of Appellant, unanimously concurs in the findings of facts of the Hearing Officer, with one exception, namely that the Hearing Officer found that Appellant "instigated" a concerted job action in Ward B-11 and B-12 on June 2, 3, 1973. The Board in its entirety however finds no evidentiary grounds whatsoever for the Hearing Officer's finding that Appellant "instigated" this job action, and therefore, such comment and finding as is made to that effect in the Hearing Officer's recommendation has not been given weight by the Board in its consideration of this Appeal.

9.   That the Board, in its entirety, places great weight on the Hearing Officer's finding that there did occur a concerted job action involving both Appellant and the five other employees assigned to this Ward on the weekend of June 2, 3, 1973, because the record discloses a sufficiency of evidence to justify the conclusion that in fact the paraprofessionals joined together with Appellant in a concerted action.

10.   That the Board, in its entirety, in considering the matter of assessment of penalty is persuaded that a useful purpose will be served by noting that a "job action" and/or a "concerted job action" in any of the Corporation's 19 Hospitals is gross misconduct warranting severe discipline.

It is difficult to conceive of any act of misconduct more grave than the deliberate and conscious decision of an employee to withhold his or her essential services in a Hospital, by a "job action" or a "concerted job action," from the ill and injured who need said services.

Here the importation into a Hospital setting of a trade union practice, not uncommon in the private sector, is so clearly misdirected and inappropriate, and so misses the point as to require Board comment.

Job actions in the private sector are designed exclusively to impose an economic cost on the employer of such dimensions as to compel compliance with a particular demand, either of a union or of a group of employees.

Job actions in a hospital setting have *absolutely* no economically coercive effect on the Hospital, or in the instant matter, on the Corporation or on the City of New York for that matter. The net effect of such a job action is to deprive the ill and the injured of services, and possibly to cause deterioration of their physical condition. How such mistreatment of ill and injured patients can possibly be viewed as the "equivalent" of the coercive economic pressure of a stoppage, walkout or job action in the private sector is beyond rational comprehension.

The irrationality of this misapplication of a private sector practice is underscored by the fact that hospitalized patients have no power whatsoever to induce, persuade or compel the Hospital management to meet the demands of those who are withholding their services.

The Board recognizes, however, that "job actions" in a Hospital do have one result — namely, they impose a test of management's sense of obligation to the patients in their custody. Generally, the management either seeks replacements or management personnel themselves seek to maintain the services normally performed by those engaged in the job action. The ill and injured are at times transferred to another facility.

Thus, in such a "test of strength," the only thing tested is the degree of responsibility and integrity of the contesting parties.

In such situations, generally, management's efforts to "fill the breach" caused by the job action win the support of the patient population and the public, and those engaged in the stoppages suffer a concomitant loss.

This Board is fully aware that resentment, irritation and even rage can accumulate among employees as a result of managerial indifference or deliberate stalling and delaying tactics concerning grievances or complaints, real or imagined. Such feelings usually underlie job actions. But to understand why job actions occur is not to justify or excuse them. The only constructive result of an understanding of the dynamics which underlie "job actions" is the clear recognition that channels for expressing and ventilating complaints, grievances and appeals be so structured as to provide for the expeditious presentation, processing and appeals of these complaints, grievances or appeals. The parties share the obligation to create such procedures, and to support and promote their implementation by the allocation of the time and personnel essential to the expeditious processing of complaints, and both, by and large, have done so.

However, here there were complaints of long standing, the exact nature of which remains unknown to the Board, which festered over a long period and finally erupted into the job action here under consideration.

It appears that neither party became aware of the "problem(s)" and that neither moved promptly to submit the particular problem underlying the job action to the processes available to them for their resolution.

It is abundantly clear that both unions and management have recognized their several responsibilities to provide the procedures for resolving disputes, complaints and dissatisfactions such as those underlying the instant incident. It seems equally clear that both have not succeeded in conveying a clear understanding of these processes and their proper uses to those actually and directly concerned in the Hospitals. Accordingly, the Board concludes that a highly useful purpose would be served if the parties undertook, jointly and/or separately to reevaluate the procedures thus far developed and the educational programs whereby those procedures are communicated to their respective constituencies. The Board, if requested, would make its offices available to the parties for the furtherance of any such program the parties may decide to undertake.

11.   That the Board, considering the transcripts, evidence and findings

referred to previously, is persuaded as was the Hearing Officer, that a concerted job action took place on June 2 and 3, and that the Ward's entire complement, the Appellant and five para-professionals deliberately, jointly and in concerted action absented themselves from work for the purpose of compelling the Hospital Administration to meet certain demands. The Board sees the evidence before it as constituting proof by a preponderance of evidence of Appellant's participation in a concerted job action.

12.   As an Appellate body, the Board necessarily is concerned with the issue of discriminatory application of discipline. This is so because the Board is required to *adjudicate* appeals. In adjudication of disputes, balance, justice and fairness are of the essence. When there is just cause for penalties to be applied for misconduct, such penalties should be evenly and fairly dispensed *to all those who participate in a particular act of misconduct.* Disparate penalties are, of course, appropriate as between and among a group of persons participating in a particular act of misconduct, depending on different degrees of culpability as between the leaders and the led, differing levels of authority and responsibility, length of service, attitude of contrition, etc.

The Hospital's disciplinary action here, even though tardy in the extreme, cannot but have a positive effect on Goldwater Memorial Hospital's employees as a whole. It will tend to discourage those who engaged in the stoppage not to do so again in the future, and will tend to cause others to believe that they too will be disciplined and/or called to account for such "job actions."

The Board notes that most employees generally abide by rules of conduct, and most employees generally perform their work well and are conscientious.

There is, however, a minority of employees in any work place who commit acts of misconduct, and who need to be educated and persuaded not to do so. Corrective discipline is the method of choice because it seeks, via education, and if necessary, penalties, to achieve a change in the outlook and/or conduct of such employees.

Another method of influencing employee attitude and conduct is the creation of a *climate of certainty in the work environment,* one that is pervasive, informative and so structured that it reaches this minority and *has the effect of making clear that concerted job actions, or any other gross misconduct,* will not be condoned, and that the management will not look the other way. On the contrary, an overview of the instant matter makes dramatically clear that there is need for the creation of a *climate of absolute certainty that decisive and firm disciplinary action will certainly be taken against all participants in a "job action."* The Corporation's action, and the Board's Decision basically sustaining it, will contribute to that climate.

The policy of corrective, graduated discipline and the creation of a climate of certainty described above can serve only as deterrents. They will not eradicate misconduct, but, nevertheless, they can be quite effective. In any event, these procedures and this climate of certainty are the best that the arts of management and personnel administration have been able to devise to date, and the instant Board Decision will contribute to strengthening that climate and those procedures.

13.   Having concluded that Appellant (and five of her fellow employees) did commit the act charged against her, and having learned that Appellant's nonprofessional co-workers have each been penalized by a suspension of five days for committing basically the same act of misconduct as did Appellant, the Board has concluded that the disparity in penalty between that accorded Appellant's nonprofessional co-workers and that assessed against Appellant is excessive, in that Appellant's penalty of thirty days' suspension resulted in a loss of salary of approximately $1,100, and her demotion for one year results in a salary loss of approximately $1,100. To date, Appellant has, in effect, been fined in the amount of approximately $2,200 for her misconduct. A further harsh consequence of the demotion aspect of the penalty meted out, is the sharp reduction of Appellant's ultimate pension benefit.

While asserting previously the propriety of disparate treatment as among a group of employees committing the same act of misconduct, the Board further concludes that the total penalty applied to Appellant is excessive and harsh, especially in the face of her 27 years of service, both as a Nurse and as a Head Nurse, unmarred and unblemished by prior reprimands or warning, and thus, the Board will sustain the Appeal, but only to the extent of directing reinstatement of Appellant to her prior title, effective September 12, 1975, 18 months from the date of her demotion.

AWARD

Having weighed and considered all the testimony, evidence and argument submitted, and on the basis of the preceding opinion, the Board finds and decides that the Appeal is sustained, but only to the extent of directing that Appellant be reinstated to her previous position and title of Head Nurse, effective September 12, 1975.

Case No. 27

*Did the absence of four out of five nursing assistants
and one unit clerk constitute a concerted refusal to
work? Did their failure to present valid medical
evidence of alleged illnesses constitute at least
misrepresentations of reason for absence?*

St. Vincent Charity Hospital (Cleveland, Ohio)
and
Hospital, Convalescent and Nursing Home Employees Union, Local 10

Arbitrator: Charles F. Ipavec
Date of Award: July 12, 1974
Citation: 190 AAA 11

On August 24, 1973, the hospital suspended indefinitely, the five grievants in this case, namely, B—, F—, D—, M— and A—. On August 27, 1973, the hospital issued a suspension notice changing the indefinite suspension to a 31-day suspension, which notice, stated as follows:

Effective August 24, 1973, you are suspended for 31 calendar days for falsely calling in sick and failing to report for work on August 19, 1973.

The hospital's action in suspending grievants precipitated a greivance being filed by the five grievants. The grievance was stated as:

We the undersign fill that we were unjustly suspended indefinitely for not reporting to work on August 19, 1973. We fill an injustice has been done and steps should be taken to correct it. (sic)

Issue

The issue in this matter can be stated thusly: Did the Company have just cause for the imposition of a 31-day disciplinary suspension upon the five grievants, B—, F—, D—, M— and A—, for the reason that the said grievants did not report for work on August 19, 1973. If not, to what remedy, if any, are the grievants entitled, either jointly or severally?

Contract Provisions

ARTICLE VII — *No-Strike and No-Lockout*

Section 1 — During the term of this Agreement, the Union shall not, directly or indirectly, call, sanction, encourage, finance and/or assist in any way, nor shall any employee instigate or participate, directly or indirectly in any strike, slowdown, walkout, work stoppage, picketing or other interference with any operation or operations of the Hospital. The Union shall cooperate with the Hospital throughout said period in continuing operations in a normal manner, and shall actively discourage and endeavor to prevent or terminate any violation of this Section.

Section 2 — Any employee who violates Section 1 of this Article shall be subject to discharge or other disciplinary action. Such disciplinary action shall not be subject to review upon any ground other than whether the employee violated Section 1. In the event there is any strike, slowdown, walkout, work stoppage, picketing, or other interference with the Hospital's operations in violation of Section 1, neither party shall negotiate upon the merits of the dispute involved until such time as the illegal action is fully terminated and normal operations have been resumed.

ARTICLE X — *Official Leaves of Absence*

Section 1 — An employee shall be granted a leave of absence for a period not to exceed 90 calendar days because of personal illness or injury upon notice supported by medical evidence satisfactory to the Hospital, provided the employee has reported such illness or injury to his immediate supervisor during his first day of absence, unless the failure to do so is due to reasons beyond his control. If the illness or disability continues beyond 90 calendar days, additional sick leave may be granted by the Hospital. Employees who have been on such leave three (3) or more consecutive days may be required to submit to a physical examination before being permitted to return to work.

Section 7 — Employees who misrepresent facts to obtain a leave of absence or secure a leave of absence on the basis of such misrepresentation may be dismissed by the Hospital. Failure of an employee without a sufficient excuse to report for employment as of the expiration of his leave or to secure an extension of his leave shall result in the termination of this employment by the Hospital.

ARTICLE XI — *Discipline*

Section 1 — The Hospital shall have the right to discipline or discharge any employee for just cause. It is agreed that the Hospital will maintain its present procedure of oral and written warnings, but that the Hospital will send written notification to the Union of such warnings so that the Union may have an opportunity to caution its members and protect them.

Position of the Hospital

The Hospital alleges that it had just cause for suspending the five grievants in this case for a period of 31 calendar days. On Sunday, August 19, 1973, the Hospital had scheduled, among other employees, for duty in Department 3C, five nursing assistants and one unit clerk. Four of the five nursing assistants and the unit clerk, did not work on August 19, 1973, although scheduled to do so. The four nursing assistants and the unit clerk are the grievants in this case.

The grievants indicated that they would furnish medical certificates to substantiate their absence however, the so-called medical certificates which the grievants furnished are not valid.

This was a unique situation which called for a penalty to be imposed upon the grievants. Never before has such a large percentage of employees not reported for work in any one unit. The Hospital was convinced that this was a concerted activity on the part of the five grievants to effect a work stoppage. Calling in sick has become a tactic for work stoppages. The Agreement prohibits work stoppages and the penalty imposed is justified. Hospital staffing is keyed to the number of patients and each individual scheduled to work is needed in order to provide the proper care for the patients.

The grievants in this instance were aware that the patient care requires that there be a sufficient staff on duty and when all five of the grievants did not report to work on the same day the hospital interpreted it to being a move to engage in a work stoppage.

The hospital has stated, "It is patently incredible that 85% of the scheduled personnel for Department 3C, on August 19, 1973, would be simultaneously absent from work without such action being the result of concerted planning and activity."

The medical certificates which were submitted by four of the five grievants at the arbitration hearing are suspect and even taken on their face value the so-called medical certificates have no real probative value.

The grievance should be denied.

Position of the Union

The Union in its brief has accurately summarized the evidence, testimony and argument as presented by the Union at the hearing, as follows:

As stated by the Union in its closing argument, the case heard by the Arbitrator is a rather simple and straightforward case. The Hospital suspended for 31 days, five long-term Hospital employees. The Hospital failed completely to conduct even a semblance of an investigation, as illicited from the Hospital during the arbitration. Instead of investigating the case or even bothering to talk to the five individuals who had over four years apiece of employment at the Hospital, the Hospital convinced itself that some plot must have been afoot; since never before had there been this number of absences at one time from one department. In fact, as pointed out by counsel for the Union, the only real investigation of the circumstances surrounding the August 19 absences was the detailed questioning of the individuals by counsel for the Hospital at the arbitration hearing.

Let us briefly examine each of the five individuals who were suspended:

First, D— testified that she had a severe rash on her arm and that nurses at the Hospital were aware of the rash and prescribed medication for it on Saturday, August 18. Early in the morning on Sunday, August 19, Mrs. D—'s family called in to indicate she had gone to the emergency room at University Hospital for treatment. The record before the arbitrator indicates that not only was Mrs. D— in the emergency room on the 19th, but that she was advised to return on an out-patient basis on the 21st, which she did. The slight confusion as to whether Mrs. D— was at the emergency room on the 19th was caused by the fact that St. Vincent, in preparation for the arbitration, requested verification of her attendance at the emergency room under her married name, whereas all of the University Hospital records are in her maiden name. Mrs. D— and all of the other individuals in sworn testimony, indicated that they had no knowledge of anybody else being absent, made no plans of absence, and were not in contact with each other at all during the 19th.

Secondly, B— testified that she was too ill to come into work due to an attack of gastritis. However, Mrs. B— did call in and indicate she had stomach problems; and she called nursing services in the required manner. Mrs. B— testified that she had been under doctor's care for some period of time and had been troubled by gastritis since March of 1973, when all of her teeth had been extracted. Mrs. B— further testified that although she was troubled by gastritis almost daily, she was generally able to come to work, although there had been several times when she had called in sick when the attacks were the most severe. The only thing that the Hospital could say about her was that when she got an attack at work she usually was able to finish the shift. This, obviously, should be to her credit rather than to her detriment. Further underscoring the problem, however, Mrs. B— testified that on one occasion she became so ill during work that a nurse requested that she sit down, and the nurse gave her something for the condition.

Thirdly, F— testified that she called in ill with a toothache on Sunday; that she stayed home all day and tried home remedies; that she came to work even with the toothache on Monday, because she could not get a dentist appointment; and on Tuesday the tooth was extracted. Certainly it must be clear that this would be a rather gross measure to take in order to cover up a "plot" to stay home.

The fourth person involved is M—. Mrs. M— was the individual with the injured wrist. She testified that she had injured her wrist on Monday, August 13. She came into work during the week of the 13th with her wrist bandaged. On Saturday the 18th she was shaking down a thermometer that seemed to stick and reinjured her wrist. The wrist was actually rebandaged on Saturday by one of the nurses on the floor; and the Hospital's own witnesses testified that they knew of the injury. It is further interesting to note that Mrs. M— called in later *Saturday* night to tell the Hospital that she would not be in on Sunday, many, many hours before any of the others called in.

The final individual involved is A—. Miss A— testified to having been hit on Sunday with menstrual cramps. When she awoke the cramps were so severe that she called in and that she had to take Edrisol, which had been prescribed to her because of severe menstrual cramps by one of the doctors at the Hospital. Miss A— testified that she generally works during her period, except on occasional days when the cramps are so severe that she feels that she cannot work. The Hospital introduced time sheets which show her good work record during the two weeks surrounding August 19; but an examination of the Hospital records for the months prior would clearly indicate occasional absences during the menstrual periods and support Miss A—'s testimony.

Of special importance is the fact that on August 19, a sixth person, a Miss Smith, also was scheduled to work and did not come in. However, the Hospital did not suspend Miss Smith as it did the other five. The Hospital, at the hearing, seemed to indicate that the reason that they did not suspend Miss Smith was that they called her back, said they were shorthanded, and asked her to please come in and she did. The Hospital, however, also admits that they *never* called any one of the other five girls to see if they were feeling better and could come in because of the shorthanded situation.

Against this testimony, all the Hospital could offer was testimony of Mrs. Collins who did a statistical survey in October and November of 1971; and she testified, based on her knowledge for that two-month period, that there had never been a similar absence in one department. First, there is no guarantee that this is a statistically relevant period. Secondly, Ms. Collins' study was based on the night shift. Thirdly, and most importantly, however, Ms. Collins admits that her statistics were never examined, nor was she ever consulted at the time the suspensions were made, thus further underscoring the fact that although the Hospital originally suspended the employees indefinitely and agreed to investigate the matter, they never investigated it until the arbitration hearing. The Hospital's only other testimony came from two other nurses who indicated that the absence was unusually high. The grievants do not doubt that the absence was high, but the only testimony in the record substantiates legitimate medical excuses and a coincidence. Where is any shred of evidence of a plot or a work stoppage? Where is there even a theory advanced of a dispute?

It is for this reason that the arbitrator must overturn the suspension, have the disciplinary action removed from the subject employees' files and award them the pay that they lost for the 31 days in question.

Decision

Generally an arbitrator is empowered to view the labor dispute in the light of the entire Agreement between the parties. The parties may however restrict the arbitrator as to the portion or portions of the Agreement which are applicable to the controversy. In this case the parties made no such limitation upon the arbitrator and accordingly then, the arbitrator is permitted to decide the controversy after a consideration of the entire Agreement between the parties.

When four out of the five nursing aides scheduled for work on Sunday, August 19, 1973, did not report for work and when one out of one unit clerk scheduled to work on the same day did not report for work on the same day it does seem somewhat incredulous that it was by mere coincidence. The Arbitrator agrees with the Hospital's first reaction to the situation; however, the Hospital failed to realize that there is a difference between what seems incredulous and what is incredulous. To bridge the gap between what seems incredulous and what is incredulous there must be some evidence other than averages and past experience. Whenever a concerted work stoppage is suspected, for which the employer may be justified in imposing discipline, a thorough and searching investigation must be made. There is always a reason for a work stoppage and it is incumbent upon the employer to make some attempt to determine the reason for the alleged work stoppage. In this case no evidence was presented which would indicate grievants had a reason for engaging in a concerted action to create a work stoppage, such as a dispute with management over working conditions or other reason.

In the opinion of the arbitrator the Hospital failed to make a proper investigation concerning the alleged work stoppage. This is not to say that the hospital was incorrect in its conclusion that a work stoppage did in fact exist. The grievants, in their own minds, know whether they were engaging in a work stoppage or whether it really was coincidence that all five happened to be sick on the same Sunday for which they had been scheduled to work. As the hospital's evidence concerning a concerted action to create a work stoppage is weak, the Union's evidence is by no means strong, especially when it presents the argument that the five grievants were not in contact with each other at all during the 19th, as part of the Union's defense that there was no such concerted action. Naturally if there, in fact, was a concerted action to create a work stoppage by the grievants, the contacts would have been made before the 19th in order to plan a work stoppage on the 19th. In the opinion of the arbitrator, there is insufficient evidence to conclude that the five grievants in this case acted in concert to create a work stoppage.

The suspension notice states the reason as being, "for falsely calling in sick and failing to report for work on August 19, 1973." Such charge was made to each grievant individually and there is no allegation of a concerted effort among the five grievants.

Once the suspension notice was issued and the grievants were aware of the exact charge, it became incumbent upon the grievants to substantiate their illnesses. The Agreement between the parties in Article X refers to a leave of absence due to personal illness or injury, for a period not to exceed ninety calendar days, which, in the opinion of the arbitrator, means a period from one to ninety days, so that a request for a leave of absence for personal illness is covered under this Article even though such request is for one day only, in this instance, Sunday, August 19, 1973. Said Article X provides that the employee is to provide medical evidence satisfactory to the hospital.

In Article VI of the Agreement between the parties, entitled Grievance Procedure, in Section 2, it is provided that, "within two weeks after a grievance is filed, such grievance shall be submitted to a meeting between representatives of the Union and the Executive Director or his designee, for full discussion, and, if possible amicable settlement." The grievants should have presented proper medical evidence, acceptable to the hospital, concerning their illness on August 19, 1973, at the time that the grievants were confronted with the allegation that they had falsely called in sick. If proper medical evidence was not presented immediately then the grievants should have had available such medical evidence to be made available to the representatives of the Union for use in their discussion with the Executive Director or his designee when this grievance was being discussed under the terms of the Agreement between the parties.

Grievant D— testified that she went to the University Hospital on the morning of August 19, 1973, for emergency treatment for a rash upon her arm. Grievant D— presented a certificate, (Union Ex-1), from University Hospitals to the effect that a D— was seen by the doctors on August 19, 1973, however, grievant D— also testified that she did not use her name of D— but used her maiden name, yet the documentation from University Hospitals is in the name of D—. In the opinion of the arbitrator, grievant D—'s own testimony seriously diminished the evidentuary value of the certificate from University Hospitals.

Although the letter from Richard A. Parrish addressed to Thomas J. McDermott, Esq., of June 10, 1974, after the oral hearing in this matter, is self serving and certainly not the best evidence of what the medical records at University Hospitals do in fact contain, nevertheless it appears to substantiate grievant D—'s testimony that the hospital would have no record under the name of D—.

In the opinion of the arbitrator, grievant D— did not substantiate her personal illness as the reason for her absence on August 19, 1973.

Grievant A— offered no medical evidence substantiating her personal illness on August 19, 1973, and the hospital is not in violation of the Agreement between the parties, in refusing to accept grievant A—'s personal statement concerning her illness and in requiring some satisfactory medical evidence.

In the opinion of the arbitrator grievant A— did not substantiate her personal illness as being the reason for her absence on August 19, 1973.

Grievant F— testified that she stayed home because of pain caused by a toothache on August 19, 1973. Grievant F— worked on August 20, 1973, and had her tooth extracted on August 21, 1973. Grievant F—'s dentist, Dr. Lester indicated on the back of one of his calling cards, that Mrs. F— had tooth extracted on August 21, 1973 (Union Ex-2). In the opinion of the arbitrator, Dr. Lester's note does not medically substantiate an illness on August 19, 1973, which can be given as an excuse for not reporting for work.

In the opinion of the arbitrator, grievant F— did not substantiate her personal illness as her reason for not reporting to work on August 19, 1973.

Grievant B— testified that she was ill at home with gastritis and resorted to home remedies. On September 6, 1973, her physician, Dr. John R. Hickey, did furnish grievant B— with a disability certificate stating that a B—

was totally incapacitated on August 19, 1973. There was no evidence submitted as to the manner in which Dr. Hickey would be, on September 6, 1973, aware of the fact that grievant B— was completely incapacitated on August 19, 1973, especially in the light of grievant B—'s testimony that she did not visit the doctor or talk with the doctor on August 19, 1973. The probative value of the disability certificate presented by grievant B— (Union Ex-3), would have been increasingly enhanced as the date of the certificate would have come closer to the date of the disability.

In the opinion of the arbitrator grievant B— has not substantiated her personal illness as being the reason for her absence from work on August 19, 1973.

Grievant M— testified that her right wrist was sprained and that she was not able to work on August 19, 1973. To substantiate her disability grievant M— introduced a certificate (Union Ex-4) from Doctor Harold J. Hertz. The certificate does not state that Dr. Hertz saw or talked with grievant M— and the certificate is dated December 2, 1973.

In the opinion of the arbitrator grievant M— did not substantiate her personal illness as the reason for her absence from work on August 19, 1973.

When the hospital realized that all five of the grievants reported as being sick on the same day, Sunday, August 19, 1973, it could logically make a temporary conclusion that a concerted action to create a work stoppage was being made by the five grievants. At that point it would become incumbent upon the grievants to offer the hospital acceptable medical evidence that each one was in fact ill on the date in question. Had the grievants presented acceptable medical evidence of their illnesses to the hospital, the arbitrator is confident that the hospital would have abandoned its allegation of a concerted work stoppage by the five grievants, and of falsely calling in sick.

Under Article X of the Agreement between the parties, Section 7, the hospital is permitted to discharge an employee who misrepresents facts to obtain a leave of absence, which, in the opinion of the arbitrator, would include a leave of absence for personal illness for a period of one to ninety days.

All five of the grievants claimed to be ill on August 19, 1973. Four of the grievants presented unacceptable medical evidence supposedly supporting their claim of illness on August 19, 1973. One grievant presented no medical evidence of illness whatsoever. In the opinion of the arbitrator, and based upon the symptoms of illness testified to by each of the five grievants, it would appear that the best place for each of the grievants to have been on August 19, 1973, was in the hospital, where they could have received immediate medical attention, if in fact such medical attention was required.

If in fact this was a concerted action to cause a work stoppage on the part of the five grievants and should the grievants again engage in such a concerted action, the arbitrator would warn the grievants that they are travelling on a collision course which will surely result in the loss of their employment. In this case, the arbitrator does not say that there was no concerted action to cause a work stoppage on the part of the grievants, for it is only the grievants who really can answer that question, but rather that the hospital presented insufficient evidence so that the arbitrator could reasonably conclude that the five grievants were in fact engaged in a concerted action to cause a work stoppage. On the other hand, however, there is insufficient evidence for the arbitrator to reasonably conclude that in fact each of the five grievants were too ill to work on Sunday, August 19, 1973. In the opinion of the arbitrator, each of the five grievants, acting singly, decided to take Sunday, August 19, 1973, off, called in and gave as their excuse for not reporting to work, a personal illness, which could not be substantiated later on. The grievants misrepresented to the hospital, their reason for not reporting to work on the day in question.

In the light of the fact that there was no testimony as to prior discipline being imposed upon any one of the five grievants in this case, the arbitrator gave serious consideration to a mitigation of the penalty; however, because the Agreement between the parties gives the hospital the right to impose a discipline of up to discharge for misrepresenting facts to obtain a leave of absence, it would not be proper for the arbitrator to substitute his judgment for that of the hospital in the severity of the discipline imposed upon the five grievants. Any leniency shown to the grievants must come from the Hospital and not the arbitrator.

AWARD

The grievances of D—, F—, B—, M— and A— are denied.

Case No. 28

*What was the proper discipline to be taken against
two off-duty nurses aides who returned to the
Facility and engaged in intra-union activity which
was disruptive of operations?*

Lafayette Extended Care Facility (Flint, Mich.)
and
American Federation of State, County and Municipal Employees,
Local 1918, Chapter P

Arbitrator: E. V. Ott
Date of Award: August 20, 1974
Citation: 194 AAA 13

Employer's Position

The aggrieved employees were properly discharged because they violated Article 5 — Representation, Section D, and Article 7 — Management Rights of the Labor Agreement. In addition, they were guilty of acts of sabotage and dishonest actions which are cause for immediate discharge.

Union's Position

The Employer improperly suspended the aggrieved for violation of Article 5, Section D, which action was protested by the Union. The Employer compounded his improper action of suspension by adding charges of sabotage and dishonesty and discharging the grievants. The Union maintains Employer could not sustain his charges "beyond a reasonable doubt," that Employer's actions are based on conjecture and not fact, and requests that the grievants be reinstated, awarded back pay, and their disciplinary records cleared.

Contractual Provisions Involved

ARTICLE 5, SECTION D — *Representation*

The Steward and alternates have no authority to take strike action or any other action interrupting the Employer's business, except as authorized by official action of the Union.

ARTICLE 7 — *Management Rights*

The management of the business and the direction of the working force, including the right to plan and direct operations, hire, suspend or discharge for proper cause, transfer or relieve employees from duty because of lack of work or other legitimate reasons only, the right to study or introduce new or improved production methods or facilities, and the right to establish and maintain reasonable rules and regulations covering the operation of the business, a violation of which reasonable rules and regulations shall be among the causes for discipline or discharge vested in the Employer, provided, however, that such rights shall be exercised with due regard for the rights of the employees and subject to the provisions of the Agreement, and without discrimination against any employees.

ARTICLE 10 — *Discharge or Suspension*

A.   The Employer shall not discharge or suspend any employee without just cause, but in respect to discharge or suspension shall give at least one (1) warning notice of complaint against such employee to the employee in writing, and a copy of same to the Union and job steward affected, except with cases of dishonesty, drunkeness or patient abuse.

The article continues with Sections B, C, D, E, F, G, and H, which for the sake of brevity are not re-stated herein.

APPENDIX D — *Use of Past Records*

"C," being the pertinent section is re-stated. A, B, D, E are omitted again for the sake of brevity.

"C.   The following actions shall be considered cause for immediate discharge.
. . . 3. Sabotage
. . . 5. Proven dishonesty."

Discussion

After discussion between the parties it was agreed that the actions of grievants on March 17, 1974, gave rise to the Employer's charge of violating Article 5, Section D, and Article 7 of the contract, which resulted in a seven (7) day suspension pending final determination.

The employer on March 27, 1974, after investigation issued a termination on the grounds that the rules, Appendix D, Item 3 (sabotage) and 5 (dishonesty) "as defined in Webster dictionary (Appendix D does not provide for this definition of these items.)"

The Union, contending it was the moving party, proceeded first. The Employer had no objection to this.

Grievant A— testified on her own behalf. Briefly her pertinent testimony is as follows: She has been a nurses aide for five years and 3 months; she has no disciplinary record. She attended the meeting of March 19, 1974, at which she was given her seven (7) days suspension. She received her discharge through the mail. She admitted she was in the building on Sunday, March 17, 1974, her prime purpose being to give some house slippers to a patient. She has visited many patients in the past, to the best of her knowledge there was no rule against this and "no one told me I couldn't do it." On the day in question, she could not find the patient she came to visit, looked for her from floor to floor, talked to some employees and patients, assisted in the care of patients, and helped feed some. She left the facility and came back shortly to find the patient for whom she had bought the house slippers. She stayed for a while and then left to see her hospitalized husband. She did not work March 18, 1974, because of Union meeting; she is not a steward or alternate, but is an officer of the Chapter.

She returned to work on March 19, 1974, worked to 3:20 p.m. when she was informed by her supervisor to report to the administrator's office, where she was informed that she was circulating a petition for the removal of the Chapter chairman and was suspended for seven (7) days. She denied circulating the petition, but did admit she had a list of complaints in regard to change of schedule hours.

During cross-examination, she testified she is not presently employed. She was in the building from "a little after one — left — returned in a short while and stayed until a little after 4:00 p.m." That she had a folder with her, but she did not discuss the Chapter chairman's removal with the girls, she had no knowledge of the possibility of a strike. She admitted talking on the telephone with Mrs. Adams following her suspension, about two days later, as to "what choices do I have" and that Mrs. Wilson's (Chapter chairman) position was wrong, she was making deals and something should be done about it. Mrs. Adams was present at the meeting of March 19, 1974, as was her chief steward.

She discussed her suspension with the other grievant at Union meeting, as well as her list of complaints with all members present, including the Chapter chairman.

W—, the other grievant, was treated in the same manner as grievant A—. She testified that she came to work on March 19, 1974, and even though she was sick, worked to 5:30 p.m., when she went home because she was too ill to continue. On March 20, 1974, she called Mrs. Adams to inquire about her sick days and was informed that Mr. Rabidoux wished to speak to her about a meeting. She reported at about 2:00 p.m. and a disciplinary hearing was held. She was charged with circulating a petition and was given her seven (7) days suspension, subsequently changed to a discharge. She denied the charge at the hearing.

On cross-examination, she again denied she had circulated a petition, for the simple reason that "I didn't have one."

She was questioned as to a reprimand that she received in January, 1973. She responded that she was so reprimanded, but that the reprimand was removed from her record as a result of a grievance settlement.

Ruthie Vincent, chief steward, testified that she represented grievant A— at the disciplinary hearing, wherein A— was charged with circulating a petition. She testified that Mr. Rabidoux stated he had knowledge of this act from his nursing staff. A— denied the charge and was sent out of the room. Vincent and Rabidoux discussed the matter with Vincent requesting that A— be permitted to return to work while Rabidoux investigated the charge. In addition, Vincent asked what the petition was about. She was advised by Rabidoux "because of her long standing as an employee not to get involved in the matter." A— was then brought back into the room and was issued her seven (7) day suspension, which was subsequently changed to a discharge.

On March 20, 1974, Vincent testified that she had forwarned grievant W— as to what she was being charged with, that W— denied she had committed such act. A disciplinary hearing was held and grievant W— was treated in the same manner as grievant A—.

During cross-examination, Vincent, in response to questioning, testified that on the day in question (March 17) the "floor was going quite well," and she "had no knowledge" of any petition being circulated around. The charge of sabotage was added during a grievance meeting of April 9, 1974, the basis being that circulating of the petition during working hours "disrupted his (Rabidoux) business."

The Employer's President, Mr. Ken Rabidoux, testified to the effect that he was not present in the building on the day in question, but on March 18, 1974, he was asked about the "disruption on March 17, 1974" by Mrs. Wyatt, L.P.N., who informed him that A— was "in the building for a considerable length of time with a document seeking signatures." That employees were gathering in groups and ignoring patients.

Following this report, Mr. Rabidoux talked to various employees in this regard and while he got "mixed answers," he was satisfied that grievants were in the building. He then decided to "confront these employees point blank." He questioned A— first in the presence of Mrs. Adams and the chief steward. His testimony in this regard is that when he asked A— "if she was in the building" her first answer was "No," but later she admitted she was in the building to see a patient. Further, that she was in the building a very few minutes and not a matter of hours. Finally, she did not circulate a "petition, bill of complaint, or document of any kind."

He then informed grievant A— that based on the information he had, he could terminate; however, he was giving her a seven (7) day suspension to further investigate the matter, and if the investigation proved that grievant A— was not in violation of Article 5, Section D, and Article 7, he would reinstate her and make her whole.

Grievant W— came to his office at his request, and again in the presence of Mrs. Adams and the chief steward. He asked her the same "general questions" based on the general information he had. In view of the fact that Grievant W— "denied any knowledge of a petition" or of "any activity," he in order to be consistent, treated her in the same manner that he had treated grievant A—.

Mr. Rabidoux then made a further investigation which consisted of "talking to the employees and making careful records" of what they informed him. At the conclusion of this investigation, he felt he had no other "alternate than to terminate," adding the charges of "dishonesty and sabotage," contending that dishonesty occurred when both grievants answered his questions, and sabotage because of the "underhanded interference" with the operations which could have resulted in a loss of business for the facility if patients were neglected in that friends, family and relatives would take the patients out of the home.

He concluded that the main thrust of his action was based on violation of Article 5, Section D, and Article 7, of the Labor Agreement. The notice of suspension had been prepared by Mrs. Adams, which he signed.

Mrs. Adams, payroll and personnel clerk, testified to the effect that Mr. Rabidoux's testimony was substantially correct. She did not assist in any investigation, however, some of the employees talked to her and from what she heard, there was a petition to remove Mary Wilson "going around on the night shift." She had a telephone conversation with A— which in substance revolved around Mary Wilson's performance as Chapter chairman, in which grievant A— said she "would take care of her." Mrs. Adams advised her that "you would only get hurt in the long run." There was no talk of a strike.

She was present at the disciplinary hearing of March 20, 1974, and testified that grievant A— denied circulating any petition, but that she did have a list of complaints.

She had no conversation with grievant W—, but was present at her disciplinary hearing. She prepared the notices of suspension and discharge for Mr. Rabidoux's signature.

On cross-examination, she testified that she did not hear the complaint from Mrs. Wyatt. She does not have the authority to recommend disciplinary action. One of the girls who signed the complaint list told her she was sorry she signed it.

Dymple F. Wyatt, L.P.N., testified she was on duty on March 17, 1974, and she saw grievant A— in 2 South with some slippers in her hands. A paper was being circulated around and the charge aide let her read it. She talked with grievant A— and advised her she would get into a "great deal of difficulty" if she took any action. A— responded that "she was only doing what the girls asked her to do." Mrs. Wyatt then went on to testify that A— stayed in the corridor and talked to most of the girls. Later in the day she saw A— at the desk on the first floor, but she did not hear the conversation. She left a little after 3:00 p.m. and was off of work for several days. When she returned, she informed her supervisor of A—'s action on March 17, 1974.

On cross-examination, she testified that grievant A— handed the paper to her, she read it, and asked A— "if all these things are true." A— responded that she got the complaints from the aides. All she did was put it together. Wyatt testified that A— did not interrupt the work force. She never directed A— to leave the building, and the aides dispersed when she directed them to do so.

The Employer then called ten additional witnesses, two of whom testified that grievant A— was in the building on March 17, 1974. One of these testified that A— attempted to read "some paper" that she was not interested in anything but the "schedules." The others, that A— had "some slippers in her hands as well as her folder." She read some comments about Mary Wilson, but that "no one signed the paper."

Three witnesses testified that grievant W— had a petition on March 18, 1974, about the new schedule. One of these did not read or sign it; another signed her name to a blank piece of paper; the third testified she was approached by W— just before the start of her shift to sign "a piece of paper" about the schedules, which she signed.

A third shift steward testified that while she did not work on the 18th, she worked the next day, and several of her constituents told her about the petition. She informed them they should not have signed it.

Mary Wilson, Chapter P Chairman, testified that she was aware of the activities of A— and W—; that she did not see A— in the facility on March 17, 1974; however, she knew that she was in the building. She had been informed of a threat against her made by A—. She did not see W— in the facility on March 18, 1974.

The remaining witnesses were supervisory personnel. One did not work on the day in question, but testified that she saw a "group of girls in a room talking about getting rid of Mary Wilson, and maybe A— was with them." The atmosphere in the place was bad. Another testified she got some "feed back" from her aides following the suspension of the grievants, but had no personal knowledge of the grievants' activities of March 17, and 18. The third testified that she worked on March 17, 1974, saw grievant A— on 3 North with a male companion, and that A— talked to three aides: She did not see A— with petition or paper. She saw aides standing together, but did not give them any orders to go back to work.

Opinion

I have purposely reported the testimony in great detail because of the gravity of the charges against the grievants and the arguments made in summation by the parties.

In regard to Article 5, Section D, the language of this section is quite clear. It refers only to "stewards and alternates" and while neither grievant is a steward or alternate, it was shown that A— is the recording secretary and W— a trustee of the Chapter. Common sense dictates that officers of the Chapter would not take any "strike action or any other action interrupting the Employer's business except as authorized by official action of the Union;" as W— put it, "this would violate Article 8, No Strike" provision of the Agreement. Both grievants are knowledgeable in regard to the provisions of the Agreement, and because of this, I cannot permit them to excuse their actions on a technicality; specifically, that they are not "steward or alternates." While there was "no strike action" there was, in my opinion, "other action interrupting the Employer's business," which I will deal with later. Suffice it to say that the Employer, because of a technicality, failed to show a violation of Article 5, Section D.

I fail to find how Article 7 — Management Rights, is involved in this matter. Here, management exercised its right to take disciplinary action and the Union exercised its right to grieve under the grievance procedure. An Employer has the right to bring out the facts discovered in his investigation, while an employee is suspended, which will substantiate the reason for suspension and possibly lead to a more severe penalty than suspension or lead to a withdrawal of the suspension and make the employee whole. Here the Employer seeks to add additional charges, dishonesty and sabotage, either one of which could be a dischargeable offense. Procedurally, this is improper, but notwithstanding, what act of dishonesty or sabotage occurred?

In regard to dishonesty as it is known in labor relations, what illegal activity did either of the grievants commit? Was there a destruction of reports? Was there any fraud committed against the Employer? Was there any falsification of any records? The application for employment? Was there any misuse of equipment? Was there any deliberate misrepresentation? It may well be argued as the Employer did, that grievant A— did not immediately tell the truth when he asked her about the "petition, bill of complaint, or paper;" however, it has long been held in arbitration that there are varying degrees of dishonesty and the test to use in levying a penalty is: What is the effect on the efficiency of the operation? It is obvious that A—'s answer at the suspension hearing had no effect on the efficiency of the operation.

In my opinion, the charge of proven sabotage is without merit. What act of sabotage occurred? To mention a few: Was there any physical damage to the facility? Were the washing machines or dryers in the laundry damaged? Were any of the patients' charts destroyed? Were any of the dinner trays upset? Were any of the hand rails or windows broken? None of these acts attributable to the grievants was shown. The Employer argues that because of the grievant's activities, there was a possibility of the loss of business. This argument stretches the meaning of sabotage as understood in labor relations, and in my view is at the best, speculation.

It has long been established that a discharge cannot be based on conjecture, surprise, suspicion or anything but hard material and known facts. These are determined by material evidence and not by the sheer weight of a great number of witnesses. In my view, all the testimony established was that the grievants were in the building, A— on off-duty hours and W— during duty hours, both were engaged in an activity which interfered with the efficiency of operations. Supervisors who were on duty took little or no action to correct this situation. Finally, there is no doubt that intra-Union politics have been brought into the facility.

In regard to Union politics, I feel that an Employer should not concern himself with such activity unless it is brought into the work place and seriously interferes with the efficiency of the operation. In such event, the Employer has the right to take appropriate action which will get such activity out of his facility. However, in doing so, he must maintain a posture of neutrality. In my view, a suspension of those engaged in such activity followed by a special conference as provided for in Article 27, would have been the procedure to follow.

Arbitrators have often been criticized for the dicta in their opinions, often times the dicta is an expression of their experience and a desire to assist the parties in avoiding similar errors in the future. To that end, may I say this is the first facility I know of which permits employees to come back in on their off duty hours. In addition, the maintenance of discipline is a function and responsibility of management which should be assumed by its supervision. Why supervision would permit employees to interfere with the efficiency of their department and permit their employees to loiter and congregate with an off duty employee is beyond my understanding.

I am not persuaded that grievant A—'s visit was for the sole purpose of "giving some slippers to a patient." Nor am I persuaded that grievant W— "didn't know anything about a petition." On the other hand, A— has been an employee for five years and three months and has an unblemished record. W— has been an employee since July 25, 1965, and she, too, has an unblemished record.

Both grievants are officers of the Chapter, both testified that they have been attending courses in labor relations. It follows that both should know and should exercise good judgment in pursuing their Union activity, in this case their Union politics, in such a manner so as to not unduly interfere with their Employer's business. This they did not do, nor did they indicate at the hearing that they will refrain from doing so.

AWARD

The Employer failed to meet the burden of proof required to sustain the charges brought against both grievants. The grievants, officers of the Chapter, displayed poor judgment and engaged in activities which interfered with the normal operations of the facility. However, in view of supervision's failure to take action at the time grievants engaged in such activity, the grievants' long seniority standing and unblemished records, discharge is too severe. They are to be reinstated with no loss of seniority or other fringe benefits, and are to be awarded back pay from April 28, 1974. Back pay is to be computed at eight (8) hours per day, five (5) days per week, less the usual deductions for unemployment compensation benefits and earnings earned elsewhere. Reinstatement to be effective as soon as possible from date of this award.

Case No. 29

*In an effort to prevent patients from becoming
involved in internal hospital–union affairs, did the
Hospital have the right to prohibit employees from
engaging in union activities on its property? Did the
Hospital's action infringe on the employees'
Constitutional right to freedom of speech?*

Metropolitan Hospital and Health Centers (Detroit, Mich.)
and
Office and Professional Employees International Union, Local 42

Arbitrator: George T. Roumell, Jr.
Date of Award: August 26, 1974
Citation: 63 LA 378

In September, 1972, the Hospital (Metropolitan Hospital and Health Centers) promulgated a work rule prohibiting employees from passing out unauthorized literature. This rule was enacted following a history of the distribution of literature in the Hospital from unknown sources which challenged certain Hospital policies and resulted in the Hospital believing it was obliged to answer such literature.

In August, 1973, this rule was again reviewed by the Hospital's Board of Directors following the receipt of union literature by a member of the Hospital Board who received same while a patient in the Hospital. As a result, on August 31, 1973, the Hospital promulgated the following rule:

> Periodically unauthorized literature has been distributed at Metropolitan Hospitals and its Health Centers. All employees are advised that the continuing policy of the Hospital on the distribution of literature is as follows:

1.   No employee is permitted to distribute literature or participate in the distribution of literature in any area of the Hospitals or Health Centers without the express written authorization from Administration for each item to be distributed.

2.   No employee is permitted to bring in or distribute at any time on Hospital and Health Center property, literature which may be libelous, defamatory, scurrilous, abusive or insulting or any literature which would tend to disrupt order, discipline or patient care at the Hospitals or Health Centers.

Any employee who brings in or distributes literature or participates in the distribution of literature in violation of this policy is subject to discipline up to and including discharge.

In August of 1973, the office of the Professional Employees International Union Local 42, AFL–CIO ("Union") caused an education committee to be formed to serve the employees represented by the union at the Hospital. The Education Committee held meetings for union membership at the Hospital using the cafeteria with the first meeting being held on September 20, 1973. There were two meetings held in October and one each in November and December, 1973. The Hospital granted permission to use the cafeteria for the second October meeting and the December meeting. A meeting was scheduled for January, 1974; however, the Hospital withdrew permission for said meeting and the meeting was not held on the Hospital premises.

In connection with the meetings that were held on Hospital premises, the committee distributed literature which included material concerning objections to the wage controls suggesting they were unfavorable to hospital employees and raising questions concerning sex discrimination.

On January 12, 1974 the Hospital wrote the following letter to Mrs. Mabel Holleran, President of Local 42, objecting to the Education Committee's distribution of literature on Hospital premises and in so doing, said in part:

On Friday, January 11, copies of a publication entitled "Lets Get Together," published by OPEIU, Local 42's Education Committee (Metropolitan Hospital Unit) were distributed widely throughout the Hospital to employees and to patients. Such action is in complete violation of Hospital rules and, theoretically, it would make the members of the Education Committee of the Hospital unit be subject to immediate discharge. Members of the Committee, however, may not be aware that our policy refers to the Committee members as well as to individuals. This letter will serve as a warning that if such literature is distributed in the future by the Education Committee or any other committee, the members of that committee will be subject to immediate discharge.

Because the action of the Education Committee in distributing the above mentioned literature is contrary to the interests of the institution, no further meetings of the Education Committee will be allowed on any Hospital or Health Center premises effective immediately. This confirms the conversation that you and I had over the telephone on January 11.

As a result, the union on January 28, 1974 filed the following grievance and requested the following relief:

NATURE OF GRIEVANCE: On 1-14-74, the employer issued a letter to the union barring the Education Committee of the Union from using the premises of the Hospital for its education sessions; specifically banning the literature of the Education Committee in the Hospitals; and threatening to dismiss members of the Education Committee if their literature appeared in the Hospital, regardless of how it got there. This action interferes with the freedom of speech, press and activity required by the union for effective functioning. It violates the relationship between the parties established by past practice as an implication of union recognition, Article I, Section 1, and deprives employees of effective union representation. Furthermore, the action lowers working conditions for the entire membership, violating Article XIII, Section 14; unjustly disciplines the entire membership in violation of Article VI, Section 10; and discriminates against the entire membership for its union activity, in violation of Article XIII, Section 1. Finally, the action represents discipline of the members of the Education Committee without cause (Article VI, Section 10) and discrimination against them for their union activity (Article XIII, Section 1), as well as threats of further such action.

SETTLEMENT DESIRED: The letter of 1-14-74 must be rescinded, and the employer must cease and desist from interfering with meetings and literature of the Education Committee. Education Committee meetings on Hospital premises must be reinstated. Members of the Education Committee must not be disciplined or threatened for carrying out their legitimate education functions including the production and distribution of education material.

At page 10, of its post hearing brief the union states the issue of its rights as follows:

The central issue in the present grievance is the right of Union employees, collectively organized in the Union and acting through their duly-elected Education Committee, to freedom of speech, press and assembly on Hospital premises. The Union contends that the Employer's "property rights" and "management rights" must yield to the employees' democratic rights in the present case, under the terms of the Agreement and in the light of the practices hithertofore followed by the parties and the general practice in labor-management relations.

From the beginning, it is plain that no provisions of the Agreement directly permit the Union to distribute Union literature and hold Union meetings on Hospital premises, nor does any provision forbid the Union to do so. Likewise, no provision directly requires the Employer to permit such distribution and such meetings, nor does any provision permit the Employer to refuse such permission. However, in the view of the Union, several provisions of the Agreement, taken in light of the practices hithertofore followed by the parties and the general practice in labor-management relations, do add up to a guarantee of the Union's right to distribute Union literature in non-work areas on non-working time, and to hold meetings of established Union bodies on Hospital premises.

The Hospital frames the issue by referring to its alleged rights under the management rights clause, Article II, of the collective bargaining agreement which provides as follows:

The Employer shall retain the exclusive right to direct and schedule the working force and hours of work, plan, direct and control operations, discontinue or reorganize any department, promulgate and enforce reasonable rules and regulations except where the same may be in conflict with the terms of this Agreement. However, Management agrees to discuss with the Union the discontinuance, and/or reorganization of any department, and/or the elimination of any job within the bargaining unit before such actions are taken.

The Hospital takes the position that its no distribution of literature rule is consistent with the rights of management to promulgate and enforce reasonable work rules.

In their excellent book, How Arbitration Works (3rd Ed.) BNA 1973 at 415-417 Professor Frank Elkouri and Edna Elkouri recognize the basic proposition that in negotiating a collective bargaining agreement management retains its managerial rights unless it gives rights up in the contract. In so recognizing this principle the Elkouris note the following statements:

In any study of arbitration the view taken by arbitrators in regard to management rights is of great interest and importance. Many arbitrators have expressly recognized that the residual powers are in management. To illustrate the variations in arbitral statements recognizing the "residual" or "reserved" rights doctrine, we may note the following:

Arbitrator Harry J. Dworkin: "It is axiomatic that an employer retains all managerial rights not expressly forbidden by statutory law in the absence of a collective bargaining agreement. When a collective bargaining agreement is entered into, these managerial rights are given up only to the extent evidenced in the agreement."

Arbitrator Lewis E. Solomon: "Collective bargaining agreements, generally, are devised to establish and grant certain rights to employees, which rights they would not otherwise have under common law. It is also a normal and well recognized principle in the interpretation of such Agreements that the rights of management are limited and curtailed only to the degree to which it has yielded specified rights. The right of Management to operate its business and control the working force may be specifically reserved in a labor agreement. However, even in the absence of such a specific reservations clause, as is the case here, those rights are inherent and are nevertheless reserved and maintained by it and its decisions with respect to the operations of the business and the direction of the working forces may not be denied, rejected, or curtailed unless the same are in clear violation of the terms of the contract, or may be clearly implied, or are so clearly arbitrary or capricious as to reflect an intent to derogate the relationship."

Arbitrator John Day Larkin: "Initially before unions came into the picture, all power and responsibility in all aspects of personnel management were vested in the company and its officials. Except for certain limitations imposed by Federal, state or local legislative enactments, there were no limitations on management's prerogatives. When a union is formed, and a collective bargaining agreement is entered into, the original power and authority of the company is modified only to the extent that it voluntarily and specifically relinquishes facets of its power and authority. * * * In short, the Company does not have to bargain with the Union to get 'rights' which are inherent in the management function; but it may relinquish certain of those rights in the course of bargaining with the Union."

In recognition of the "residual" or "reserved" rights discussed above, the Hospital in Article II of the collective bargaining agreement has retained its management rights "except where the same may be in conflict with the terms of this Agreement." Specifically, the Hospital reserved what some consider as residual rights, to wit: the right to "promulgate and enforce reasonable rules and regulations." Thus, this Arbitrator finds a contract that reserves management rights and specifically reserves to management the right to promulgate and enforce reasonable rules. This Arbitrator, however, finds no prohibition against limiting distribution of union material or any requirements to provide union meeting space in the Hospital except as provided in Article VI, Section 14, providing for meetings between the Grievance Committee and the Stewards, and as provided in Article VII, Section 5, providing for an office for the Unit Chairman.

The test of the reasonableness of a work rule "is whether or not the rule is reasonably related to legitimate objectives of management." *Robertshaw Controls Co.*, 55 LA 283, 286 (Block, 1960).

The Hospital alleges that the no distribution rule is related to the Hospital's ability to manage its institutions. The Hospital claims that in the past material distributed has come into patients' hands while they have been confined to the Hospital. Furthermore, literature of the Education Committee has currently been found not only in the employees locker room, but in the emergency room where patients frequent. The Hospital maintains that as it is a private institution, it has the right to insist that its patients be isolated from any union-management dialogues or concerns or for that matter any other type of activity nonrelated to health care. Likewise, the Hospital maintains that except as it has agreed to by contract, it is not obligated to provide meeting rooms to the union.

The footing of the union's claim that it should be permitted to distribute the material of the Education Committee rests on the decision of the National Labor Relations Board in *Stoddard–Quirk Mfg. Co.*, 138 NLRB 615, 51 LRRM 1110 (1962). The Board held that although an employer has a legitimate interest in cleanliness, order and discipline, as a property right, these rights are diminished to permit the distribution of literature in nonworking areas in an organizational situation. The *Stoddard–Quirk* decision is an extension of the United States Supreme Court decision in *Republic Aviation Corporation* 324 U.S. 793, 16 LRRM 620 (1945) which recognized that under Section 7 of the National Labor Relations Act[1] employees had the right to solicit during working time on the employer's premises regardless of the employer's property right claim.

There have, however, been recognized limitations of *Republic Aviation* and *Stoddard–Quirk*. The National Labor Relations Board has found that in an organizational situation a rule barring distribution "in such manner as to litter the plant" was valid despite *Stoddard–Quirk*. *Litton Industries*, 192 NLRB 119, 78 LRRM 1041 (1971). Only recently the National Labor Rela-

---

[1] Sec. 7. Employees shall have the right to self-organization, to form, join, or assist labor organizations, to bargain collectively through representatives of their own choosing, and to engage in other concerted activities for the purpose of collective bargaining or other mutual aid or protection, and shall also have the right to refrain from any or all of such activities except to the extent that such right may be affected by an agreement requiring membership in a labor organization as a condition of employment as authorized in section 8(a)(3). [49 Stat. 452, 29 U.S. Code, Sec. 157, as amended by P. L. 101, 80th Cong, 1st Sess.]

tions Board upheld a company rule prohibiting employees from entering or remaining on the employer's premises when not on duty or scheduled to work for the purpose of solicitation or distribution. *GTE Lenkurt, Inc.*, 204 NLRB 75, 83 LRRM 1684. The courts have even gone so far as to deny union representatives access to the employer's two ships which were constantly on the sea even though the courts acknowledged that there was "great practical difficulty" faced by the union in communicating with the employees in their organizational attempt. The Eighth Circuit held that the employer's property rights and production facilities would be impaired. *NLRB v. Sioux City & New Orleans Barge Lines*, 472 F.2d 753, 82 LRRM 2488 (CA 8, 1971).

Finally, the courts have recognized that no solicitation and no distribution rules may be valid in retail stores and other business where the public co-mingles with the employees as contrasted to a *Republic Aviation* situation where there is no such co-mingling. Thus, the courts have recognizes that even in organizational situations retail department stores may ban distribution and solicitation on selling floor and selling areas. *May Department Stores Co.*, 316 F.2d, 797, 53 LRRM 2172 (CA 6, 1963). Because of the co-mingling of patients with employees the principle as set forth in *May Department Stores* applies to the Hospital here. The employees in the Hospital are not isolated from the public as they would be if working in a manufacturing situation.

The purpose of the above discussion is to illustrate that even if this was a situation involving the statutory rights of employees under the National Labor Relations Act in organizational situations, there would be serious question as to whether or not the union could insist on the broad distribution rights that it claims here. But the point here is that the Arbitrator is not dealing with a statutory right. There is no organizational situation here. The union has been recognized. There is a collective bargaining agreement. This is the critical point.

In *NLRB v. Magnavox Co.*, 415 U.S. 322, 85 LRRM 2475 (U.S. Supreme Court February 1974) the Court found that the National Labor Relations Board properly held that an employer violated Section 8(a)(1) of the Labor Management Relations Act by maintaining a rule forbidding distribution of literature in nonworking areas during nonworking time, notwithstanding the union's contractual waiver of any objections to the rule. The case arose in an organizing situation. The decision of the Board 195 NLRB No. 40, 79 LRRM 1285 (1972) contains the following footnote:

> As our holding is concerned solely with the exercise by employees of their Section 7 rights, it is not to be taken as licensing in any way the distribution of institutional — as distinguished from purely organizational — literature of a labor organization which has acquiesced

in an employer's promulgation of maintenance of a broad non-distribution rule.

The above footnote at 195 NLRB No. 40, 79 LRRM 1285 emphasizes the point. The *Stoddard–Quirk Manufacturing Co.* case and its progeny deal with statutory rights or organization rights as contrasted to institutional distribution. Thus, for the reasons already pointed out this is an institutional distribution case involving an already established union and not a case involving organizational rights.

The question here is what does the contract say and what are the rights of management? Although the union relies on the First and Fourteenth Amendments Rights of the United States Constitution, alleging free speech, the union did not contest that this is a private hospital involving private property. The Supreme Court of the United States in 1972 answered the union's claim here. In *Central Hardware Co.* v. *NLRB*, 407 U.S. 539, 80 LRRM 2769 (1973) the court upheld the company's rights in an organizational situation to prevent the union from distributing on a company parking lot and in doing so said at 547, 80 LRRM at 2772:

> Before an owner of private property can be subjected to the commands of the First and Fourteenth Amendments the privately owned property must assume to some significant degree the functional attributes of public property devoted to public use. The First and Fourteenth Amendments are limitations on state action, not on action by the owner of private property used only for private purposes. The only fact relied upon for the argument that Central's parking lots have acquired the characteristics of a public municipal facility is that they are "open to the public." Such an argument could be made with respect to almost every retail and service establishment in the country regardless of size or location. To accept it would cut Logan Valley entirely away from its roots in Marsh. It would also constitute an unwarranted infringement of long-settled rights of private property protected by the First and Fourteenth Amendments. We hold the the Board and the Court of Appeals erred in applying Logan Valley to this case.

Based upon *Central Hardware* it is clear that the constitutional rights alleged are not applicable for this is a private property situation. Furthermore, there is a serious question whether these rights are being abridged. There is nothing prohibiting the union through its own newsletters or through distribution outside of the Hospital from disseminating the information it wishes, other than distribution within the Hospital.

The union's reference to the General Motors contract is not appropo as it is a contract between another employer and another union. The fact that the General Motors Corporation and the UAW saw fit to verify management's rights as to no distribution rules has no bearing here. The contract here reserves the rights of management unless modified by the contractual language. Here the contract specifically gives the right to management to promulgate and enforce real rules and regulations.

Even using the criteria that the courts have used in organizational cases [i.e. *May Department Stores Co.*, 316 F.2d 797, 53 LRRM 2772 (6CA, 1963)] the Hospital was reasonable in promulgating a no distribution rule which among other reasons was designed to prevent patients from becoming involved in internal hospital-union affairs or for that matter involved in anything not related to the patient's purpose for being in the hospital. Furthermore, there is no showing here that the union did not have other methods of communication available to it which would not involve Hospital premises.

As to the right to have a meeting room the answer is clear. Certainly management has reserved the right to control its own property. This contract verifies this point for it specifically provides only two instances whereby the Hospital gives up certain use of the property for the benefit of the union. Nowhere has the Hospital given up the absolute right of the use of its property to the union other than for meetings between the Grievance Committee and Stewards and an office for the unit chairperson. Absent such language which would obligate the Hospital to provide meeting space for the Education Committee, the claim of the union for meeting space is unfounded. Furthermore, the record reveals that space for meetings other than grievance meetings and chairperson office space has only been given with permission to use this space.

Finally, in support of the grievance the union alleges that there has been a binding past practice permitting distribution of literature. The union specifically refers to campaign literature, union election information, some newsletters and literature distributed with the apparent consent of the union and the hospital concerning contract negotiations.

The record reveals that the hospital had no direct knowledge of the union campaign material and of similar union distributions. The record further reveals that the negotiations and contract ratification material was distributed with the permission of the hospital in circumstances whereby the Hospital and the union were attempting to resolve a contractual dispute.

Generally, in order to establish a past practice as binding there must be an element of mutuality as stated in Arbitration & Collective Bargaining by Prasow & Peters at p. 109.

> If the employee benefit is minor, then the practice is a basic management function and the element of mutuality is irrelevant. If the practice was initiated or administered unilaterally, the burden is on the party asserting its validity to establish a sufficient element of mutuality to make

the practice binding. Mutuality or its absence may be proved by conduct in negotiation. The incidence of the practice may be so rare, or its duration so short, or its form and content so fragmentary, that employees can hardly be said to have relied upon it, and therefore a claim of mutuality is specious.

The union certainly cannot show a claim of mutuality under the present circumstances or maintain that the rather infrequent occurance of the distribution of literature established a binding past practice.

In *Jacob Rupert* v. *Office Employees International Union*, 35 LA 503, 504-505 (B. Turkus, 1960). Arbitrator B. Turkus, enumerated the following criteria to determine whether a practice was binding:

1. Does the practice concern a major condition of employment?

2. Was it established unilaterally?

3. Was it administered unilaterally?

4. Did either of the parties seek to incorporate it into the body of the written agreement?

5. What is the frequency or repetition of the "practice"?

6. Is the "practice" a longstanding one?

7. Is it specific and detailed?

8. Do the employees rely on it?

This case does not show that the recognized and requisite criteria appear with sufficient cumulative force and criteria to sustain the position of the union.

The key here is that there must be mutuality in order to establish a binding past practice, particularly when there is no reference in the contract giving the union the right to distribute this material and there is a management rights clause reserving the rights of management that are not modified by the contract. Here, there is a work rule limiting the right of distribution. The predecessor to the present rule was promulgated prior to the existing contract. Now the interesting point is that the union never objected to the predecessor rule nor did it in fact raise objection to the current rule when it was first promulgated. Furthermore, there is no evidence that the Hospital acquiesced in what distribution was going on or that this matter was ever brought up during contract negotiation.

Under the criteria discussed above concerning past practice it is clear that mutuality has not been established to even consider applying the doctrine of past practice particularly in light of Article II which gives the employer the right to promulgate reasonable rules.

Nor can it be said that management is attempting to censor the union's material. The union has other avenues of distributing its material. There has been no showing, even if relevant, that the union could not invoke other methods of distribution *NLRB v. Babock & Wilcox*, 351 U.S. 105, 38 LRRM 2001 (1956). Neither is this a case of a company town where the company controls places and other avenues of communication. *NLRB v. Stowe Spinning Company*, 336 U.S. 226, 23 LRRM 2371 (1949). Finally, this Arbitrator notes that arbitrators in the past, although not faced with the exact situation as here, have, by implication recognized in general the rights of management to limit any activity on company premises absent any contractual provision to the contrary in an institutional situation as contrasted to a statutory organizational situation. *Armour & Co.* 10 LA 43 (Gilden, 1948); *Continental Airlines, Inc.* 56 LA 503 (Ross, 1960).

For the reasons set forth above the grievance must be denied.

AWARD

The grievances are denied.

Part V

Discrimination
and Bona Fide
Job Qualification

Case No. 30

*Could a female employee's application for an
Orderly vacancy be rejected solely on the basis of
sex? Were the business and medical reasons for
placing a male orderly on the night shift
sufficient to overcome the Hospital's obligations
under the nondiscrimination provision?*

**Jackson Osteopathic Hospital (Jackson, Mich.)
and
Hospital Employees Division of the Service Employees
International Union, Local 79**

Arbitrator: Howard A. Cole
Date of Award: June 15, 1974
Citation: 193 AAA 2

This matter has arisen under the parties' Agreement dated January 23,
1973. Article IV, Section 9 thereof provides for posting of notices of job
vacancies in the bargaining unit, and with respect to selection of employees
for transfer it states:

(a)   An employee shall be selected for transfer to another classification
on the basis of his ability to perform the work of the other classification.
An employee's written attendance and productivity record will be
evaluated in considering his ability to perform the new classification. In
cases where ability is judged to be equal the transfer will be given to the
employee within the department with the most seniority. If no employee
within the department applies for the transfer then the employee with
the most seniority will be given the transfer where ability is judged to be
equal.

Article XII provides:

> There shall be no discrimination under any circumstances because of
> race, creed, age, sex, proper union activity, marital status or national
> origin. On questions of promotions, only an employee's seniority and
> ability shall be considered. There shall be no discrimination on any of the
> points listed above. Notwithstanding the above the Hospital retains the
> right to retire any employee at age sixty-five (65) or to continue the
> employment of any employee past age sixty-five (65) if the employee is
> rendering satisfactory service to the Hospital.

The Agreement's Appendix "A" — Wage Schedule sets forth seven different
hourly rate ranges, arranged in seven different columns. One of the columns
bears the following heading:

NURSE

AIDES

ORDERLIES

There is a written job description for "Nurse Aide — Nursing
Department," dated February 12, 1974, and signed by Hospital Personnel
Director Gordon L. Dillingham and Union Business Agent K. A. Davis. This
superseded an earlier written and undated job description for "Nurse Aide —
Nursing Department." There is also an undated written job description for
"Orderly." The Union states that the latter two job descriptions were never
approved by it.

*   *   *   *   *

In November 1973, the Hospital posted a notice of a job vacancy for
Orderly on the 11 A.M. to 7 P.M. shift. On November 30, 1973, Betty Bradley
applied for the position. Ms. Bradley was a Nurse Aide on the 7 A.M. to 3
P.M. shift. She had been employed by the Hospital as a Nurse Aide since
August 1970. According to her, she applied for the position because it was on
the 11 P.M. to 7 A.M. shift — this shift being more convenient for her and also
carrying a shift differential of fifteen cents per hour.

The Hospital rejected Ms. Bradley's application. It is agreed that the
rejection was because of her sex. The Hospital contends that one of the
legitimate qualifications of the Orderly job is that the job's occupant be a male.

Ms. Bradley proceeded to file the instant grievance under date of
December 10, 1973, citing Article XII and charging discrimination because of
her sex.

*   *   *   *   *

The arbitrator's function is to decide duly processed grievances involving claimed violations of the Agreement. He must make his decision in accordance with the Agreement. He is expressly prohibited from adding to, subtracting from, changing, modifying, or disregarding any of the provisions of the Agreement (Article V, Section 1, Step 3).

Thus, just as Article XII of the Agreement is binding upon each of the parties, so is it binding upon the arbitrator. Aritcle XII states, broadly and plainly, that "There shall be no discrimination under any circumstances because of. . . sex. . ." It is noted that this is a general prohibition; it appears to be applicable to all transfers, whether or not they involve promotion.

Clearly and admittedly, the Hospital refused to consider Ms. Bradley for the here involved Orderly job vacancy because of her sex. Her application was rejected, because she was female. If she were male, she would have been considered. As the arbitrator sees it, there is simply no reasonable way of escaping the conclusion that this constituted discrimination because of sex. This being so, an Article XII violation must be found, unless it can somehow be inferred that a here applicable exception is attached to the article.

The term "Orderly" does not of itself provide a valid and adequate basis for such an exception. The Hospital has cited *Taber's Cyclopedic Medical Dictionary*, which defines "orderly" as a "male" hospital attendant who performs certain work and has certain responsibilities. On the other hand, the "male" element does not appear in the definition of "orderly" in dictionaries such as *Webster's Third New International Dictionary* and *Black's Law Dictionary*. Moreover, whatever the overall dictionary score might be, and whatever may be the image customarily evoked by the word "orderly" in the mind of the average hospital employee, it seems too strained to find an exception to the clear and simple language of Article XII on the basis of a job title alone. It is interesting to note that the Hospital's job description of Orderly, although setting forth responsibilities and qualifications of the job in considerable detail, says nothing about the sex of the job occupant.

The Hospital has relied upon practice. The evidence does show that all past occupants of Orderly positions at the Hospital have been male. However, this is too slim a reed to support the notion that the parties intended an Article XII exception with respect to Orderlies. For, among other considerations, there is no indication that any female ever applied for an Orderly job prior to the instant situation; accordingly, the issue never came up, and the parties' intentions were never tested. Furthermore, in this particular collective bargaining relationship, practice has been significantly downgraded by Article XVII, Section 1 of the Agreement, which reads:

This Agreement constitutes the entire collective bargaining agreement between the parties. Accordingly, all past or present, oral or written, express or implied agreements, practices or understandings between the

Hospital and employees or Union not specifically included in this Agreement are of no further force and effect.

The Hospital's principal contention has been stated by it as follows: "The anti-discrimination provision of the Agreement permits the Hospital to discriminate because of sex regarding transfers and promotions when sex is a bonafide occupational qualification reasonably necessary to the normal operation of the Hospital's business." It urges that the arbitrator apply to Article XII the "bonafide occupational qualification" exception contained in Title VII of the Civil Rights Act of 1964. In response, the Union maintains (1) that the arbitrator should confine his decision to the four corners of the Agreement and not read a "bonafide occupational qualification" exception into the Agreement from the existing law, and (2) that the here involved sexual classification is for mere administrative convenience and not supported by existing law.

In the opinion of the arbitrator, the Hospital has shown strong reasons, both business and medical, for having a male Orderly on the 11 P.M. to 7 A.M. shift. However, he fails to see how a "bonafide occupational qualification" exception can be read into Article XII of the Agreement, simply because such an exception is contained in the law. Actually, the presence of the exception in the law serves to emphasize its absence in Article XII. If the parties had intended such an exception, why did they not write it into Article XII, just as it was written into the law? It must be presumed that they did not write such an exception into Article XII, because they did not mean it to be there. This view is strengthened by their use of the heavy words "under any circumstances." If Article XII's sex discrimination ban is to apply "under any circumstances," then it must apply even in circumstances where a particular sex may in fact be a bonafide occupational qualification.

In keeping with all of the foregoing, and notwithstanding his sympathy with many of the Hospital's concerns in this matter, the arbitrator is constrained to find that the instant grievance is contractually well founded and must therefore be sustained.

The arbitrator does not understand, either from Ms. Bradley's grievance or from the Union's arbitration presentation, that any retroactivity is being requested by way of remedy. Further, he notes that the Hospital refrained from filling the job which was the subject of the here involved posting. From the date of the posting until the date of the arbitration hearing, there was in fact no Orderly on the 11 P.M. to 7 A.M. shift. It appears that the Hospital's November 1973 determination to post such a job was premised upon its honestly held (albeit mistaken) belief that the male qualification was legitimate and enforceable. It does not seem unreasonable to permit the Hospital to reevaluate its 11 P.M. to 7 A.M. staffing needs in the light of this arbitration decision. Under all of the presented circumstances, the remedy set forth in the award seems reasonable and appropriate.

AWARD

The Hospital violated Article XII of the Agreement by refusing to consider Bradley's application for the job vacancy of Orderly on the 11 P.M. to 7 A.M. shift posted in November 1973. If there is another posting for such a vacancy during the term of the current Agreement, and if Ms. Bradley duly applies for the opening, her application shall be duly considered and shall not be rejected because of her sex.

Case No. 31

*Did a Hospital wrongfully discriminate against male
Licensed Vocational Nurses (LVN) by refusing to
assign them to "sensitive personal care" of female
patients? After determining that two male orderlies
should not have been promoted to LVN because
there were not enough male patients for them to
work with, did the Hospital have the right to demote
them to orderlies again?*

**Kaiser Foundation Hospitals and Medical Center, et al. (Bellflower, Calif.)
and
Hospital, Institutional and Professional Division, Local 399, BSEIU**

Arbitrator: Edgar A. Jones, Jr.
Date of Award: June 26, 1967
Citation: 48 LA 1138

Two male employees, each presently classified as Orderly, have filed grievances against their employer, Kaiser's Bellflower hospital, complaining of discrimination based on their sex. Each is licensed by the State of California as a Licensed Vocational Nurse (LVN). Admittedly, the hospital refuses to allow them to work in the LVN classification because they are men. This is because the male LVN at Bellflower would have to perform "sensitive personal care" for female patients in situations where he would frequently have to be alone in a hospital in intimate physical contact with a female patient. The hospital emphasizes that it does not in the least impugn the professionalism of Grievants. Its management is simply convinced that American female patients will not tolerate men tending to their intimate physical care who are not physicians. That being so, it reasons, male LVN's could not perform a significant percentage of the duties required of LVN's in its Bellflower facility. Therefore, it would be economic waste, a needless surcharge on hospital costs, were it compelled to classify Grievants as LVN's.

It is the specific policy of the Kaiser Foundation that, "No Kaiser Hospital utilizes male LVN's to administer personal female medical care." (Employer Brief, pp. 4, 10-11)

Grievants have also filed charges with the Equal Employment Opportunities Commission, alleging that they have been discriminated against because of their sex, contrary to the Civil Rights Act of 1964. An EEOC investigator has conducted an investigation in Los Angeles and has quite recently filed his report and recommendations with the Commission in Washington. There is no indication of how soon or in what manner the Commission may react to the charges.

The collective agreement (operative August 1, 1966 to August 1, 1969) provides in Article IV, "Management," that:

> The Union recognizes that there are rights and responsibilities belonging solely to the Employer such as, but not limited to, the authority to determine the type and scope of work to be performed and the services and products, if any, to be provided, to establish schedules of operation and workload, and to decide the methods, processes, means and places of providing services and products, except where specifically limited in this Agreement.

Similarly, Section 2 vests exclusively in the employer, "except as may be specifically limited by this Agreement," the "authority to select, direct, adjust, transfer, increase and decrease the working force, to remove employees and to maintain discipline among, and efficiency of, employees."

Section 2 of Article VIII requires that no employee covered by the Agreement "shall, as a result hereof, suffer a reduction in wages or other benefits," the "hereof" referring to the establishment of minimum wage scales.

Section 1 of Article XIX, "Seniority," requires that, in respect of reductions in force, rehiring and promoting, "the principle of seniority in each department and craft shall govern, providing that merit and ability are approximately equal." Section 3 also provides that employees may submit requests "in advance" for higher rated jobs "or equal classifications which may subsequently become vacant within the region covered by this Agreement." Such employees "shall be given first consideration, providing they possess the necessary qualifications for the job." The clause, "within the region covered by this Agreement," was incorporated in the 1966 agreement as a Union proposal because of the previous refusal of the employer to allow transfers from one hospital to another. The language was not intended to relate to intra-hospital transfers.

The LVN is an occupational classification requiring greater skills and a higher order of responsibility than is expected of an Orderly. But the LVN must undergo significantly less training and education than does a Registered Nurse. In California, as in other states, the LVN is an occupation licensed by the state. The license is issuable only upon proof of the completion of a certain program of training and experience. The evolution of the LVN category reflects both the national shortage of registered nurses and the sense in the medical profession and among hospital administrators of a need for professionally trained personnel to replace the nonprofessional aides once commonly used.

Kaiser Foundation Hospitals operates five hospitals in Southern California, four of which are covered by a collective agreement with the Union. That at Bellflower, the hospital involved in these two grievances, numbers 176 beds in a multi-storied building. It opened its doors on July 19, 1965. Expansion is now planned to 300 beds, possibly 400. Its Harbor hospital has 169 beds housed in a single story. Its Sunset hospital, a multi-storied building, has 350 beds and 100 additional are planned in a new wing. The fourth is located in Panorama City.

The Bellflower hospital is organized around modules of twelve patients each. To each module is assigned a nursing team of one Registered Nurse (RN) and one Licensed Vocational Nurse (LVN). Six patients are assigned to each, but presently the RN also has the responsibility of issuing medications as prescribed by the attending physicians. Shortly, however, the LVN's, now being trained to do so, will also issue medications. This modular approach to patient care is designed around twelve-bed blocks in order to increase the efficiency and direct contact of the nursing personnel with the individual patient. It requires the LVN member of the team to handle female as well as male patients. At Bellflower the sixth, seventh and eighth floors of the hospital contain medical, surgical and pediatric patients. There is no separate orthopedic area where a male LVN would be needed to manhandle the weights and hoist mechanisms. Nor is there a distinct geriatric area comprised of older male patients.

In contrast, the Kaiser Harbor hospital in the San Pedro area has a substantial number of older male patients, many of whom are Longshoremen pensioners. It has employed a male LVN on the afternoon shift since September of 1965. He is a middle-aged man who teamworks along with an RN. They routinely divide 16–20 patients, men and women, between them. He testified that he gives and removes bed pans; distributes medications and food trays; feeds the patients where necessary; prepares female as well as male patients for hernial operations; changes dressings affecting the "personal areas" of female patients and is authorized to give them douches but not enemas. As to the latter, he calls the female RN to take over. He also runs the post-operative forced inhalation pneumonia-preventative machine (IPPB) and administers oxygen therapy.

Male LVN's also are employed at Kaiser's Sunset hospital. This is so, the employer declares, because the size and configuration of that hospital enable male LVN's to be efficiently utilized without assignments to personal female patient care. Indeed, as a settlement the employer offered to transfer Grievants to that hospital in the LVN classification. This was rejected by them since they preferred working in the Bellflower facility and felt they were contractually and legally (aside from the collective agreement) entitled to work there as LVN's.

Each Grievant is an Orderly. The employer's expectations of the duties of an Orderly, as expressed in the "Position Description" prepared by it for its own use (i.e., not negotiated), are that he transports patients from point to point in the hospital; obtains or delivers items; "preps" male patients for surgery; assists in the physical moving of patients; performs catheterizations of male patients; serves meals to and assists in feeding patients; instructs and assists in the use of crutches and the like; prepares deceased patients for and takes corpses to the morgue. The general description of the "primary purpose" of the position is stated to be as follows:

> Under direct supervision, performs various services not involving patients, to assist in providing patient care; provides limited patient care as directed; and performs related duties as required.

The classification of LVN-Medical contains a statement of its "primary purpose" as follows:

> Under supervision and within defined limits, gives competent nursing care to assigned medical unit patients.

According to the Position Description this entails taking and recording temperature, pulse, respiration and blood pressures; reporting symptoms and complaints; preparing and giving vaginal, colonic or colostomy irrigations; preparing and giving enemas and catheterizations; collecting and recording excretion specimens; assist physicians in examinations and treatments; "preping" patients for surgery; "apply and remove dressings for selected 'cases' ; "give "direct nursing care" to assigned patients (e.g., bathe; clean and change "incontiment" patients; perform oral hygiene; make beds; serve meals; assist in and out of bed; dress and undress; teach use of needed devices, etc.); do requisite paper work, including charting.

Grievant William Gatzke was hired in June of 1965, as an Orderly. In 1960–63, having been trained as a medical aid man, he had served in the army in an aid station in Korea, working with male and female patients, and then in Fort Leonard Wood, Missouri. In early July of 1966, having received his LVN certificate in May, 1966, he notified the Bellflower Director of Nursing, Mrs. Dolsen, that he had obtained his LVN certification. She congratulated him for upgrading himself and then telephoned personnel to notify them of that fact and that she okayed his license and directed them to put his photostat of it in his record. She then told him to go to the personnel office and show them his license. This he did and changes were recorded in his file. His classification at that time was changed from Orderly to LVN, effective July 25, 1966. He was aware of this because in the next pay period the labor code of 572 (Orderly) was changed on his pay check to that of 576 (LVN), a change requiring the approval signatures of both the Director of Nurses and the hospital's Administrator. At that time, the rate of pay for an LVN was the same as for an Orderly. But, effective August 1, the LVN pay rate for a one-year employee was increased so that a two-cent per hour differential was created. On October 1, 1966, the rate increased so that the differential became 14 cents per hour.

Grievant Andre Boutin served four years in the Navy, becoming a Hospital Mate 2nd Class, including service on Sick Officers Quarters in the naval hospital at Newport, Rhode Island, on a male-female, medical-surgical intensive care unit. He then attended Operating Room school at Chelsea, New Hampshire, preparatory to spending two years in an OR on board ship. He was hired by Kaiser as a Surgical Technician at the Harbor hospital 18 months before requesting transfer to the lower paid but regular hours job of Orderly in Central Supply. He went to work in that capacity at Bellflower in October of 1965. On September 5, 1966, he was reclassified from Orderly to LVN after speaking to the Director of Nursing, Mrs. Dolsen, who okayed his LVN license for the personnel office when they were unable to find his name on the hospital's LVN registry. Before he had had the opportunity to discuss the matter with her but after he had sought to make an appointment for that purpose, she observed to him in the hall one day that, "I hear you want to make a penny more an hour." His duties in Central Supply continued unchanged after he was reclassified to LVN.

Sometime in October of 1966, Mrs. Dolsen, on rounds, spoke to Grievant Boutin in the hall, telling him that she couldn't afford to pay him the new LVN raise just negotiated by the Union retroactive to August 1, 1966. Discussion followed between Grievant Boutin and Mrs. Dolsen with Mr. Vernon Brammer, the hospital administrator in charge of the Bellflower facility. He explained to Grievant that an on-rolls study had turned up the fact that both Grievants were paid the newly boosted LVN rate although their duties continued, necessarily, to be those of Orderly, since they could not perform "sensitive female care." Mr. Brammer acknowledged their LVN certificates but said possession of the certificates could not automatically mean classification at the higher rate irrespective of the duties they were to perform. If he were to hire a lawyer to do gardening work, he reasoned to them, he could only pay him the gardener's rate irrespective of his lawyer's license to practice law. At that time, he offered to promote Grievant Boutin to Surgical Technician, but he rejected it for the same reasons that he had left that job earlier, lack of free time and night calls.

Grievant Gatzke was given substantially the same explanation by Mrs. Dolsen, namely, that the hospital could not afford to maintain them in the LVN classification at the new increased rates when their duties could only be those of Orderly. She said that there was no justification at Bellflower for a male LVN, in her judgment and that of her superiors.

Both men were reclassified from LVN to Orderly on November 9, 1966. The Union protested on November 17 and requested they be restored to the LVN classification and paid retroactively. "If the demotion occurred because of their sex," wrote Mr. Mike McDermott for the Union to Mr. Brammer, the Administrator of the Bellflower hospital, "I must point out to you that the Civil Rights Act prohibits discrimination because of sex." The Union relies on the Seniority Article which establishes seniority by department and craft for promotions, reductions in force and rehires. It also privileges requests for transfer to higher or equal rated jobs "within the region covered by this Agreement." (Article XIX, Sections 1 and 3) It also involves the provision which prohibits "reduction in wages or other benefits" by virtue of the execution of the Agreement. This, it argues, bars reduction of Grievants from LVN to Orderly due to the increased wage cost of the LVN category.

The employer responds that an administrative error resulted in the original upgrading, that management has the right to withhold male employees from engaging in sensitive female care and that, therefore, Grievants have no justifiable complaint.

Analysis and Conclusions

It is necessary at the outset of this analysis to recall some distinctions which are crucial to the resolution of this difficult and delicate problem. It is difficult because it is necessary to relate the accommodation of important aspects of public policy to the effectuation of private contractual intent. It is delicate because its disposition involves matters of intimate concern to feminine patients.

We confront the problem in the context of an arbitration conducted in accordance with a contractual obligation voluntarily undertaken by the parties to a collective bargaining agreement. Thus, contractually, we have a dispute between the Union and the Employer, pitting their institutional interests one against the other. But it is one which also (and typically) affects the employment rights and the welfare of two employees. As a matter of law, the decision here will be final and binding as between the parties to the collective agreement. It is an aspect of national labor policy, repeatedly affirmed by the Supreme Court, that arbitral awards normally be accorded a degree of finality making them immune to judicial review on the merits.

In this case, however, the decision may not in fact result in finality because of the existence of employee interests which are legally cognizable independently of the collective bargaining relationship. Essentially, those interests are describable in terms of the public policy against invidious discrimination based on racial, religious or ethnic grounds. They have thus far had their chief legislative expression in the Civil Rights Act of 1964. But they have for a number of years been increasingly indicated in federal and state courts, most notably in the past dozen or so years in the United States Supreme Court. Perhaps less visibly but nevertheless in reality, however, the public interest in eliminating discriminatory retaliation against citizens has had a counterpart expression in labor arbitration. When called upon in the operation of grievance procedures arbitrators routinely have not hesitated to remedy proven instances of discriminatorily motivated employer action. Since this is a known pattern of arbitral decision it may be anticipated that finality is likely to be accorded to arbitral awards in this problem area as in others, whether before the federal Equal Employment Opportunities Commission or a reviewing court, so long as it is apparent that the matter was carefully considered and resolved.*

There is currently a good deal of discussion of whether a labor arbitrator should concern himself with public policy factors extraneous to the contract. It is unnecessary for the purpose of this decision to confront that complex matter. This is so because there is such a marked identity of issues when an employer's discrimination is alleged to exist in a bargaining unit covered by a collective agreement containing an arbitration provision. The coincident existence of the proscriptions of the Civil Rights Act superimposes no discrimination policy on the bargaining relationship which has not already been rather widely recognized for some time by arbitrators to be an incident of the employment relationship to be vindicated through the arbitral tribunal

---

*Arbitrator's hindsight footnote (June 1974). In a unanimous decision in early 1974, the Supreme Court in *Alexander v. Gardner-Denver, Inc.*, decided that an aggrieved employee complaining of racial discrimination, disappointed in an arbitrator's decision, may still press his Title VII claim in a later judicial proceeding without being barred by the contrary arbitral award. The Court did, however, in footnotes 15 and 21 to its opinion, suggest that "great weight" might be given an arbitrator's award as a matter of judicial discretion, depending on the arbiter's professional standing (a new element in the equation of review), the factors considered by him, and the state of the record before him. So the question now is whether the Court may yet adopt a modified deference of the type applied in its *Steelworkers Trilogy Cases* and reaffirmed in another 1974 decision in *Gateway Coal* (concerning safety problems).

created by the parties. Indeed, the Equal Employment Opportunities Commission is not nearly so expeditious a tribunal as that created by the collective bargainers themselves.

Under the collective agreement, the inquiry is: have the Parties reserved to the hospital's management the exclusive exercise of that kind of experiential judgment which predicts and seeks to avoid adverse reaction among female patients to the use of male LVN's? Under the Civil Rights Act, the issue is: does this preclusive action of the hospital, based on its view of the relevance to institutional nursing care of male-female sexual differences of temperament and disposition, constitute the proscribed "discrimination"? Actually, the answer to the first question is bound to be significant to the second.

It is reasonable to conclude that neither the collective agreement nor the Civil Rights Act proscribes all instances of discrimination based on sex. The evil arises when the discrimination is invidious, when it derogates from the dignity of the man or woman affected. No one is apt to argue that a regulation is proscribed under either agreement or Act which accurately assesses the physical strength of women to be typically less than that of men and therefore bars utilization of women to perform work which foreseeably would be harmful to them.* That is protective rather than invidious discrimination. Thus reasonableness of the act or omission to act may privilege the discrimination effectuated. We turn then to inquire into the reasonableness of Kaiser's policy of assigning male LVN's.

Our society is pluralistic in its moral beliefs and its notions of esthetic propriety. We tolerate, indeed we encourage, a wide spectrum of beliefs and unbeliefs. We do share a very basic commitment, however, to the preservation of the dignity of each individual among us. Although, in the human tradition, we by no means consistently observe that precept, the vast majority among us do affirm its necessity and rightness and regard deviation from it as at least deplorable and often as outrageous. Enactment of the Civil Rights Act of 1964 is but one more reflection of that basic national concern since invidious discrimination based on race, color or creed is a gross affront to the humanness of a man or a woman.

Another aspect of the philosophical attachment to observance of the dignity of the human person is relevant here. It is to be seen in the federal constitutional requirement that governmental officials refrain from acting so as to disturb the "penumbra where privacy is protected from governmental

---

*Arbitrator's hindsight footnote (June 1974). Not only has someone since so argued, a course of decision has now emerged which requires that individual capacity rather than stereotypical conclusions shall govern. Some women, after all, are stronger of mind or body than most men, even as some men similarly excel relative to most women. Individual assessment thus makes a more fair approach to the elimination of stereotypical discrimination.

instrusion."[1] The various amendments of the Bill of Rights "create zones of privacy,"[2] Under their aegis, there is protection against governmental invasion of each individual's "living rights . . . to privacy and repose."[3] This is attributed to "the sanctity of a man's home and the privacies of life" which are based on "his indefeasible right of personal security, personal liberty."[4] Particularly sensitive in this regard is the individual's physical being. The Court has recently barred intrusion by governmental officials into "the notions of privacy surrounding the marriage relationship,"[5] and has sought effectively in recent years to insulate accused or suspected persons from physical manhandling in the course of investigation of suspected wrong doing by them.[6] It has done this by excluding from evidence the fruits of wrongful searches and seizures. At the same time, however, the Court has cautioned that, at least in the investigation of suspected crime, the test cannot be what is considered offensive by the most delicate. Due process, the Court reasoned, "is not measured by the yardstick of personal reaction . . . of the most sensitive person, but by that whole community sense of 'decency and fairness' that has woven by common experience into the fabric of acceptable conduct."[7]

The constitutional emphasis upon individual privacy suggests that there is a sound basis for the concern of the hospital in this case, that its female patients not be subjected to what many of them, in the experience of the hospital's administration, would regard as a highly offensive indignity. This reaction is what it foresees if either the collective agreement or the Civil Rights Act be deemed to compel the hospital to assign male LVN's to perform nursing care of an intimate nature for female patients. That assessment of the proclivities of its female patients is entitled to considerable weight in this proceeding.

The Union asks the Arbitrator to set aside a practice of the hospital and an attitude of its patients, each of long standing, on the ground that they ought no longer to be indulged because progress and equality have outmoded them. But the hospital offers a service for pay and must anticipate what those who must avail of nursing care in its beds will be willing to tolerate. The reasoning must be the same, however, whether the concern is for the sensibilities of female poverty patients or for those who are able to pay for their own way.

[1] *Griswold* v. *Connecticut*, 381 U.S. 479, 483 (1965).

[2] *Id.* at 484.

[3] *Breard* v. *Alexandria*, 341 U.S. 622, 626, 644 (1951).

[4] *Boyd* v. *United States*, 116 U.S. 616, 630 (1886).

[5] *Griswold* v. *Connecticut*, 381 U.S. 479, 486 (1965).

[6] See *Rochin* v. *California*, 342 U.S. 165 (1952).

[7] *Breithaupt* v. *Abram*, 352 U.S. 432, 436 (1957).

Management of the hospital has adopted a policy of discrimination which is related to its anticipation of the desires (and revulsions) of its female patients. It is not an invidious discrimination on the face of it. Nor has evidence been adduced which rebuts the inferences it has drawn from its experience and that of other hospitals. Its judgment is reasonable in the circumstances. It is difficult enough for a sick person to preserve a sense of personality in the necessarily antiseptic atmosphere of a hospital. To be confronted also with the necessity to defend against an unwanted, professionally unnecessary, and traumatically intimate exposure need not be demanded of the many women who would react with embarrassment to the prospect. The hospital has sought to balance the claims of its male LVN's to unbiased treatment with the entitlement of its female patients to as much personal privacy as their straitened circumstances can allow. Its choice to insulate the latter rather than promote the former is an exercise of discretion based on expert judgment which must be upheld. It is discriminatory, indeed, but that actually says little in these circumstances since a decision to the contrary would often result in discrimination against the female patients subjected to the routine but unwanted ministrations of male LVN's.

Thus the conclusion here is that Kaiser Foundation does not wrongfully discriminate against male LVN's by refusing to assign them to tend female patients in the circumstances of intimate personal care. It is evident also that the job functions performable by male LVN's would typically thereby be significantly truncated as against those done by female LVN's. But male-type LVN work is available in some hospitals covered by this collective agreement in sufficient quantity to warrant promotion of qualified male employees to do the work. This reasoning would then be inapposite. Allowable discrimination in one facility of the Foundation means that it must be attentive in other facilities in the bargaining unit to the legitimate interests of male LVN's, even if that means on occasion preferring a male to a female, since it is discrimination within the bargaining unit, which is to say among all the employees, that is proscribed both by the agreement and by the Act.

But the claims of the these particular Grievants are not foreclosed by these conclusions. It is possible, of course, for Kaiser to promote male Orderlies to the LVN classification despite its policy of withholding them from the intimate care of female patients. The decision in this case justifies the administration in refusing a promotion to LVN where the work mix, with that factor deleted, would not warrant full time for a male LVN. But it by no means follows that the demotion of employees already promoted to LVN can be contractually justified.

In the circumstances of this case, authorized hospital personnel participated in the promotion of Grievants to LVN. It was a routine administrative matter routinely effectuated. Their labor codes were appropriately altered to reflect the reclassification. While the administration apparently didn't care two cents about the promotion when it was accomplished, fourteen cents later, after the wage negotiations, the decision began to look like a mistake. It was then too late. A "mistake" under the agreement, warranting return to an erroneously "promoted" employee to his true classification, has to amount to more than a lately recognized act of earlier economic imprudence. For the employer to prevail, the alleged mistake must at the least qualify as a ministerial error not involving judgment but comprising something like mistaken identity, garbled instructions, or the like. And even then it will have to pass muster as balanced against any actual inconvenience or detriment experienced by an employee disadvantaged by the employer's mistake. All this is simply to say that equities rule remedies when mistakes are alleged as the basis for winding the clock backward.

So it is that the ultimate dispositions of the issues raised in this arbitration are, *first*, that the Kaiser Hospital Foundation can properly discriminate against male employees by refusing to promote them to LVN wherever in the hospital system which is encompassed by the bargaining unit that intimate care of female patients is a routine requisite of employees working as an LVN; and, *second*, that these two Grievants, having been duly promoted with none of the indicia of mistake, as they were, cannot now be demoted except for cause other than increased cost or fragmented job function.

AWARD

Grievants Boutin and Gatzke shall be reinstated in the LVN classification and be paid the applicable differential between the Orderly and LVN rates for all time worked at the Bellflower hospital.

Case No. 32

*Did the Clinic have the right to refuse to recall an
X-ray technician from layoff because she was
pregnant? Does a pregnant women who has accepted
the risks of an X-ray technicians job have the
additional right to risk the safety of her unborn
child?*

Centerville Clinics, Inc. (Centerville, Pa.)
and
Office Professional Employees International Union, Local 457

Arbitrator: Alice B. Grant
Date of Award: May 1, 1973
Citation: 60 LA 691

The Issue

Both parties agreed to the following submission:

Did the employer violate Article X of the Agreement when it refused
to recall Mrs. Susan Hoy because of her pregnancy?

As a remedy the Union asks that Mrs. Hoy receive back pay and
allowances from May 10, 1972 to the end of August which was one week in
advance of the birth of her child. The allowances include coverage she would
have received for doctor and hospital bills ($185 for the Doctor's bill and
$497.00 for the hospital bill).

Background

The relevant contract provision is as follows:

ARTICLE X — *Seniority*

Seniority is defined as the employee's length of service with the Employer from the date of most recent employment, except that an employee who terminates employment and is re-hired within one (1) year after the termination shall be given seniority credit for all time accumulated prior to the termination but shall not accumulate seniority during the time away from the Employer. The Employer recognizes the principle of seniority in layoffs, recalls, and promotions within the organization as a whole provided that the employee has the qualifications and ability to efficiently perform the required work.

Seniority shall be broken by: (1) Discharge for just cause, such as, absence from work for a period of two (2) consecutive working days without permission from management or without a reasonable excuse. (2) Voluntary quit (except as qualified above). (3) Layoff of 12 months. (4) Failure to report back to work within ten working days when recalled after a layoff.

Mrs. Hoy, the grievant was employed as an X-Ray Technician for approximately two years before she was laid off on October 26, 1971. In March 1972, about six months later, Mrs Hoy's supervisor in the X-Ray Department phoned to ask her to return to work. Mrs. Hoy was denied the job, however, when the supervisor learned that she was pregnant, and on May 10, 1972, a new person was hired. Following this Mrs. Hoy filed a grievance which was carried through the steps of the grievance procedure ending in this present Arbitration hearing.

Contentions of the Union

The Union charges that the employer acted in a discriminatory manner when it denied Mrs. Hoy the job for the reasons that she was pregnant and that work in the X-Ray Department might constitute a danger to her unborn child. The Union argues that the 1964 Civil Rights Act provides that women receive equal treatment with men and that pregnancy cannot be treated differently from other medical disabilities. The Union cites the case, *Cohen vs. Chesterfield County School Board* (Union Exhibit #1) in which the Court ruled that "since no two pregnancies are alike, decisions of when a pregnant teacher should discontinue working are matters best left up to the woman and her doctor."

In arguing that women must receive equal treatment with men, the Union points out that the danger of radiation in the X-Ray Department also applies to men who may receive damage to chromosomes which may affect unborn children. Although these dangers exist, precautions are taken to guard against radiation, and, in the Union's opinion, it is the right of the individual to decide whether or not to run this risk by working in the X-Ray Department.

The Union also introduced an article (Union Exhibit #2), "Abnormalities In Children Exposed to X-Radiation During Various Stages of Gestation: Tentative Timetable of Radiation Injury to The Human Fetus, Part 1," by Anatole S. Dekaban[1], who concludes that the greatest danger from radiation to the fetus occurs in the first trimester of pregnancy. Since Mrs. Hoy's doctor dates her pregnancy from December 12, 1971, she would have been in her fifth month of pregnancy by May 10, 1972, the date on which the X-Ray Department employed a new person. Since Mrs. Hoy enjoyed a healthy pregnancy, the Union reiterates that it should have been her option to decide whether she wanted to return to work.

As a further argument the Union cited two precedents where pregnant women had been allowed to continue working in the X-Ray Department. One woman had worked through two pregnancies and although she was not permitted to do fluoroscopy, she performed related duties. The Union also stated that there are other institutions which allow women to work in X-Ray departments during pregnancies and that some of those institutions even allow them to do fluoroscopy.

Finally, the Union contends that it suggested a compromise solution to the grievance which the Employer turned down. Under the Contract an employee loses seniority rights after a layoff of one year or more. If the Employer had been willing to extend Mrs. Hoy's recall rights to one year and nine months, the Union suggests that Mrs. Hoy might have accepted these terms. According to the Union this offer was made to the Board of Directors which turned it down.

Contentions of the Employer

The Employer argues that the precedents cited by the Union do not apply to this case since the situations were not comparable. The other two employees who were allowed to continue working through their pregnancies were currently on the payroll. The Employer states that it has never laid off a full time regular employee because of pregnancy, but instead has changed the working conditions. This case is different in that the employee was on layoff status at the time it was determined that a temporary employee was needed in the X-Ray Department.

The Employer points out that a particular set of circumstances brought about the need for a temporary X-Ray technician to work through the summer months of 1972. First, the staff of the Department had been reduced from

1. Journal of Nuclear Medicine, Vol. 9, No. 9, pp. 471-477 (September 1968).

eight and one half in 1969, to six technicians in 1972. Second, an emergency situation was created both by summer vacation schedules and by an emergency leave of absence required by one technician. For these reasons the Employer argues that it could not afford to change the duties of the job which would be necessitated by the dangers of radiation to a fetus, but instead needed a temporary technician who could handle all aspects of the job.

To point out the dangers of radiation, the Employer presented substantial medical testimony through two radiologists on the staff of the Clinics, Dr. Bastacky and Dr. Kunkle. Both doctors explained the hazards of radiation and the precautions taken by the Clinics to protect the employees. Although the radiation level in the Clinics is below the permissible dose, both doctors testified that ideally a pregnant woman should not be in the department because the fetus is particularly sensitive to radiation. Although research in medical science has not determined what the maximum permissible amount of radiation is for a fetus, it is known that radiation can cause genetically irreversible changes which can affect future generations. Both doctors agreed that the first trimester of pregnancy was the most dangerous period in which to be exposed to radiation (Union Exhibit #2), but, even so, this does not minimize the danger to the fetus in the latter months of pregnancy.

On the basis of this medical knowledge, the Employer contends that the decision to work while pregnant is not that of the pregnant mother alone. The Employer also has the moral responsibility to protect the fetus, and further suggests that it may have a legal responsibility, subjecting it to suit if a defective baby were born.

Opinion

According to the medical testimony presented at the hearing, it is clear that there is danger from the effects of radiation to the fetus of a pregnant woman working in an X-Ray department. Moreover, the Doctors testified that the work is hazardous to all individuals working in the department, and for this reason every possible precaution is taken to ensure the safety of all employees.

Since both men and women train specifically to work in this field and do so with knowledge of the possible risks involved, the question appears to be whether a pregnant woman, who has the acknowledged right to determine for herself whether she will take these risks, has the additional right to take the risks for her fetus. The measure of the potential risk to the fetus depends, however, on extensive knowledge of medicine, a field in which the Arbitrator is concededly not an expert. It would therefore be impossible for the Arbitrator to reach any conclusive judgment regarding the hazards of this work for either adults or unborn babies.

The Arbitrator's function is to judge this case by the standards established in labor relations which include the language of the Contract which was agreed to by both parties and by their past practices in administering it.

To look at past practice first, it should be noted that the Employer concedes that there were three instances in which a pregnant woman continued to work in the X-Ray Department throughout her pregnancy. The Employer contends that while no pregnant women should work in the Department, it nevertheless made concessions in these instances out of consideration for the personal and financial needs of these employees.

In justifying the position in the instant case, the Employer makes two other points: 1) there is a difference between keeping a present employee and recalling a laid-off employee, and, 2) the present situation is different in that the department was larger in the past and it was therefore possible to divide the work so that the pregnant employee would be exposed to the least possible risk.

In regard to past precedent, the Arbitrator credits the Union's claim that the grievant also had financial reasons for continuing to work. Since the Employer was willing in the past to consider personal necessity, in the Arbitrator's judgment it has shown no reason why it should not have applied the same standard to the grievant's situation.

The Arbitrator also finds it difficult to accept the Employer's differentiation between retaining a currently employed pregnant employee and recalling a laid-off pregnant employee. Laid-off employees have protected right to recall under the Contract. Furthermore, the Employer agrees that it is in the early months of pregnancy that the danger of damage from radiation is most serious. To follow this reasoning, it is less hazardous to call back an employee in the later stages of pregnancy than to continue the employment of a pregnant employee in the first trimester.

The most cogent argument of the Employer is that the size of the Department no longer permitted the flexibility in arranging work duties necessary to permit the pregnant employee to avoid the most dangerous functions, such as fluoroscopy. The Employer, however, provided insufficient evidence to support its claim that it would have been completely impossible to work out a rearrangement of job duties in the Department.

Finally, and most important to the Arbitrator, is the Contract language itself. Article X spells out specific rights of seniority in layoffs and recalls modified only by the provision that the "employee has the qualifications and ability to efficiently perform the required work." There was no question raised as to the competence of the grievant to perform the job in the X-Ray Department. The problem according to the Employer, arises out of its sincere concern based on medical evidence, as to whether a pregnant woman has the sole right to decide to work in the X-Ray Department during her pregnancy. Instead the Employer believes that it has the obligation to make this decision.

If the Employer is confident of the validity of its opinion that pregnant women should not be exposed to the dangers of radiation while working in an X-Ray Department, then the Employer has the obligation to negotiate such a provision in the Contract. Carried to its logical conclusion, this might mean that no woman of child bearing age should work as an X-Ray technician, since genetic changes are most likely to occur within the first trimester, a period in which many women are uncertain of pregnancy.

Whether such a clause might be illegal under the Civil Rights Act of 1964 would have to be determined by the Equal Employment Opportunity Commission and the Courts. Many of these questions concerning pregnancy remain to be decided. The Union cited the *Cohen vs. Chesterfield County School Board* case, but this was later reversed on rehearing by the Court of Appeals for the Fourth Circuit. Just recently the Supreme Court agreed "to decide whether school systems that require female teachers to quit their jobs four or five months before they expect children are engaging in unconstitutional discrimination based on sex" (New York Times, April 24, 1973). The decision is not expected until 1974.

Since the law in this area remains in doubt, the Arbitrator is confining her opinion to the language of the Contract and the past practice of the parties.

AWARD

Based on these considerations, the Arbitrator finds that the Employer violated Article X of the Contract and that the grievant is entitled to back pay and allowances for the period from May 10, 1972 to August 31, 1972. She is to be credited with accumulated seniority for this period and her present date of layoff will be September 1, 1972.

Case No. 33

Was it discriminatory for a Nursing Home to require male employees in the food service department to cut their hair so that it would not "extend below the collar" while female employees were required only to wear hairnets?

St. Paul's Towers (San Francisco, Calif.)
and
Hospital and Institutional Workers, Local 250

Arbitrator: James R. Lucas
Date of Award: October 18, 1974
Citation: 195 AAA 14

Facts

The collective bargaining agreement in effect between the parties contains the following pertinent provisions:

Preamble [para. 2.]. "It is mutually agreed that it is the duty and right of Employer to manage itself and direct its employees, and Employer reserves all of its rights, powers and authority in connection therewith, which includes, but is not limited to, the right to hire, transfer, promote, reclassify, lay off and discharge employees, except as limited by express provisions of this Agreement."

Section 4 — Discharge for Cause. "Employer shall have the right to discharge any employee for just and sufficient cause which includes but is not limited to: proven dishonesty, insubordination, insobriety, incompetence, willful negligence, failure to perform work as required, or violating Employer's house rules. Employer agrees to exercise fair and reasonable judgment in the application of this Section."

"Employer may draft such reasonable house rules as may be necessary in its judgment for governing the conduct of employees in matters affecting fire protection, safety of property, sanitation, care of the sick and all other appropriate matters in connection with the proper operation of St. Paul's Towers. Such rules when drafted shall be forwarded by registered mail to the Union before being posted. Employer reserves the right to change such rules whenever it deems appropriate or necessary, providing that any such changes or amendments shall be forwarded in writing to the Union prior to posting and posted as hereinabove set forth and shall not be implemented by the Employer until so forwarded to the Union. House rules will not conflict with the provisions of this Agreement."

Section 19 — Discrimination. ". . . Neither Employer nor the Union shall discriminate for or against any employee . . . on account of race, color, religious creed, sex, or national origin. All provisions of this Agreement shall apply to all employees covered hereunder regardless of race, color, religious creed, sex, or national origin."

Section 23 – Grievance Procedure and Arbitration. D. "Employer shall also have the right to submit grievances with reference to the interpretation or application of, or compliance with this Agreement . . ."

E. ". . . the arbitrator shall have no power to add to, subtract from or alter any provisions of this Agreement."

HOUSE RULES: In March, 1974, employer issued house rules with respect to grooming standards. These included the following:

Women:	1)	Hair — clean and pinned up. Completely covered by a hairnet . . .
Men:	4)	Hair — clean, neat, completely covered by a hat or hairnet, if beyond the collar. Kitchen personnel — all times.

On or shortly before June 14, 1974, employer issued revised rules with respect to grooming standards. These included the following:

Women:	1)	Hair — clean and pinned up. (completely covered by a hairnet in Food Service Department).
Men:	4)	Hair — clean, neat. No one may wear hair length below the collar.

Chronology of events

Grievants P— and W— had been employed, respectively, for four and one-half years and three and three-fourths years prior to a strike that began April 12, 1974, and lasted until June 14, 1974. P— worked continuously in the food service department on a regular 40-hour week. W— also worked in the food service department, but on a part-time basis, averaging 17½ hours per week.

Grievant P— was written up by R.A. Burke, then Food Service Supervisor on March 11, 1974, and April 10, 1974, both times for long and unruly hair.

Grievant W— was similarly written up on March 13, and 18, and April 5, 1974. The March 18 write-up includes the following: "Since he was wearing a hair net and not working in D.R. we decided to let it go till a decision could be reached as we were already short of help."

All of the write-ups were countersigned by Isaiah Rhodes, Kitchen Supervisor, and all but one were also countersigned by Emil Del Carlo, who was then Assistant Food Service Manager. Mr. Burke testified that both Rhodes and Del Carlo were present, together with P—, when P— was "correctively interviewed," in person, on March 11 (Tr. 34), and that he thought Rhodes had been present during the April 10 corrective interview. The purpose of the countersignatures was to attest that the employee had refused to sign. However, Mr. Rhodes testified that he didn't remember being present when the forms were made out and that he did not have first hand knowledge that the grievant had refused to sign. (Tr. 73) Mr. Del Carlo also testified that he was not actually a witness to the interviews or to the refusal to sign. (Tr. 76). Mr. P— testified that he had never seen the corrective interview forms until the hearing in arbitration. Essentially the same set of facts apply to the "corrective interviews" with grievant W— except that in this case Mr. Burke did not testify that Rhodes had actually been present during the interviews. Mr. W— also testified that he had not seen the forms before the hearing.

The weight of the testimony indicates to the arbitrator that these forms were used to build a record and were not gone over with the grievants. However, it is not substantially disputed by the grievants that each of them was told on one or more occasions prior to the strike to cut his hair, and that they had been talked to about wearing hair nets or caps. Therefore the inference drawn by the arbitrator is not that the grievants had not been told to cut their hair shorter, nor that they had not been told to wear hats or hair nets, but that the corrective interview exhibits have little if any probative value as to what degree or kind of warning of possible disciplinary action was given prior to the strike.

At the end of the strike grievants were notified to report back to work. This they did. Upon reporting each was given a copy of the newly promulgated rules and told he would not be allowed to return to work until he had complied with the new rule on hair length. They were allowed forty-eight hours to comply with this demand. Neither did so and both were discharged.

Mr. Dillard, the administrator of St. Paul's Towers since January 21, 1974, testified at some length as to the nature of the Employer's business, which is to provide living accommodations and medical care to the elderly. The current vacancy rate is considerably more than desirable or economic. The average age of the clientele is in excess of eighty. People in this age group are more prone than the average, according to Mr. Dillard, to take a conservative view of such things as the currently popular longer hair styles affected by younger men. He stated that there had been complaints by the clients, through the residents' council, about slovenly appearance on the part of both male and female employees. Mr. Dillard recalled specific residents' council complaints in early February, 1974, about the appearance of grievant W — and two other employees.

According to testimony, there was a significant problém with grievants and with other employees in getting them to keep hair nets or caps on.

Mr. Rhodes, as kitchen supervisor, supervised Mr. P— but not Mr. W—.

He testified that he had never had occasion to criticize either one for his appearance.

Mr. W— had previously worked in the dining room and had been told by Mr. Del Carlo he would have to either have his hair cut or covered. He chose to do other work instead, primarily storeroom work but including some tray delivery. According to Mr. Del Carlo, "He was still getting in the food, it seemed, so every now and then he was told to put on a hair net which he would do sometimes and sometimes he wouldn't." (Tr. 78).

In response to a question as to what Mr. Del Carlo found to criticize about Mr. P— he said: "His general appearance and mostly the fact that his hair was too long and he didn't have a hair net on or a hat, and when I would tell him to do it, he would put it on and some time later he would have it off again. It was a constant battle of having the hair covered." (TR 78).

Issue

The issue to be decided is: Whether or not grievants P— and W— were discharged for just cause under the terms of the collective bargaining agreement, and if not, what remedy is appropriate?

Employer Argument

1.   The employer has a right unilaterally to establish working rules which bear a reasonable relationship to the efficient and orderly conduct of the business, and such right may only be curtailed by provisions of a collective bargaining agreement. This right is specified in both the Preamble and in Section 4 of the Agreement. Therefore the employer was fully empowered to promulgate the revised rules of May, 1974.

2.   The May, 1974, rules fully met the test of reasonableness for grooming rules as set forth in *Monroe Concrete Company* 71-1 ARB 8144.

3.   The employer is in the business of providing living, dining and medical facilities for more than 250 elderly residents whose average age exceeds 80 years. Residents of St. Paul's Towers complained about long hair to an extent that there is clear evidence that failure to comply with employer's grooming standards was damaging to business.

4.   Proper grooming standards are a legitimate health and safety concern.

5.   If the grooming rules of May, 1974, are reasonable, whether other and different rules might have been reasonably applied is irrelevant.

6.   The rules for grooming promulgated by the Employer in May, 1974, are lawful and not in violation of Title VII of the Civil Rights Act of 1964.

7.   The grievants were properly terminated for their refusal to report for work with hair cut in accordance with employer's rules. They were put on notice on June 14, and later given another two days in which to comply.

8.   For the foregoing reasons the grievances should be denied.

Union Argument

1.   Violation of a house rule does not *per se* constitute just cause for discharge.

2.   Employer changed its rules concerning men's hair during the strike, aimed at the grievants; this is a denial of due process.

3.   The rule in question is inconsistent with the treatment of female employees.

4.   Changing hair styles for men have been the subject of much recent arbitration, and the Union's position is supported in a number of decisions.

5.   The Employer's action raises serious questions under the Civil Rights Act of 1964.

6.   Nothing on the record indicates that either grievant had anything but a good work record. There is no evidence that either grievant had any knowledge of the pre-strike corrective interviews.

7.   There is no direct evidence that Employer's clients were concerned with grievants' hair styles, and no evidence that their hair styles interfered with their job performance or resulted in food contamination.

8.   Employer failed to carry its burdenof proof to show that the discharges were for just cause. Grievants should be reinstated with back pay to June 14, 1974.

Conclusions

1.   The citations of arbitral precedent given by both parties were given careful and respectful consideration. It would burden this opinion unduly to attempt a discussion of each citation; also, it is self-evident that no two cases are precisely on all fours: three fours is probably the best one can hope for.

2.   For reasons that will become evident, this arbitrator chooses to by-pass argument pro and con applicability of Title VII of the Civil Rights Act of 1964. The agreement itself, incorporating reasonable house rules by reference, in Section 19 forbids discrimination on account of sex and further states: "All provisions of this Agreement shall apply to all employees covered hereunder regardless of . . . sex . . . ." Since the rules can reasonably be construed as part of the agreement it follows that insofar as is biologically practical the rules should be the same for male and female employees alike.

3.   Because attitudes with respect to men's hair styles are still in the process of change, the arbitrator researched more recent decisions than those cited, with the following results:

In *City of East Detroit and East Detroit Police Officers Association*, 61 LA 485, Case No. 342, September 25, 1973, Arbitrator: Maurice Kelman, summary quoted:

> City was not justified in suspending policeman who failed to comply with grooming code by having his hair partially covering his ears and his mustache extending beyond the corner of his mouth, since there is controversy between City and union regarding propriety of grooming code and it would not serve equity considerations to single out grievant for "test case" purposes; real controversy here is between City and union, and grievant as pawn in that dispute should not be made to suffer.

While it was not argued that in the instant case the real controversy was between the Employer and the Union, it is nonetheless a fact that the strike casts an aura over the entire proceeding. Mr. Burke testified:

> Frankly, I was on the verge of terminating them. I didn't want to make any additional problems when we were on the verge of a strike, so I prolonged that decision until we could see if the strike would perhaps

dissipate and not come about. I felt it would aggravate the situation since we already had a termination just prior to that. (Tr. 60).

Remembering then the fact that the new rules were not effectively promulgated, insofar as the grievants were concerned, until June 14, the day they reported back to work following the strike, there is some cause to suspect that there was a punitive aspect having to do more with the strike than with the length of grievants' hair.

At 61 LA 645 Arbitrator James R. McCormick struck down a grooming rule the City of Detroit sought to apply to firefighters while at the same time upholding the imposition of a 30-day suspension on the grounds that the rule was promulgated as a safety rule and could not be considered an exception to the "obey now and grieve later" precept.

At 57-B-9, American Arbitration Association, ARBITRATION IN THE SCHOOLS, Arbitrator William J. Fallon strikes down a school rule on hair and mustaches on First Amendment grounds, citing the U.S. Supreme Court in *Tinker v. Des Moines Independent Free School District*, which held that: the wearing of hair and beards were manners of free expression and First Amendment rights (Quoted from summary: full text not yet available).

4.   Arbitrator Arthur Jacobs, in the case cited by the Union, at 60 LA 1198, while upholding the grievant in a grooming discharge case, had this to say:

> If in fact there is a safety hazard inherent in the use of this particular baler involving length of hair . . . the Company would have been within its rights in requiring Grievant to have worn a cap or hairnet . . .

and

> Certainly a rule which requires that hair be clean, neat and well-groomed is a reasonable rule [*and nothing in this decision should be construed to mean that this Arbitrator believes otherwise.*]*

5.   The original rules were reasonable. The revised rules are, in this opinion, unreasonable to the extent only of discriminating against male employees in the matter of hair grooming. The rule in question is also in conflict with the provisions of Section 19 of the collective bargaining agreement between the parties.

6.   The Employer's case is vitiated by the lack of direct testimony from clients as to their feelings about long hair on male employees or direct

---

*The emphasis has been added to signify that this arbitrator concurs fully. Arbitrator Jacobs also made the point that unkempt hair and long hair are not one and the same thing.

testimony as to the possible effect on occupancy. A direct showing of business loss on a cause-and-effect basis would possibly have had an impact on this opinion. This is not said to discount altogether Mr. Dillard's testimony; there is no reason to doubt his veracity, but there is the fact that the testimony was hearsay and some of the opinions were subjective in nature.

7.   The Employer erred seriously (giving full credence to testimony by Messrs. Burke and Del Carlo) in not enforcing the house rules promulgated in March. Despite this arbitrator's dislike for such hypothetical formulations, the instant case compels the statement that if grievants were indeed guilty of continuous violation of the rule pertaining to hair covering, and if the type of progressive discipline customary to other than gross malfeasance cases had been applied, namely: written warning with a copy to the Union, followed by disciplinary suspension for a repeated violation of the same rule, followed by discharge for a successive violation, the arbitrator would have little difficulty sustaining the Employer's position. Employer not only had the right to enforce that March rule, but a duty as well, under the State Code.

8.   Employer has the right, under the collective bargaining agreement, to file grievances. In a case such as this, where no immediately irreparable damage was being done to the Employer, it would seem that this avenue could have been utilized, either to secure agreement with the Union or to obtain a declaratory opinion from an arbitrator, rather than resorting to what the late Arthur Ross termed the capital punishment of the industrial world: discharge.

9.   As indicated previously, the strike casts its own aura over the entire discharge procedure. The terms of the strike settlement agreement not being in evidence, the arbitrator can say no more than that a suspicion exists that attaching a new condition precedent to the offer of reemployment is questionable.

10.   The question remains: were the grievants entitled to self-help, or should the rule of "obey now, grieve later" be applied? Had the order to the grievants involved no more than a temporary inconvenience, and absent any jeopardy to personal health or safety, the obey now, grieve later rule probably would have applied. It could be argued that no more than a temporary inconvenience was involved, but to accept that premise would be to ignore the fact that there is a large segment of our populace to whom the right to individualized hair styles is more than just a passing fancy. To many young men this right is an important First Amendment right and many young men have taken considerable risks and suffered great indignities to uphold this right, just as grievants took a great risk by laying their jobs on the line. A line is of course drawn where such expressions of personal freedom infringe on the rights of others, e.g., grievants may have the right to wear long hair; they do not have the right to get it in my soup. Some of the limits on the extent to which food handlers may infringe on the rights of others are set forth at Section

28636 of the State Health and Safety Code, and there are obviously other limits.

AWARD

1. Grievants are to be reinstated, with back pay to June 14, 1974, less five working days, and less earnings from substitute employment and/or nonreimburseable unemployment compensation benefits, if any.

2. Back pay shall be based on the work schedules last in effect for the grievants prior to the 1974 strike and on the wage rates in effect since June 14, 1974.

3. There shall be no loss of seniority or any other benefits related to length of service for the period from June 14, 1974, to the date of reinstatement.

Case No. 34

When the State Department of Health recommended that the Hospital establish a new position, was it reasonable for the Hospital to assume that failure to do so immediately might jeopardize its certification? Having unilaterally established the new position, could the Hospital require that it be filled by an LPN?

Benzie Medical Care Facility (Benzie County, Mich.)
and
Benzie Medical Employees Chapter of Local No. 1084, AFSCME

Arbitrator: Samuel S. Shaw
Date of Award: January 18, 1975
Citation: LAIG 1277

The following policy Grievance was filed on September 5, 1974, relative to job posting and bidding procedure:

"The employer has violated the agreement between the parties by not posting a job vacancy. This is Article XVII, violations of Articles XVI, para. B, Article XXXVIII, Article XXXIX, Article XLIII."

Remedy: "The Facility stop violating the agreement between the parties, and post the vacant posission in accordance with the Agreement. Also the senior employee who bids on the possission be given all back pay to the date the vacancy occured.

/s/ E. Merrill, Steward
9/5/74"

In a meeting on July 23, 1974, the Parties attempted to resolve the issue. However, no satisfactory agreement could be reached, and the Parties mutually agreed to waive the grievance procedure and appeal directly to arbitration.

The Hearing was held at the Benzie County Medical Facility on November 13, 1974, before Samuel S. Shaw, Arbitrator, mutually selected from a panel submitted by the American Arbitration Association. The Parties were fully represented and given full and ample opportunity to submit all pertinent documentary evidence, to introduce and cross-examine witnesses, and to present arguments in support of their respective positions. Witnesses were not sworn. No court reporter was present; however, the proceedings were tape recorded by the Arbitrator.

Both Parties elected to file briefs to be mailed postmarked no later than December 10, 1974. The brief from the Union was received as agreed; however, the brief from the Facility was not received until January 8, 1975. At the direction of the American Arbitration Association, the Hearing was not closed until this later date.

Facts and Background

The Benzie Medical Facility, established in 1965, is a skilled care facility of 42 beds. The Benzie County Medical Facility Employees Council 55, AFSCME has represented the nonlicensed employees for approximately five years.

During this period, the Restorative Nursing Department of the Facility was manned by an Aide, Mrs. Allyn Storr. Immediately prior, the Department was operated by Eugene Allen, LPN.

The administrative activities of the Facility are directed by an Administrator, and the medical policy by a Medical Director and Director of Nurses. As the Facility has an SNF certification from the Michigan Department of Health, its patient policy must conform to the specifics established by this licensing agency. As far as the State is concerned, this certification is issued by the Michigan Department of Public Health and is re-issued annually.

In June, 1973, Miss Agnes Fredericks, RN, from the Michigan Department of Social Services, visited the Facility for the purpose of assessing the adequacy of the licensed staff. In her report following this visit, she made the following comments and recommendations:

Employ a R.N. or L.P.N. in the Restorative Nursing Department who has the advantage of Rehabilitation Nursing and/or Restorative Nursing. If no one is available, make some arrangements, to secure this preparation at an institution which offers such a course. (Contact Helen Millen, R.N., Kenny Michigan Rehabilitation Foundation, 6131 W. Outer Drive, Detroit, Michigan 48235. Telephone 342-5500).

a.   A Nurse Aide is limited in effectiveness since the background knowledge limits transfer of knowledge from one situation to another. The potential positive effects of the RPT are seriously limited by the present arrangement.

b.   The Nurse Aid-Ord. is also limited in service since his/her orientation is to basic nursing skills, hence limiting a broader scope of services.

c.   There is a further limitation when using unlicensed persons as the primary co-ordinator for Restorative Nursing since licensed persons seldom follow the "Lead of an unlicensed person."

It is my "feeling" that Benzie County Medical Care Facility has provided adequate patient care through the years, but with recent advances and necessary changes the accepted pattern of "adequacy" assumed by the Facility has been constant which makes the care inadequate now. The acuity of illness and the older population now served changes the needs manifested by patients and personnel and as a result the type of care required.

On June 30, 1973, Mr. Herbert E. Harrington, then Administrator of the Facility, wrote to Mrs. Helen Millen, R.N., of the Kenny Michigan Rehabilitation Foundation, with the following comments relative to the Physical Therapy problem in the Facility:

One of the areas of concern for both Miss Fredericks and me is the Physical Therapy Department. Although Mr. Edward Axman, R.P.T., does an excellent job for us, he is somewhat limited in time as a consultant, thus Miss Fredericks suggested I contact you for information on a course in Rehabilitation Nursing or Restorative Nursing.

In June of 1974, the Michigan Department of Public Health made a survey of the Facility and subsequently issued the following recommendation:

The facility will be in compliance when a new contract is written, since the present arrangement is questionable. At present, Mr. Axman is under contract with an independent physical therapy agency, Nedervett & Knoll, and they have released him under a sub-contract to serve the hospital and Medical Care Facility at Frankfort. Therefore, the owners have no responsibility in the facility to insure the delivery of physical therapy. It would be preferable to make a new arrangement with Mr. Axman, which was discussed at the time of my visit. I suggest that an R.N. supervise the activities of the nursing aide when she renders extended physical therapy type services in the absence of the R.P.T.

In May, 1974, Miss Fredericks RN from the Michigan Department of Social Services, made an evaluation visit. Her report, relative to the Physical Therapy problem, was as follows:

Restorative Nursing/Physical Therapy

There continues to be a need for a concerted effort to improve the utilization of restorative–rehabilitation nursing in collaboration with the skills and knowledges of the Registered Physical Therapy Consultant, Mr. Ed Axman.

In a letter dated June 20, 1974, to the Facility's Administrator, Dr. James Kaufman, M.D., Medical Director of the Facility, recommended that the services of Mr. Axman, RPT, be increased and that a nurse or trained PT Assistant be employed on a full-time basis. In his letter, Dr. Kaufman stated the reason for his recommendation:

. . . because the physical therapy is more effective in the hospital in terms of time of treatments and quality of treatments.

In early July, 1974, Mr. Axman, RPT, recommended to the Facility Administrator that consideration be given to up-grading the Restorative Aide position, inasmuch as the present Aide, Mrs. Allyn Storr, had notified the Facility that she was leaving to attend LPN School. In his recommendation, Mr. Axman also stated:

The solution to this problem is to fill this present position with a Physical Therapy Assistant, Registered Nurse or Licensed Practical Nurse who have all had formal training in the aforementioned sciences and skills, with the exception of therapeutic exercise by the R.N. or L.P.N. Even more practical would be an L.P.N., since to locate a P.T. Assistant is impossible at this time and using an R.N. would not be feasible as yet.

The advantages in using an L.P.N. would be numerous. They have had a formal program in the basic medical sciences, and it can be proven by certificate. There is a foundation for teaching therapeutic exercise and the indications and counter-indications of treatment. The authoratative manner and liaison skills for teaching and promoting Restorative Nursing can be realized. Even a basis is present for criticizing their performance.

As the result of the survey reports from the Michigan Department of Public Health, the Michigan Department of Social Services, Dr. Kaufman's and Mr. Axman's recommendations, the Facility decided to employ a LPN to fill the vacancy created by Mrs. Storr's resignation. Therefore, a new classification was established for a Restorative Care Nurse, and a job description written defining the qualifications and job responsibilities.

In a letter dated July 23, 1974, Mr. Van Hoose, Administrator, advised Willard Howes, Representative of Local 1804, Michigan Council 55, that Mrs. Storr was leaving her employment, and would be replaced by a Licensed Practical Nurse. Subsequently, the Facility hired Miss Shelly Goddard, who, although not as yet licensed, was a graduate of a Licensed Practical Nursing School.

Pertinent Contractual Provisions

RECOGNITION

Pursuant to and in accordance with all applicable provisions of Act 379 of the Public Acts of 1965, as amended, the Facility does hereby recognize the Union as the exclusive representative for the purpose of collective bargaining in respect to rates of pay, wages, hours of employment and other conditions of employment for the term of this agreement of all employees of the Facility included in the bargaining units described below.

UNIT 1. All regular full-time and part-time Nurses Aides, Orderlies, Maintenance, Food Service and Laundry and Housekeeping, excluding Administrative Personnel, Office Clerical, Registered Nurses, Licensed Practical Nurses, Registered or Licensed Physical Therapists, Registered or Licensed Lab Technicians, Registered or Licensed Pharmacists, the Medical Director, and Supervisors as defined in the Act.

C. Powers of the Arbitrator. It shall be the function of the arbitrator, and he shall be empowered, except as his powers are limited below, after due investigation to make a decision in cases of alleged violation of the specific articles and sections of this agreement.

1.   He shall have no power to add to, subtract from, disregard, alter or modify any of the terms of this agreement.

5.   There shall be no appeal from an arbitrator's decision if within the scope of his authority as set forth above. Each such decision shall be binding and final on the Union, its members, the employee or employees involved, and the Facility.

ARTICLE XVII — *Job Postings and Bidding Procedure*

A.   All job vacancies and newly-created positions within the bargaining unit shall be made on the basis of seniority and qualifications. Job vacancies and newly-created positions will be posted for a period of four

(4) days setting forth the requirements for the position at the time clock within seven (7) days before or after the vacancy occurs or the newly-created position is established. The senior employee applying for the position and who meets the qualifications shall be granted a four (4) week training period to determine:
1.   His desire to remain on the job
2.   His ability to perfom the job

ARTICLE XIX — *Rates For New Jobs*

When a new job is placed in a unit and cannot be properly placed in an existing classification, the Facility will notify the Union prior to establishing a classification and rate structure. If the Union does not agree with the classification or rate, it shall notify the Facility within five (5) days after receipt of notice.

ARTICLE XLIII — *Work Performed Outside Bargaining Unit*

Supervisory employees and other employees not covered by the bargaining unit shall not regularly perform work which is performed by the bargaining unit, except in case of an emergency. Nothing herein contained shall be construed as a limitation on the existing and past practice of such personnel in the performance of their work.

Although the Grievance cited Article XVI, Paragraph B, Article XXXVIII and Article XXXIX, the Arbitrator did not feel that they were sufficiently pertinent to the issue to necessitate their being reproduced.

Discussion

Although the Grievance was directed primarily at the failure of the Employer to post the vacancy, at the Hearing the Union added the issue that the Employer has failed to fill the vacancy with a member of Local 1804.

In the opinion of the Arbitrator, the issue here is whether or not the Facility was in violation of the Contract by not filling the classification of Restorative Care Nurse with a member of the Unit. Once this issue is resolved, the question of posting becomes axiomatic.

It was the position of the Facility that the classification of Restorative Care Aide was not eliminated, but a new classification of Restorative Care Nurse established. Further, that in the event a Restorative Care Aide was needed, it would be filled by an employee of the Unit.

It was the Union's basic contention that even though the Restorative Care Nurse's classification was new, it was not substantially different from that of Restorative Care Aide and as such, should properly be filled by a member of the Unit.

In the opinion of the Arbitrator, there are two questions that have to be resolved — first, does management have the right to establish a new classification, and second, are the job requirements of the new classification sufficiently higher to justify its establishment, and removing it from the former classification structure?

In labor/management contractual interpretations, it has been a long and well-established principle that, providing the action is not capricious, arbitrary, or discriminatory, management retains the right to establish new, combine, or eliminate classifications when based upon sound business reasons. This assumes, of course, there is no specific contractual provisions barring such action, or stipulation that management has waived this right.

After reviewing the evidence, particularly the documents submitted as exhibits, the Arbitrator is satisfied that Management has not waived its right to establish a new classification. In fact, in this particular case, it is apparent that the Facility established the classification of Restorative Care Nurse because of outside pressure, and was not a result of any capricious or discriminatory thinking on the part of the Administration.

In 1973, a representative of the Michigan Department of Social Services criticized the physical therapy treatment provided by the Facility, and specifically recommended the Employment of an RN or LPN, suggesting that an Aide was limited in effectiveness by background, knowledge and training.

In 1974, the Michigan Department of Health recommended that the physical therapy treatment be up-graded, and improvement made in personnel. Also, in the same year, the Michigan Department of Social Services again pressed for improvement in the Physical Therapy Department. When it is considered that the Michigan Department of Public Health is the Facility's certification agency, it has to be concluded that any recommendation they might make is almost in the form of a request, and must be implemented.

It is true that nothing in these reports specifically referred to the certification, but it is not unreasonable to assume that continued failure to comply might jeopardize its continued renewal.

On the basis of the above, the Arbitrator has to conclude that the action taken by the Facility in establishing the classification of Restorative Care Nurse was based upon sound business reasons.

The second question is whether this new classification had to be filled by a LPN as a minimum requirement. Although the Arbitrator would not be considered an expert in this field, he does believe that the testimony of Dr. Kaufman and Mr. Axman, when coupled with the reports from the two state agencies, is convincing. The agency reports both directed their attention to this recommendation, and both Dr. Kaufman and Mr. Axman stated that the formal education acquired by a LPN was necessary, if the physical therapy treatment was to meet the standards required.

The Arbitrator agrees that some of the treatment given by the LPN would be the same as that previously given by Mrs. Storr, the former Restorative Care Aide. However, according to the evidence, a substantial addition has been made to the responsibility and knowledge requirements of the new classification to set it apart from the classification of Restorative Care Aide.

In arguing its position, the Union pointed out that the person hired to fill the new classification, Mrs. Stoddard or Goddard, was not licensed. Although this is technically a fact, it was established that she had completed her formal training at the Northwestern School of Nursing and was now operating under a temporary permit pending the actual receipt of her license. It was further established that prior to her LPN training, she had had two years experience in an orthopedic ward of a hospital.

Inasmuch as, in the Arbitrator's opinion, the classification of Restorative Care Nurse must be held by at least a LPN, the question of whether she should or should not be a member of Local 1804 is resolved. The Facility recognizes the Licensed Practical Nurses Association as the exclusive representative of the LPN's.

Under the Agreement with this organization and the Facility, in addition to "licensed nurses," the Agreement provides: ". . . persons who are awaiting Michigan licenses and who are employed as nurses in the categories described above under a valid temporary permit issued by the Michigan Board of Nursing, shall be included in the Unit." On this basis, there can be no question that the LPN now occupying the classification of Restorative Care Nurse cannot be a member of Local 1804, inasmuch as she is required to be a member of the Licensed Practical Nurses Association.

In summary, it is the Arbitrator's conclusion, after due consideration of all of the evidence, that the Facility is not in violation of the Agreement as alleged by the Union. The Facility was required to up-grade its Physical Therapy Department to a level satisfactory to its certifying agency. This Agency's agent, in addition to the Facility's medical personnel, were of the opinion the Department must be staffed by an LPN as a minimum. As a result, the job content of the position in question had to be changed to reflect the added duties and responsibilities required in this new position, even though some of the duties were transferred from the former classification. Further, particularly under these circumstances, the Administration cannot be held in violation of the Agreement, inasmuch as there is no provision specifically denying them this right. Further, as the LPN hired to fill this new classification is covered by a valid agreement between the Facility and the Licensed Practical Nurses Association, she is automatically barred from membership in Local 1804.

In view of the above, the Facility cannot be held in violation of the Agreement for failure to post the classification of Restorative Care Nurse, as this new classification is not covered by the Agreement between the Facility and Local 1804.

AWARD

The Arbitrator concludes from the evidence the Facility had no alternative but to up-grade its Restorative Nursing Department. This was the result of strong recommendations of the Michigan Department of Public Health, the licensing agency for the Facility.

Competent medical authority determined this up-grading could not be accomplished through the knowledge and skill level specified in the existing job of Restorative Care Aide, a decision that was supported by the Michigan Department of Social Services. Therefore, a new job classification was established raising the knowledge and skill requirements to that of an LPN. Although this new classification included some of the duties performed by the classification of Restorative Care Aide, sufficient and substantial new requirements and responsibilities were added to qualify it as a new classification.

In the opinion of the Arbitrator, an employer has the right to establish a new job classification when the action is not arbitrary or capricious, but dictated by sound business needs. Therefore, as this criteria was met in this case, the Employer cannot be held in violation of the Agreement because this new classification was established.

In accordance with the requirements of the new classification, the job was filled by a LPN, who, although not actually licensed, holds a valid temporary permit while awaiting her license.

Inasmuch as all LPN's at the Facility are represented by their own Union, the LPN filling the new classification could not be represented by Local 1804.

Further, as the Arbitrator finds the Facility had the right to establish a new classification, and that the minimum requirements of this new classification was for the skill and knowledge level of an LPN, the job is not properly within the jurisdiction of Local 1804.

Therefore, the Employer's failure to post the job was not a violation of the Agreement.

Case No 35

*Were the lack of ability to perform the required
secretarial functions of the employee health nurse
position and unfamiliarity with rules and regulations
pertaining to safety and compensation adequate
reasons to deny the bids of otherwise qualified
employees and fill the vacancy from the outside?*

**Cooley-Dickinson Hospital (Northampton, Mass.)
and
Massachusetts Nurses Association**

Arbitrator: Robert F. Koretz
Date of Award: July 12, 1972
Citation: LAIG 627

The issue for determination was stipulated as follows:

Whether the Hospital violated the Agreement by rejecting all of the
employee applicants who bid for the position of Employee Health Nurse and
by hiring an employee from the outside. If so, what shall the remedy be?

Provisions of the Agreement

Reference was made to the following provisions of the parties' Agreement
as pertinent to the dispute:

ARTICLE IX

Section 2. Promotions.
1. Vacancies in position above staff nurses shall be posted on the
approved bulletin board for a period of five (5) days. Any nurse interested

in said vacancy shall make application to the Director of Nursing. The position shall be filled on the basis of qualifications and, where qualifications are relatively equal, seniority shall be the determining factor in filling said positions.

*   *   *   *   *

ARTICLE XI

Section 3.   Arbitration.
   1.   If the dispute is not resolved in the foregoing Sections of this Article, either party may submit the matter to arbitration within thirty (30) days after the receipt of a written answer in Step 3. The party desiring arbitration shall satisfy the other party, and they shall thereupon attempt to agree upon an arbitrator. In the event the parties cannot reach agreement, the dispute shall be submitted to the American Arbitration Association under its voluntary Labor Arbitration rules and regulations. The decision of the arbitrator shall be final and binding on all of the parties. The costs of the arbitration assessed by the American Arbitration Association and the arbitrator shall be borne equally by the parties.

   A.   The arbitrator shall have no authority to add to or subtract from or modify any of the terms of this agreement . . .

*   *   *   *   *

ARTICLE XIII

Section 1.   Management Rights.
   1.   The Association recognizes that the Hospital has the obligation of serving the public with the highest quality, efficient and economical medical care and in meeting medical emergencies. The Association further recognizes the right of the Hospital to operate and manage the Hospital including but not limited to the right to require efficient standards of performance and maintenance of discipline, order and efficiency, the right to determine medical and nursing care, standards and methods to direct nurses and determine professional assignments, to schedule work, to introduce new methods and facilities, to determine efficient staffing requirements, to determine the number and location of facilities, to determine whether the whole or any part of the operation shall continue to operate, to select and hire employees, to determine qualifications for nursing positions, to promote, to demote, suspend, discipline or discharge employees for just cause, to lay off employees for lack of work or other legitimate reasons, to recall employees, to determine that nurse employees shall not perform certain functions, to require reasonable overtime work, to promulgate reasonable rules and

regulations provided that such rights shall not be exercised so as to violate any of the specific provisions of this Agreement.

*   *   *   *   *

Facts: Contentions of the Parties

On October 18, 1971, the Hospital posted a notice as follows:

EMPLOYEE HEALTH NURSE

Position available in Employee Health Service for a Registered Nurse starting sometime in December. Normal working hours, Monday through Friday, 7:30 a.m. to 3:30 p.m., 37½ hour week. If you are interested, please submit your written request to the Personnel Office.

The notice remained posted until November 3, 1971.

As the Union points out, neither of the two prior occupants of the position of Employee Health Nurse had previous occupational nursing experience; both had come from the Hospital nursing staff. The Job Description in effect at the time of the posting was dated November 16, 1965, and read as follows:

Assists the Employee Health Physician in the administration of the Employee Health Service, and the rendering of employee medical services. Assist in the planning, organizing and directing of an employee health and safety program. Assist in orientation of new personnel, working in close cooperation with all departments. Provides necessary nursing care for employees as prescribed by the Employee Health Physician's standing orders. Maintains the necessary records and handles clerical duties involved in the proper operation of the department. Insures the availability of supplies and equipment. Works in close cooperation with the Personnel Director.

Six registered nurses, four of whom were in the bargaining unit, bid for the position. They were as follows:

V.H.	on 10/19/71
M.D.	on 10/20/71
E.B.	on 10/21/71
S.D.	on 10/26/71
P.C.	on 10/27/71
C.S.	on 11/10/71

V.H., E.B., and P.C. were currently in an employment status. M.D. had been terminated but was placed on reserve status. S.D. and C.S. were nonemployees with no affiliation with the Hospital.

All applicants were interviewed by Paul Dextrader, Director of Personnel, between November 8 and November 12, 1971. Prior to the interview of each employee-applicant, their files were reviewed. At the interview each applicant was told the requirements of the position. All the applicants called as witnesses testified that there was little discussion about the nursing functions of the position, and that the discussion of the position related substantially to the nonnursing duties of the position, e.g., record keeping, statistics, typing and knowledge and understanding of the laws and regulations relating to industrial accidents and occupational health and safety programs.

When Dextrader explained the position to each applicant, he used as a basis of his explanation a job description and evaluation which had been reviewed and updated. It was formally dated November 1, 1971, and replaced the job description dated November 16, 1965. The new job description reads as follows:

> Assists the Employee Health Physician in the administration of the Employee Health Service, and the rendering of employee medical services. Assists in the planning and executing of health and safety programs designed to improve efficiency and reduce absentee and accident rates. Provides necessary nursing care for employees as prescribed by the Employee Health Physician's standing orders. Maintains the necessary records and handles clerical duties involved in the proper operation of the department. Insures the availability of supplies and equipment. Works in close cooperation with all departments and in liaison with the Personnel Director, reporting to and keeping him informed of department activities and making recommendations for improvements or changes.
>
> Perform other related duties as necessary.

The Employee Health Nurse position at the Hospital was initiated in 1963 or 1964. The function of the nurse was to assist the physician in pre-employment physicals only. Prior to 1963 a part-time nurse was available to assist on pre-employment physicals. In 1965, with the writing of a formal job description, the Employee Health Nurse was required to take on additional duties which came with the expansion of the employment at the Hospital from about 200 employees to approximately 800 employees. It was also anticipated that with the expansion of workmen's compensation to the health care field in 1966, there was the need to develop and coordinate a health and safety program which in turn necessitated record keeping and statistical data and an increased need to follow up on employee illnesses, leaves of absence and to reduce sick time.

Up to about 1970 the Hospital felt that a general duty nurse could handle the job. However, the Hospital states that it became apparent, as the position became less nursing oriented, that there was difficulty on the part of the Employee Health Nurse to carry out the administrative functions of the job; and that with the passage of the Employment Security Act of 1970 and the Occupational Safety and Health Act of 1971, both of which laws were made applicable to health care facilities, the complexity of the Employee Health Nurse position changed dramatically. In addition, the Hospital initiated a major program in tuberculosis control. The Hospital found that the general duty nurse in the Employee Health Nurse position was unable to keep up with the expansion of the functions of the position. She was not replaced until 1971 because her retirement was imminent. She actually retired as of January 1, 1972.

Personnel Director Dextrader testified that the position of Employee Health Nurse came under his supervision as a personnel function and that the growing problems relating to the Employee Health Program concerned him because of the vast increase in the quantity and quality of the work required and the health and legal penalties involved in various health programs. He accordingly undertook in September, 1971, to review and update the Employee Health Nurse position. Dextrader testified that he considered three areas of major importance in the filling of the position under the new description: (1) the individual have training in secretarial work, (2) have familiarity with "those rules and regulations on safety and compensation as they affect Health Care Institutions," and (3) have at least one year's experience in occupational nursing. Dextrader further testified that the qualifications for the position involved more than technical and administrative proficiency, and that an essential qualification was dependability and ability to get along with other people, including Dr. Hogan, the Employee Health Physician.

S.D., a nonemployee, was selected by the Hospital for the Employee Health Nurse position. Dextrader's testimony as to the basis of selection, as accurately reflected in the Hospital's brief, was substantially as follows: Dextrader testified that none of the employee-applicants met the qualifications of the job but that S.D. did meet the qualifications. None of the applicants except S.D. fulfilled the technical qualifications. One applicant, V.H., was considered unqualified in technical and administrative experience and also was eliminated from consideration because of an apparent lack of interest and an apparent lack of dependability. For example, she was 15 minutes late for her interview and made her application to the Director of Nursing although the posted notice specifically requested that applications be made to the Personnel Office. Dextrader sent four of the applicants, M.D.,

E.B., P.C., and V.H., employee-applicants, to Dr. Hogan for interviews. Dextrader testified, and Dr. Hogan's testimony agreed, that these interviews were for the purpose of ensuring compatability with Dr. Hogan. And Hogan found all satisfactory. Dextrader further testified that he sent the three employee-applicants to Dr. Hogan, although unqualified in the technical sense with the belief that with extensive training they could meet the qualifications. Dextrader also testified that although only S.D. met the technical qualifications, there was the possibility that she would not get along with Dr. Hogan or vice versa, or that she may have decided to turn down the job offer; and that the other applicants would be considered for training if a qualified applicant was not found.

Under the date of December 1, 1971, Dextrader wrote the following letter to each of the employee-applicants:

> This is to notify you that an applicant has been selected for the position of Employee Health Nurse.
>
> The receipt of your application and others equally qualified made our selection difficult. Unfortunately, there was only one position available, and we therefore had to make our decision in favor of the applicant who had the most experience in the field of occupational nursing and the clerical aspects of the position.

As the Union points out, none of the employee-applicants had ever been advised either orally or in writing that they were considered unqualified for the position; the first time this assertion was made was at the hearing.

The heart of the Association's position is reflected in the following portions of its brief:

> It is evident that (1) the posting and bidding procedures provided in the agreement are limited to nurses in the bargaining unit; (2) that the comparative qualification test comes into play only when there is more than one qualified applicant from the bargaining unit and (3) the Hospital may only go outside the bargaining unit to fill a vacancy when there are no qualified applicants from the unit . . . .
>
>   The Hospital does not dispute these propositions but asserts that none of the applicants from the unit were qualified for the Employee Health Nurse position and therefore it could hire from the outside. We contend that the evidence establishes that this defense was formulated for the arbitration hearing and that in fact the employer had previously determined that three of the unit applicants — E.B., P.C., and V.H. — were qualified but had hired the outside applicant because it felt that she was even better qualified. It was only after the Hospital learned that the comparative qualification test could not be used between qualified unit

applicants and an outsider did it assert that the unit applicants were unqualified.

The Association cites certain evidence in support of its position, in brief as follows: (1) During his initial interview with the applicants, Dextrader gave no indication that any were deemed unqualified because of a lack of prior experience in occupational nursing. (2) The text of the letter advising the applicants that someone else had been given the job is consistent with a finding that he deemed the applicants to be qualified. (3) When the grievance was discussed at step two of the grievance procedure, Dextrader argued his right to select the most qualified applicant and never claimed that all the unit applicants were unqualified. (4) The Association states that although in his original testimony Dextrader sought to convey that the decision was jointly made by him, Dr. Hogan and the Director of Nurses, Dr. Hogan's testimony makes clear that the decision was that of Dextrader.

Finally, the Association contends that assuming arguendo that the Hospital did reject the unit applicants as unqualified, it has the burden of establishing that all the applicants were unqualified and failed to sustain that burden. In particular, the Association challenges Dextrader's contention that a nurse could not qualify for the position unless she had prior experience as an occupational nurse. The Association points out that no such requirement was contained in the job description that was in effect at the time the position was posted, and argues that "the circumstances strongly suggest that the new specifications were tailored to Mrs. D.S.'s background." Further, although the Management Rights clause of the Agreement provides for certain rights of the employer including the right to determine qualifications for nursing positions, it also provides that such rights shall not be exercised so as to violate any provisions of the Agreement, and it accordingly "may not establish requirements that do not reasonably or fairly relate to the position" and the Union states that the new specifications are unreasonable and do not fairly relate to the position, and accordingly that their imposition violates the seniority and bidding provisions of the Agreement.

The heart of the Hospital's position, as I understand it, is reflected in the following portion of its brief:

> Under the terms of the collective-bargaining agreement the MNA has agreed that the Hospital retains the right to determine the qualifications of all registered nurse positions. This is so provided in the Management Rights clause and in the Promotions clause. Accordingly, the MNA has waived its right to challenge the determinations of qualifications made by the Hospital for the position of Employee Health Nurse. In addition, the language of the contract does not preclude the Hospital from choosing applicants for a position who are non-bargaining unit members. The

Management Rights clause provides that the Hospital shall retain the right to hire, and this right is not limited by the language of the Promotions clause . . .

The Hospital states that it has made a reasonable determination that the four employee-applicants were unqualified for the position. Specifically, it states that "the nursing aspects of the position are more limited than that of a general nurse duty," that "the primary emphasis of the position is more administrative and personnel oriented," and that the ability to administer the Employee Health Service program "as an entity is the crucial aspect of the position." The Hospital also asserts that "attitude and personality are as essential qualifications as are the technical aspects" of the position.

In its brief the Hospital has reviewed in detail the evidence concerning the qualifications of each of the employee-applicants, and states that "in reading the *total* qualifications of each of the employee-applicants, the Hospital was justified in its determination that none of them had the qualifications for the position." It contends that:

> In the light of past experiences with having general duty nurses fill the Employee Health Nurse Position the Hospital was amply justified in rejecting them and accepting a new hire that met the qualifications in all aspects. The employee-applicants would have required extensive training in order for them to handle the position with the desired and necessary proficiency. In comparing the past history with the present situation where there is now a person with the appropriate qualifications filling the position, the reasonableness and justification for the Hospital's determination is borne out.

Discussion and Conclusions

The foregoing facts and arguments present a close and difficult question, indeed. And while I agree with much that the Association states in its counsel's excellent brief, I nevertheless believe that the grievance must be denied. My reasons follow.

At the outset, I agree with the Association, as stated in its brief, (1) that the posting and bidding procedures provided in the Agreement are limited to nurses in the bargaining unit; (2) that the comparative qualifications test comes into play only when there is more than one qualified applicant from the bargaining unit; and (3) that the Hospital may only go outside the bargaining unit to fill a vacancy when there are no qualified applicants from the unit.

However, and although the case is an extremely close one, I believe that the Hospital has established that there were no qualified applicants from the unit, as the term "qualifications" is used in the Agreement.

As the Hospital points out, Article XIII, the Management Rights clause of the Agreement, clearly gives the Hospital the right "to determine qualifications for nursing positions." And I am unable to find that the Hospital's determination of qualifications for the Employee Health Nurse position violated any specific provision of the Agreement. In particular, I find nothing in the Agreement which barred the Hospital from making prior experience as an occupational nurse one of the qualifications for the job. I am unable to conclude, in the light of the evidence as to the development and changes in the nature of the work required, that this qualification, or the other qualifications involving secretarial training and familiarity with rules and regulations on safety and compensation, were unreasonable or unrelated to the position or otherwise violative of the Agreement.

The question remains as to whether the applicants or any of them were qualified for the position as so defined by the Hospital. There is not, and cannot be, the slightest question that all the applicants are professionally qualified to perform the nursing duties of the position. But given the primacy of the nonnursing attributes of the position, which, I have found, was a determination within the Hospital's rights, a much more difficult question is presented. Counsel for the Association indeed has pointed to facts which tend to cast doubt on the Hospital's assertion that the unit applicants are unqualified: the fact that during his initial interviews Dextrader gave no indication that they were unqualified for lack of prior experience in occupational nursing, the absence of such a statement in his letters of December 1, 1971, and his argument in the grievance procedure of his right to select the most qualified applicant. But upon all the evidence as to the nature of the position as defined by the Hospital I cannot conscientiously find that the Hospital erred in its determination that the unit applicants were not qualified for the position. This is not to denigrate the competence, training or intelligence of the unit applicants. As stated above, they clearly qualified in the nursing aspects of the position. And they obviously are employees of competence and intelligence, and undoubtedly all or some of them could be trained for the nonnursing aspects of the job, as the Hospital apparently concedes. But the Agreement makes no provision for a training period. It refers only to existing qualifications.

AWARD

It is concluded, then, that the Hospital did not violate the Agreement by rejecting all the employee-applicants who bid for the position of Employee Health Nurse and by hiring an employee from the outside. The grievance will be denied.

Case No. 36

*In view of the fact that a nurses aide's slight
physical stature was apparent at the time she was
hired, did the Hospital have the right to
subsequently terminate her on the ground that she
was not physically capable of performing the
duties of her job? What restraints are properly
placed on management in the exercise of its
discretionary power to terminate an employee
during the probationary period?*

Jackson County Medical Care Facility (Jackson, Mich.)
and
American Federation of State, County and Municipal Employees, Local 139

Arbitrator: M. David Keefe
Date of Award: December 19, 1973
Citation: LAIG 1014

The Grievant was hired on 6-4-73, as a Nurse's Aide I on the Second Shift. Section 12 (a) of the Labor Agreement between the parties dated 1-1-73 (Joint Ex. #1), provides that:

12. *Seniority–Probationary Employees*
(a) New employees hired in the unit shall be considered as probationary employees for the first ninety (90) days of their employment. The ninety (90) days probationary period shall be accumulated within not more than one hundred and eighty (180) calendar days. When an employee finishes the probationary period, by accumulating ninety (90) days of employment within not more than one hundred and eighty (180) calendar days, he shall be entered on the seniority list of the unit and shall rank for seniority from the day ninety (90) days prior to the day he completes the probationary period. There shall be no seniority among probationary employees. (Note: If an

additional thirty (30) days are needed, the Employer and the Union may agree mutually in writing.)

The Grievant was severed on 8-24-73 (Joint Ex. 2b), 76 calendar days after her date of original employment. The grievance protesting the termination (Joint Ex. 2a) was filed on 8-27-73, and processed through the Grievance Procedure to arbitration under representation authority granted the Union by Section 12 (b) of the contract, which reads:

(b) The Union shall represent probationary employees for the purposes of collective bargaining in respect to rates of pay, wages, hours of employment and other conditions of employment as set forth in this Agreement.

The Union asserted that the Employer's action, under the guise of *probationary severance*, constituted constructive discharge motivated by animus against the Grievant's previous exercise of the Grievance Procedure in her own behalf. Management insisted that the dismissal was routinely effected after evaluation which induced the conclusion that *probation* should be terminated.

Position of the County Facility

Basically, the Employer's position was outlined in the grievance answer rendered by the County Board of Commissioners on 9-21-73 (Joint Ex. 2c), which reads:

The Salary and Labor Relations Committee thoroughly examined all of the facts in the C— grievance, and it was the Committee's decision to uphold the termination of Miss C—.

There is no question that Miss C— was still on probation at the time of her termination and after examining the records, the Committee agreed that she was terminated solely on the basis of her work performance.

Under Section 5b of the current Agreement, "the management of business of the County is vested exclusively in it and the County reserves to itself all management functions including but not limited to . . . the right to hire new employees, to direct the work force, to discipline, suspend or discharge the work force for *just cause*.

The purpose of the probationary period is to observe the employee and to evaluate his or her work performance. Thus, the supervisors at

Medical Care Facility observed her work performance and determined that she should be terminated.

Second Shift Supervising Nurse Kirk testified to the duties required of a Nurses Aide 1. She explained that the institution practices the evaluation of probationary Employees shortly before seniority would be attained. In this case, she did fill out a report on the Grievant dated 8-24-73 (Emp. Ex #1a and #1b). The witness could not recall how the form was supplied to her or exactly when she received it. However, since it became established that Mrs. Kirk took a day-off on 8-24-73, she rationalized that she got the form on 8-23, filled it out at home on 8-24 and turned it in on 8-25-73. This evaluation read:

1.   Ability to Learn: Does he understand and remember instructions:

1.   Difficult to determine — avoids direct questions — giggles like a young school girl at all questions and situations — seems pathetically young and immature and not equal to answer directly on various nursing procedures.

2.   Teamwork and Cooperation: Does he get along and work well with others?

2.   In a shadowy and self-effacing way she got along with others — Some Nurse Aides requested not to be assigned to work with her — they would state she is willing but so slight in strength and stature, they did not feel she was able to do lifting necessary in the general run of "facility patients" and these same Aides would say to stop your work — find someone else to help you was not satisfactory to all involved. They stated they want to work with an aide who is able to lift and care for patients in such a way that is safe procedure for both patients and aide.

3.   Compliance with Instructions and Regulations: Does he readily conform to instructions and regulations?

3.   I don't know, she shadows another Aide and echoes her words and actions so it is unfair to give a direct answer on this question.

4.   Quantity of Work: Is it up to what should be expected?

4.   Again I must repeat she clings to another Aide in such a way that so far, I can not judge what she has performed by herself.

5.   Quality of Work: Is it up to what should be expected?

5.   The above statement is answer to no. 5 question.

In conclusion she appears to me as very immature, not fitted for arduous-exacting Nurses Aide work — Her physical limitations, her dependence on whoever is working with her — her avoidance of direct questions concerning the nursing of the sick to a supervisor nurse — her evident inability for charting (I have only one example of her charting which is very necessary for patient care) and I could not read what she had written and have not seen her actually charting and have not observed her looking at any charts for information etc. — so again she has depended on some one else to tell her about the patients.

I feel C—'s pleasant good nature and easy laughter and undoubtedly other talents she may possess could find her a job more suitable for her.

The witness amplified the comments entered on the evaluation form. She stated that the Nurses' Aides worked in teams for the most part, especially when rooms and patients were to be cleaned or patients assisted in or out of bed and, when necessary, in walking to their destination. The Grievant's slight stature made it difficult for larger Aides to work with her. At least two had requested not to be paired with her. However, complaints by one Aide, seeking to avoid assignment with another particular individual, were far from uncommon. Another shortcoming apparently derived from the Grievant's happy nature is that one overly sensitive patient had fancied that an Aide had laughed at her. Although someone else might have been involved and although there was no showing that derisive laughter had indeed been directed at the patient, the conclusion was that the Grievant had been the individual involved and she had been cautioned against allowing similar impressions to disturb patients. The Grievant was also suspected of not comprehending instructions. Usually, after receiving work orders, she seemed to consult with another Aide with whom she was quite friendly. There was no in-service Training program for the shift on which the Grievant worked. On-the-job experience and instructions substituted for formal job-training. Nevertheless, the Supervisor felt the Grievant should have progressed further than she did during her work-stint in the installation. She had difficulty in cleansing patients and performing follow-up chores.

Mrs. Kirk reported that the Grievant had requested the weekend off on 8-18-73. The Supervisor routinely checked with the Director of Nursing for approval before schedules were posted. In this case, the Director was out on vacation and the Supervisor posted the schedule, granting the Grievant's request. Later, the Director sent the Supervisor a note cancelling this time-off and rescheduling the following weekend: 8-25-73, and 8-26-73, to the Grievant. The witness concluded her testimony by asserting she had not recommended termination.

*   *   *   *   *

Director of Nursing Karazin related that she had gotten an oral report on the written evaluation. The witness made notes based on this conversation with Mrs. Kirk (Co. Ex. #2). These read:

Immature — negative approach — Giggles, laughs — no sensible explanations or answers to questions — stated new patient — 10 p.m. — wouldn't let her do anything for her.

Won't consult Supervisors — laughs when given direct assignments — disagrees with assignments in a negative way without saying so — just doesn't complete some — Mrs. Kirk feels that she is incapable of comprehension.

The Director stated that she had hired the Grievant, realizing her diminutive size. It was difficult to obtain Employees then and pressing need existed to fill the opening which the Grievant filled. She was assigned to the second shift. In-service training was restricted to the first shift and on-the-job learning obtained on the latter shift. When the weekend time-off was granted by the Supervisor, this left the shift short-handed. The Director rectified this with the cancellation of the time-off. A grievance resulted on Friday, 8-10-73 (Un. Ex. #1). On Monday, 8-13-73, the witness dispatched a note to the Grievant (Un. Ex. #2) stating:

I would like to see you in my office.

The witness generally leaves the premises at 3:30 p.m. and probably did on this date. The Grievant reports at 3:00 p.m. Despite the overlap, she did not contact the witness on Monday. Work schedules in the installation call for variable days off and, thereafter, either the Director or the Grievant was off except on Thursday, 8-16-73, which both worked. The Grievant did not see the witness then. The next day both were on the premises was Wednesday, 8-22-73. On this occasion, the Director sent for the Grievant. She came, accompanied by her Steward. She had no excuse for not contacting the Director previously. The Director reminded her that she was still on probation. The Grievant responded she had been in the Union after the first 30 days of employment. The witness explained why the weekend off had been changed. The Grievant volunteered that she had asked for the time so as to attend a wedding. The Director observed that, had she known, she would have made efforts to allow her the weekend. She apologized to the Grievant who then informed her the wedding had been cancelled. The witness declared that she was surprised at the Grievant's actions in this meeting. She sought out Mrs. Kirk for the oral evaluation and then decided on the termination, which was effected by mail, on Friday, 8-24-73. The grievance pending on the schedule change was not a factor in the decision. Her failure to respond to the 8-13-73 written summons was a factor; plus the opinion formed in the meeting of 8-22-73. In cross-examination, the Director revised this testimony, recollecting that the interview with Supervisor Kirk had transpired probably on Friday, 8-17-73 before the meeting and that, when the Grievant did come to her office, her mind had already been made up to effect termination. However, nothing was said about this pending action in the session on the schedule change. The witness had never personally observed the Grievant's work, but, after Mrs. Kirk's oral report, asked for the written evaluation to be submitted.

*   *   *   *   *

The Employer argued that Probationary Employees have no seniority from Section 12a. The Union's representation rights are confined to contractual negotiations where such Employees are concerned. The Grievance Procedure does not encompass them. No grievance had ever been filed for a worker in probationary status. The purpose of probation is to allow the Employer complete discretion in deciding whether a Probationer should be severed or retained. Certainly, the standards of *just cause* which apply when seniority obtains could not be utilized in this case. This Employee was deemed unsatisfactory . . . and that should suffice to cause dismissal of the grievance.

Position of the Union

The Grievant explained that she got the memo to see the Nursing Director only at 4:30 p.m. on 8-13-73. Since the Director had left, there was no chance to meet. On 8-16-73, no steward was available. The meeting then did take place on 8-22. Two days later, the Grievant was terminated.

The Union argued that the Employer's determination to sever the Grievant was triggered by the submission of the grievance against the schedule change. It was strictly a decision of the Nursing Director's. The Supervisor had not recommended the termination. The severance was effected even before the evaluation was received. It is also doubtful about when Mrs. Kirk's oral comments were given. But there is no doubt about the entire matter coming to a head only after the grievance was filed. This clearly aroused the Nursing Director's ire. Section 29 (f) of the Agreement reads:

(f) The immediate supervisor shall schedule the employees in the department concerned to provide each employee with a weekend off every third week. All schedules shall be posted one (1) week in advance, setting forth the schedule for three weeks in each department. (No schedule shall be changed once posted unless agreed between the immediate supervisor, employee or employees involved in writing.)

The Supervisor of the Grievant was Mrs. Kirk, not the Nursing Director. When this immediate supervisor posted the schedule allocating 8-18-73, and

8-19-73, as time-off for the Grievant, the contract prohibited the Director from unilaterally cancelling the schedule. The fact that the Grievant, as a Probationary Employee, protested this flagrant violation of her rights which the Director had inflicted is, obviously, the inspiration for her dismissal. This should be set aside and the Grievant should be made whole.

Discussion

The terms of the Agreement (Section 12b) provide Union representation of Probationers in the Grievance Procedure. The severance of the Grievant is subject to arbitral review. However, the standards for *just cause* cannot be required to be on an equal plane to the showing which must be made when a Seniority Employee is involved. Management does not have to prove that the terminated Probationer has necessarily been guilty of an infraction or series of violations which warrants disciplinary discharge. It is sufficient for the Employer to show that the affected individual failed to meet standards or displayed shortcomings during the period which lead to good faith doubt that the Probationer would appropriately contribute to the efficient and economical operation of the facility. It is, nevertheless, Management's inescapable necessity to have *clean hands* in exercising the discretionary judgment-latitude which the probationary period accords it. Probationers, with access to Union representation and grievance protests, cannot be terminated for discriminatory reasons or out of personal animus.

This case is one where it is impossible to credit the Administrator with *clean hands,* beyond all doubt. The doubts that do exist must be resolved in the Grievant's favor.

To begin with, when the Nursing Director hired the Grievant, she was quite aware of her stature and, presumably, was equally aware of the physical demands of the Nurses' Aide job. The Director chose to overlook the drawback because she needed new help. Thus, it cannot now be said that Management was surprised and only discovered during probation that the Grievant was not as robust as her fellow-workers. It is possible that the Grievant was hired tongue-in-cheek, with the unexpressed intent of getting rid of her during probation. But, to persuade her to start work, the Grievant was then lulled into believing her employment would be steady, at least as far as the fixed and known physical attributes which she brought with her onto the job. It is a belated and poor faith excuse, at this stage, to explain that she was too small to perform routine tasks since hiring standards could hardly overlook so elemental a factor when she was selected. But, be this as it may, the sudden decision to dismiss the Grievant fatally lacked the impersonal and objective judgment which performance-evaluations are designed to produce. After the grievance against schedule change was filed, matters moved with a kind of hysterical haste to effect the termination. A verbal report was elicited at some uncertain date and scribbled, random notes formed the basis for the decision. The reasoned, calm reports which could normally be anticipated in a fair evaluation were not at hand — and were not needed. The Employer's exhibit of the tardy document which was given following the termination has no supportive value to buttress the decision because it was after-the-fact. The conclusion is that the Director departed from usual routine to seek out adverse comments behind which to conceal her predetermined intent to get rid of the Grievant. Mrs. Kirk, who was extremely fuzzy in her recollections about how she came to fill out the evaluation form, did not testify at all to the verbal interview which the Director reported. The version given by the Director is unpersuasive as explaining the true motive underlying the termination.

AWARD

The termination of the Grievant is hereby set-aside. She is to be restored to work but must complete her probationary period. In the event that this is successfully accomplished, she is to be made whole for losses suffered by reason of the termination but minus all substitute earnings or unemployment compensation which accrued to her benefit during the interim.

Case No. 37

Where two applicants for the position of operating room supervisor had equal technical qualifications as to work and day-to-day ability, were a junior nurse's demonstrated superior ability to get along with her associates and her more advanced educational progress valid considerations in determining that she was better qualified for the open position than the grievant?

Williamsburgh General Hospital (Williamsburgh, N.Y.)
and
New York State Nurses Association

Arbitrator: Maurice C. Benewitz
Date of Award: June 7, 1974
Citation: Previously unreported

A hearing was held before the undersigned Arbitrator on May 28, 1974, at the offices of the American Arbitration Association, 140 West 51st Street, New York, N.Y., to consider the following controversy submitted by the parties:

Did the Hospital violate the Collective Bargaining Agreement when it selected Hermin Antoine as Operating Room Supervisor instead of Encelle Grosvenor? If so, what shall be the remedy?

Background and Dispute

The parties were bound at the time of the dispute by a Collective Bargaining Agreement dated January 1, 1972. A number of provisions of this Agreement are cited as relevant to the instant dispute. They include Section 4.07, which reads:

Seniority means length of continuous employment by Employer as an employee in a position covered by this agreement. There will be two basic types of seniority (a) regular, for a regular employee and (b) part-time, for a permanent part-time employee.

Section 4.11, which reads in part:

Seniority will apply to . . . (b) promotion . . . In promotion, Employer will be guided by seniority only if the involved employees' abilities and qualifications (including, without limitation, preparation, ability, dependability, skill, efficiency and physical fitness) are approximately equal.

Section 4.12, which provides that the Employer shall post and furnish the Association with seniority lists at least annually. Section 14, which reads in part:

Employer has both legal responsibility and sole right to manage its business and, except as limited in this agreement, to (a) . . . promote . . .

It is clear from the testimony that both employees here involved are able, efficient and valued nurses. The dispute is solely concerned with the question of which of them should have been promoted to Operating Room Supervisor effective January 1, 1974.

Encelle Grosvenor, the grievant, began her employment at the Hospital on September 28, 1966. According to her testimony, she was a staff nurse in the operating room for about six months. Grievant testified that she then became an assistant supervisor and held this position until the first Agreement was signed. Since there was no title of assistant supervisor in the scheme of this contract, she then, according to her testimony, became a head nurse. All of this service was in the operating room and, in addition, grievant had had previous operating room experience at other hospitals (total experience: 13 years). From time to time grievant had worked as a supervisor on relief in the Hospital as a whole and in the operating room. While some differences developed at the hearing concerning grievant's titles at this institution, there is no question that she performed ably as a full-time nurse since 1966. For the purposes of this proceeding there is no necessity for the Arbitrator to resolve the differences which arose.

Hermin Antoine, née Benn, was hired in the pay period ending August 31, 1962. Until 1971 she was primarily a part-time employee, who had had several leaves for educational purposes. (See Union Exhibit 1) In 1971 she became a full-time staff nurse in the operating room and most of her previous experience had been in the operating room. She had also, however, held positions as a head nurse and had acted as an assistant supervisor from time to time.

The Hospital does not, as Section 4.07 appears to require when read in conjunction with Section 4.12, maintain separate seniority lists for regular and for permanent part-time employees. Thus, on Joint Exhibit 2, the January 1974 seniority list, Mrs. Antoine is listed as more senior than grievant. The Union contends that this is improper. The Union further contends that because of her educational leaves, Mrs. Antoine cannot be said to have had "continuous" service within the meaning of Section 4.07.

The position of Operating Room Supervisor became vacant as of the end of December, 1973. The Hospital designated the operating room committee of its medical board as a search committee. Advertisements were placed in *The New York Times*. Both Mrs. Antoine and Mrs. Grosvenor applied. Others applied but were not interviewed.

The Board interviewed grievant in December. At the hearing, a number of areas considered by the Committee, which did not select grievant, were detailed. There does appear to be approximately 20 credits' difference in the standing of each candidate in their baccalaureate programs. Mrs. Antoine is closer to the degree which is now necessary for supervisory personnel.

A significant amount of testimony arose concerning grievant's dependability, which, upon examination, was mainly concerned with a single incident occurring about the time the search committee was sitting. By the admission of Administrator Donald Manney, this incident by itself would not have been sufficient reason to deny the promotion to an otherwise qualified employee.

The Arbitrator shall not consider the question of dependability at any length because it is clear that the decision which was made rested not upon such considerations but upon the judgment of the committee that grievant would not be able to relate effectively to fellow employees, hospital personnel in other departments, and surgeons who use the facilities of this proprietary hospital. Apparently, some doctors who practiced extensively at the Hospital had made it clear that they would use another Hospital if grievant became supervisor of the operating room. The Arbitrator was given a list of the names of the surgeons involved but can see no useful purpose in setting forth the names (or of keeping the list in his hearing notes). He will not list the persons involved, therefore.

During the grievance procedure the Association sought documentary support of any charges brought by the Hospital. There was documentation of the educational postures of the two applicants seriously considered by the search committee. The Hospital, however, contended that no evaluation records were available. At this proceeding, however, three evaluations were presented for each of the candidates. They were discovered only after the grievance proceeding and were not available to the search committee. Only the last evaluation in each set (Hospital Exhibits 3 and 4) were signed (by K. Weil) and none were seen by the employees or countersigned. The December 1973 evaluation of Mrs. Antoine indicates that her relationships with others are very good and contains the additional comment,

> Never refuses any extra requests of her. Works well with Doctors and all Hospital personal (*sic*).

The 12/7/73 evaluation of grievant rates her relationships with others as "very poor" and has the following two statements on it:

> Unable to get along with personal (*sic*). Never offers to help other personal (*sic.*)

The Hospital also produced a written report of the disputed "call-in" incident and its aftermath. While grievant had seen this report in handwritten form, it also was not produced at the grievance hearing.

The Association Position

By terms of Section 4.11, the Hospital is required to promote the senior employee if ability and qualifications are approximately equal. It is submitted that grievant was as able on all criteria as Mrs. Antoine. Furthermore, the Hospital incorrectly computed seniority and grievant is clearly senior to the promoted candidate. The search committee (composed of the Hospital Administrator, the Director of Nursing, Director of Surgery, Director of Gynecology, and Director of Anesthesiology) knew or should have known these facts. Grievant was better qualified and should have been selected.

The Hospital Position

The position of Operating Room Supervisor is essential to the workings of this institution. The Supervisor organizes and directs the work force. She schedules surgical procedures. She works with personnel in the laboratory, x-ray, and medical departments. She must not only be technically proficient but must also have traits of personality which enable her to work smoothly with all persons with whom she must have contact. Such traits of personality are a valid consideration in weighing candidates.

Section 4.11 is not the only contract article which must be considered. Section 14 affords the Hospital exclusive control over promotion so long as the terms of the Agreement are not violated.

In light of the importance of personality, the Hospital denies that the two candidates are approximately equal. In any case, their educational progress differs and a completed degree is important under State law and regulations. The Hospital further contends that Mrs. Antoine is the senior employee.

Discussion

The Hospital is incorrect in its statement that Mrs. Antoine is the senior employee. While leaves for education may be considered as part of continuous service, Sections 4.07 and 4.12 clearly provide for two seniority lists: regular and permanent part-time. The contract does not make clear which list shall be considered for promotional purposes. But at the time of the promotion both candidates were regular employees. On this list, grievant was obviously the senior employee.

However, Section 4.11 allows the promotion of the junior employee if ability and qualifications are not approximately equal. The question which must be answered is whether Mrs. Antoine was clearly superior to grievant so that the Hospital could properly conclude that the candidates were not approximately equal.

These two nurses appear to have approximately equal technical qualifications as to work and day-to-day ability. Both have some history in this institution of having worked as assistant supervisors from time to time.

There is no question that Mrs. Antoine is closer to achievement of the bachelor's degree. She, furthermore, is presently continuing her education while grievant, through no fault, has not been able to do so. Since State regulatory bodies require that supervisors soon have the degree, the difference in educational progress was a valid consideration for the search committee.

More fundamentally, the search committee was entitled to consider the differences between the candidates in their ability to work with all those involved in the day-to-day work of the operating room. In supervisory positions such ability may be vital and can often be judged only by consideration of subjective criteria. All of the members of the search committee were familiar with both candidates and had known them for some time. Even without documentary evidence, the committee could reasonably make a distinction which was not arbitrary, capricious or discriminatory. The testimony presented at this proceeding indicates that the committee determined not that Mrs. Grosvenor was incapable but that Mrs. Antoine was clearly and evidently superior in the area of demonstrated ability to work with others. This decision was apparently critical; the committee made it upon information to it known; and the Arbitrator cannot conclude that the decision was improper or violative of the Agreement.

On the other hand, this ruling should not be taken to mean that the Arbitrator feels that the Hospital's procedures in this area have been efficient or have met all of the requirements of equity. Had the Hospital made its evaluations known to grievant, she would have been on notice concerning a problem. Proper documentation of incidents requires that the records be shown to grievant and signed by her again so that grievant is aware of problems. Proper records would have made for a more effective grievance meeting and would have produced the documentation which the Association properly requested. The Arbitrator has sustained the Hospital decision because he believes a crucial supervisory promotion should not be voided on technical grounds where substantive data supports the action.

However, even recognizing that this is a small institution where contract procedures may have been observed only loosely in the past, the Arbitrator rules that this Hospital is now on notice that future actions must be properly documented or be in danger of reversal. This is an agreement between professionals and professional standards should be maintained.

In light of the foregoing discussion, I, the undersigned Arbitrator, having been designated in accordance with the Arbitration Agreement executed by the parties and dated January 1, 1972, and having been duly sworn, and having received the testimony and evidence of the parties at a hearing at which both were ably represented by Counsel, issue the following

AWARD

The Hospital did not violate the Collective Bargaining Agreement when it selected Hermin Antoine as Operating Room Supervisor instead of Encelle Grosvenor.

Subject Index

by case number

Ability. 2, 35, 36
Absenteeism. 25, 26
Aides. 7, 8, 10, 11, 12, 16, 24, 27, 28, 36
Arbitrability. 6

Bona Fide Occupational Qualifications.
  30, 31, 32, 34, 35, 37
Burden of Proof. 7, 10, 11

Constitutional Rights. 29, 33
Contract Clauses.
  Arbitration and grievance procedure.
    2, 3, 6, 12, 14, 15, 33, 35
  Discipline and discharge. 2, 3, 5, 6,
    9, 12, 14, 25, 27, 28
  Employee rights. 6
  Job posting and bidding. 34
  Leave of absence. 27
  Maintenance of standards. 19, 20
  Management rights. 2, 3, 5, 6, 7, 9,
    14, 17, 19, 20, 22, 25, 28, 31, 35
  Mutual rights. 21, 22
  Non-discrimination. 30, 33
  No-strike. 25, 27
  Probationary employees. 36
  Promotions. 35
  Seniority rights. 32
  Tours of duty. 21
  Transfers. 30
  Working hours. 19

Demotion. 5, 31, 32
Discharge and Discipline.
  Absenteeism. 25, 26
  Equipment abuse. 14
  Failure to administer proper medica-
    tion. 3, 5
  Falsification of reason for absence. 27
  Insubordination. 4, 6, 8
  Leaving work or work area. 2

Patient abuse. 3, 9, 11
Physical violence and threats. 4, 9,
  10, 11
Refusal of work order. 5, 6, 8, 18
Rules violation (not elsewhere classi-
  fied). 7, 12, 15, 33
Strikes, work stoppages and concer-
  ted refusal to work. 24, 25, 26
Theft. 13
Union activities. 28
Unprofessional conduct. 1, 2, 3, 16,
  18, 24, 25, 26
Work performance. 12, 16, 36
Discrimination. 6, 30, 31, 32, 33
Due Process. 3, 4, 9, 27, 36

Equipment Abuse. 14

Failure to Administer Proper Medication. 3, 5
Falsification of Reason for Absence. 27

Incompetence. 12
Insubordination. 4, 6, 8

Job Bidding. 34, 35
Job Evaluation. 3, 5, 12, 16, 36
Just Cause. 3, 4, 5, 6, 7, 10, 11, 12, 13,
  15

Layoff. 17
Licensed Practical Nurses. 1, 3, 4, 6,
  17, 19, 21, 31, 34

Negligence. 14
New Contract Terms. 23

Orderlies. 9, 24, 30

Part-Time Employees. 20
Patient Care. 5, 6, 7, 9, 11, 21

Patient-Employee Relationships. 3, 10, 12, 16
Personal Appearance. 15, 33
Personal Records. 7, 8
Physical Violence and Threats. 4, 9, 10, 11
Privacy Rights of Patients. 31
Probationary Employees. 36
Professional Ethics. 1, 2, 3, 16, 18, 24, 25, 26
Promotions. 5, 30, 31, 34, 35

Recall. 32
Registered Nurses. 2, 5, 17, 18, 19, 20, 25, 26, 35, 37
Rules. 1, 6, 12, 14, 15, 33

Safety and Health. 2, 12, 22, 32, 33
Seniority Rights. 32, 37

Shift Transfers. 18, 21
Strikes, Work Stoppages and Concerted Refusal to Work. 24, 25, 26

Technicians. 14, 15, 32
Theft. 13
Training. 7, 8

Union Activities and Security. 18, 28, 29, 34, 36

Vacations. 23

Wages. 24
Weekend Work. 19, 20
Work Assignments. 2, 7, 8, 22
Work Load. 2, 24
Work Schedule and Work Week. 17, 18, 19, 20
Working Conditions. 22, 26

Index of Arbitrators

by case numbers

Benewitz, Maurice C. 37

Casselman, Harry N. 7
Cole, Howard A. 30

DiLeone, Peter 4

Eigenbrod, Walter F. 22
Elson, Alex 17

Florey, Peter 16

Geissinger, Wayne T. 5
Glushien, Morris P. 23
Grant, Alice B. 32
Groty, C. Keith 2

Herman, Leon J. 1, 20

Ipavec, Charles F. 27

Jacobs, Arthur B. 25
Jones, Edgar A., Jr. 31

Karasick, David 15

Keefe, M. David 24, 36
Killion, Leo V. 10
Knudson, Douglas V. 19
Koretz, Robert F. 35
Krinsky, Edward B. 11

Lee, Donald B. 12
Lucas, James R. 33

Miller, Robert W. 21

Ott, E. V. 28

Perry, Samuel S. 6

Roumell, George T., Jr. 14, 29

Rutledge, Ivan C. 8

Sandler, Woodrow J. 3
Seinsheimer, Walter G. 9
Shaw, Samuel S. 34
Simons, Jesse 13, 26

Tive, Ralph D. 18